ILLUSTRATED GUIDE
TO
CRIME SCENE
INVESTIGATION

ILLUSTRATED GUIDE TO CRIME SCENE INVESTIGATION

Nicholas Petraco
Hal Sherman

Taylor & Francis
Taylor & Francis Group

Boca Raton   London   New York   Singapore

A CRC title, part of the Taylor & Francis imprint, a member of the
Taylor & Francis Group, the academic division of T&F Informa plc.

Published in 2006 by
CRC Press
Taylor & Francis Group
6000 Broken Sound Parkway NW, Suite 300
Boca Raton, FL 33487-2742

No claim to original U.S. Government works
Printed in the United States of America on acid-free paper
10 9 8 7 6 5 4 3 2 1

International Standard Book Number-10: 0-8493-2263-4 (Hardcover)
International Standard Book Number-13: 978-0-8493-2263-1 (Hardcover)
Library of Congress Card Number 2005041783

Library of Congress Cataloging-in-Publication Data

Sherman, Hal, 1961-
 Illustrated guide to crime scene investigation / Hal Sherman, Nicholas Petraco.
  p. cm.
 Includes bibliographical references and index.
 ISBN 0-8493-2263-4
 1. Crime scene searches--Handbooks, manuals, etc. 2. Criminal investigation--Handbooks, manuals, etc.
I. Petraco, Nicholas. II. Title.

HV8073.S429 2005
363.25'2--dc22   2005041783

Taylor & Francis Group
is the Academic Division of T&F Informa plc.

Visit the Taylor & Francis Web site at
http://www.taylorandfrancis.com

and the CRC Press Web site at
http://www.crcpress.com

Dedication

This work is dedicated to the valiant men and women of the New York City Police Department who have, for the past two centuries, devoted their lives to the service of the people of New York City.

Introduction

This work assumes that the first officer responding to the scene of a forensic inquiry has given medical aid to any injured person, searched for possible assailant(s) or witnesses, and secured, restricted access to, and safeguarded the original scene.

When processing crime scenes, one must remember that each scene is unique. Although there exist general methods and protocols that one could use in most situations, the crime scene investigator must above all keep an open mind when executing his or her duties.

The Crime Scene (CS) is generally considered the area surrounding the location where a crime or incident has occurred, and the area where evidence pertinent to the investigation may be found. An evaluation must be made as soon as possible after the crime, so that evidence relating to the crime can be obtained. Rapid CS response is imperative, so that evidentiary materials may be discovered and protected before being destroyed or lost.

A- The Goals of This Work are to:

Present straight-forward, scientifically supported, valid systematic procedures for the recognition, documentation, processing, collecting, packaging, preserving, and safeguarding of potential items of physical evidence (PE) discovered during the search of the scene.

Demonstrate how to establish an indisputable chain of custody for all items of PE collected at a scene of a forensic inquiry.

Present and demonstrate the knowledge, skills, and abilities needed by a Crime Scene Examiner (CSE) in order to achieve his or her primary function and goals: the Searching for and Collection, Recording, Initialing, Packaging, and Transporting (SCRIPT) of PE from the scene of a forensic inquiry to the forensic laboratory.

These goals will be realized in this work by means of photographic demonstration, illustration, short narrative segments, and/or appendices.

B- Reasons for Evidence Collection:

To identify and associate the people, places, and things that interacted during the crime or event.

To ascertain a timeline and reconstruct the actual crime or event.

C- General Crime Scene Procedures:

The CSE must be sure that the crime scene is properly secured and protected so that potential evidence is not inadvertently destroyed or contaminated. The security of the scene is achieved by:

Establishing a valid CS, one in which no unauthorized person(s) may enter or exit.
Allowing only essential personnel at the CS.
Keeping a chronological log of events at the CS.
Roping off the suspected CS.

The CSE will document, upon his or her arrival:

The time and date of arrival on the scene.
The address of the location where the incident occurred.
Specific scene conditions, i.e., the weather, temperature, visibility, and lighting conditions.

Then, the CSE must find out all available information relative to the crime and its location by using the following procedure:

Speak to the first officer at the scene.
Discuss the CS with investigators.
Determine specific personal investigative protection equipment (PIPE) needed for the safety of personnel searching the scene.
Ascertain the original CS conditions.
Determine whether the scene was secured prior to your arrival.
Carefully approach the CS.
Determine the entire area of the CS, including paths of entry and exit, and areas which may contain evidence.
Form a preliminary search plan for an initial walk-through.
Be watchful for potential evidence.
Look for signs of activity, e.g., signs of a struggle.
Theorize what may have occurred.
Have an open mind.
Determine specific equipment required for search and evidence collection.
Discuss the need for a specialist if available, e.g., forensic anthropologist, odontologist, etc.

The CSE will establish a chain of custody. The documentation and identification of evidence is paramount in order to establish a strong chain of custody. All persons coming into contact with the PE are potential witnesses in judicial proceedings. Therefore, each person coming in contact with items of PE must mark each item of evidence for identification. In addition, the CSE must do the following for each item of PE:

Document the location, processing, and collection of each item of PE.
Accurately document the location of each item of evidence in its original position by following proper recording procedures.
Collect, package, seal, mark for identification, and log each item of evidence using case number(s), the initials of the recovering CSE, and the time, date, and location where retrieved.

Note: Necessary additional handling of evidence, as it is processed, should be completely recorded and properly documented as to location, processes performed, and persons handling it.

The CSE will establish a command station for processing equipment, evidence recording, and packing and storage (Never make the command station inside the crime scene.):

Discuss safety issues.
Obtain necessary safety equipment.
Finalize a search plan and a pattern and or method of search.
Determine each crime scene examiner's CSE's assignment(s).
Put on safety personal investigatory protective equipment (PIPE) to prevent possible contamination.

The CSE should start the systematic search of the suspected CS:

Perform a final review of the search plan.
Photograph and/or videotape the entire CS.
Take overall, intermediate, and close-up photographs.
Take close-up photographs with and without scales.
Keep a detailed photographic log.
Record the CS and findings by means of notes and rough sketches.
Make accurate measurements using established techniques, such as i.e., triangulation, polar coordinates, rectangular coordinates, Be sure to have fixed points
Search for items of potential PE.
Collect, package, and log all items of evidence. Be mindful of maintaining a strong chain of custody
Carry out a final review of the CS processing.
Transport the evidence to the appropriate authority.
Write a detailed narrative of the CS while details are still fresh in your mind.
Prepare CS sketches while details are still fresh in your mind.
Release the CS when processing is completed.

The CSE must properly package evidence. Evidence must be packaged so that its integrity is established and maintained from its initial discovery until its presentation in court. Utmost care must be taken to:

Keep individual items of evidence in separate containers to prevent cross-contamination.
Use clean containers to prevent outside contamination.
Use proper-size containers so that the evidence will not be lost or damaged by improper packaging.
Properly seal evidence packages so as to retain contents within the package and prevent unauthorized handling. Seals should completely cover all seams and package openings; Initial and date the tape to show when container was sealed
Properly label the package as to its content.

The CSE must properly transport evidence. Once properly packaged and logged, all items of evidence must be promptly, safely, and securely transported to their proper destination so that:

They will not be lost, destroyed, contaminated, altered, damaged, or otherwise harmed.
They will be stored under the environmental conditions required for that type of material or substance, e.g., blood should be allowed to air dry, then store in a climate controlled cool environment, always keep out of direct sunlight.

A written record of each item of evidence from the time of its collection to its arrival at the proper destination, and ultimately to its presentation in court, must be meticulously and accurately maintained.

The times and dates of all transactions regarding each item of evidence must be carefully recorded.

The CSE must fill out accurate CS reports. All observations, actions, and details concerning the CS are important to the investigation. Therefore, all information regarding the CS must be precisely recorded, and a formal report must be presented in a clear, comprehensive, and succinct manner.

D- Knowledge, Skills, and Abilities for the Crime Scene Examiner:

A CSE must possess a basic knowledge of the scientific methods of inquiry, as well as the procedures used in searching for recognizing, documenting, processing, collecting, preserving, packaging, and transporting all categories of PE. Next, a CSE must possess the skills and abilities necessary to carry out all of the tasks required in processing a CS. The following is a list of the minimum skills and abilities needed by a CSE. A Crime Scene Examiner:

Must be able to think in a clear, logical manner, form a hypothesis, and collect data to prove or disprove his/her hypothesis;

Must know the various systematic methods for searching a CS:

Walk-through, Walk-in, walk-out (see Figure 1.B 1 in Chapter 1);
Strip search;
Spiral search (see Figure 1.B 1 in Chapter 1);
Wheel search (see Figure 1.B 2 in Chapter 1);
Pie search;
Grid search;
Zonal search; and,
Vehicle search.

Must know how to take basic CS photographs, including:

General photographs showing the condition of the CS before it is disturbed;
Good overall, intermediate, close-up, and distant photographs of all types of CS and PE;
Taking of photographs as the CS is being processed;
Use of the overall lens, 24–50 mm;
Use of intermediate/mid-range lens, 50–105 mm;
Use of an all-around- range lens, 24–85 mm or lens 24–105 mm;
Use of the close-up lens, l05 mm–Macro;
Use of the distance lens, 100–-300 mm; and,
Ability to videotape a CS.

Must be able to take clear, concise, copious notes, and make basic, informative, and accurate observations, and drawings of the CS (if possible, to scale would be preferable, but it is not necessary in a rough sketch) (see Figure B1.-3 in Chapter 1).

Must have knowledge of the fundamental methods for making accurate measurements:

Rectangular coordinate method;
Triangulation method;

Transecting baseline method;
Polar coordinate method; and,
Secondary reference point.
Must know the basic methods used in sketching a CS:
Rough and finished sketch;
Pecspective sketch;
Cross-projection method;
Small area sketch;
Large area sketch; and,
Elevation drawing.
Must be able to process a CS for the following types of PE: visible, latent, and plastic fingerprints and palm-prints or handprints, footprints, ballistic evidence, projectile trajectories, tool marks, footwear and tire impressions, serological evidence, trace evidence (glass, hairs, fibers, soils, paint), GSR (gunshot residue), pattern evidence, questioned document evidence, unknown inorganic and organic substances, and arson and explosive residues and evidence.
Must be able to properly collect, package, safeguard, store, and transport all the various forms of PE acquired from the CS during the processing stage.
Must be able to handle physiological fluids, chemicals, and hazardous equipment in a safe manner.
Must have the ability to safely handle and make safe all types of firearms.
Must be able to examine and recover from a firearm its caliber, make, model, and serial number, and to determine whether it is loaded or unloaded, in a fired or unfired position, or is the hammer cocked or not cocked, and the position of the cylinder and clip.
A CSE must posses good communication skills, and be able to assist the detective(s) investigating the crime; write clear and accurate reports regarding the CS processing and evidence collection phase; be able to identify all items of PE collected at the CS; and give clear, honest, and unbiased expert witness testimony during all required legal proceedings.
Finally, a CSE must know the potential obstacles he or she may encounter when processing a CS:
The limited physical contact with surfaces by the assailant(s).
The commingling of fingerprints in public places.
The limited amount of evidence due to action of attacker(s).
The wearing of protective and/or concealing clothing by the perpetrator(s) e.g., gloves, or masks.
Limited physical contact between the assailant(s) and victim(s).

Contents

Processing the Scene of a Burglary

1

The crime of burglary can be classified as the entry into a property without the permission of the owner for the purpose of unlawfully removing merchandise. Burglaries generally involve the forcible entry into premises by means of breaking, cutting, drilling, or otherwise compromising the window(s), skylight(s), door(s), wall(s), roof(s), exhaust fans, vents, and air conditioning units encompassed within the location.

During the act of forcibly entering a location, i.e., a building, house, store, or apartment, the person or persons responsible for the act usually come into contact with the objects and surfaces present at the location. It is during the times of these inadvertent contacts that a mutual transfer of trace evidence, e.g., fragments of glass, paint, wood, plaster, blood, hairs, or fibers, often unwittingly occurs. In addition, the interactions among the people, places, and things during the event can lead to the presence of other evidence in the form of tool-mark impressions, footwear impressions, residual footwear prints, visible and invisible fingerprints, etc. The systematic process of careful searching, recognizing, documenting, collecting, and packaging of items of physical evidence is essential to any successful burglary investigation and subsequent prosecution. The following is a suggested, time-proven protocol for the processing of a typical burglary scene and most other scenes of crime.

General Crime Scene Practices

Discuss the crime scene and the status of the investigation with the first officer on the scene and the investigating officer(s) present at the scene.

Examine the general area; do a quick, careful systematic but thorough walk-through of a suspected crime scene, making sure not to disturb anything prior to documentation of the scene and any potential physical evidence (PE) (see Figure 1.1).

Establish the appropriate search pattern (see Figures 1.2 and 1.3).

Photograph the overall outside location while looking for items of evidence and signs of damage to property and areas, e.g., broken windows, bypassed or defeated alarms and security devices (see Figures 1.4 to1.15).

Take multiple exposures and bracket photographs.

Determine the points of entry and exit, in addition to areas from where property was removed.

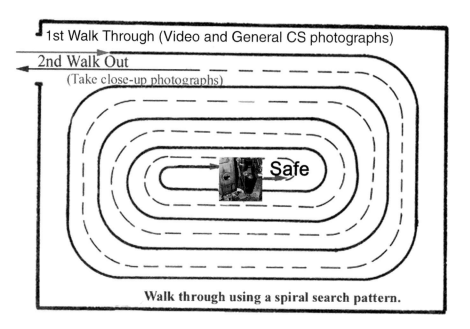

Figure 1.1   Do a quick general walk-through to determine the best search pattern.

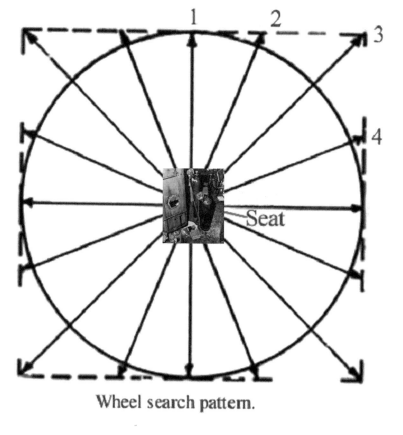

Figure 1.2   Wheel or pie search pattern.

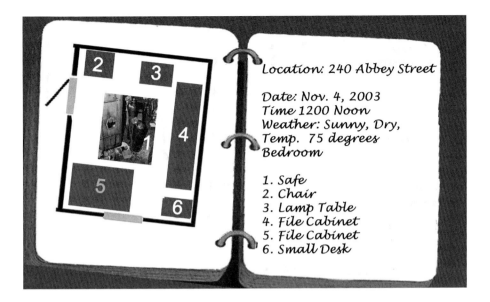

Figure 1.3 Take thorough notes.

Figure 1.4 Search and photograph the front of the premise.

(a)

Figure 1.5a

(b)

Figure 1.5b   Search and photograph the sides of the premise, front towards rear and opposite view.

Figure 1.6 Photograph multiple views of the location, both left and right, showing different perspectives.

Figure 1.7   Photograph from the location outward (top). In addition, look for and photograph identifying numbered utility poles near the location (bottom).

Figure 1.8   Search for and photograph points of entry and exit.

Figure 1.9   Continue search for physical evidence.

Figure 1.10   After locating an item of potential physical evidence, mark and safeguard it until the item can be properly documented and processed.

Figure 1.11   Search and photograph all around the outer perimeter of the location.

Figure 1.12 Continue documenting the entire area outside the location.

Figure 1.13 Locate point of entry.

Figure 1.14 Take several photographs of various views of points of interest. Vary the camera shutter speed (exposure) and f-stop settings. Remember: decreasing the f-stop by one stop, e.g., f8 to f5.6, will double the exposure time, while increasing the f-stop by one stop, e.g., f8 to f11, will decrease the exposure time by one half.

Figure 1.15 Document the suspected point(s) of entry and any physical evidence showing damage or entry.

Carefully search and record any items of physical evidence. Look for misplaced items, such as clothing, e.g., hats, and impression evidence, such as tool marks, tire tracks, footwear tracks, and fingerprints.

Photograph all items of evidence found at the crime scene before moving them (see Figure 1.15).

Prepare an accurate, detailed photographic record sheet (see Figure 1.16), and attempt to establish a modus operandi.

Look for misplaced items, such as clothing (hats, ski masks, baseball caps, gloves, etc.), and impression evidence, such as footwear and tire-track impressions. Document, collect, and package all items of physical evidence found during a search of the outer perimeter of the premises (see Figures 1.17 to 1.30).

Search and do a walk-through of the interior of the premises. Wear protective clothing to protect yourself from biological exposure and prevent cross-contamination (see Figures 1.31 to 1.37a–f).

Figure 1.16 Photographic record of crime scene.

Figure 1.17 Photograph any evidence before moving it, to show its original position when discovered at the crime scene.

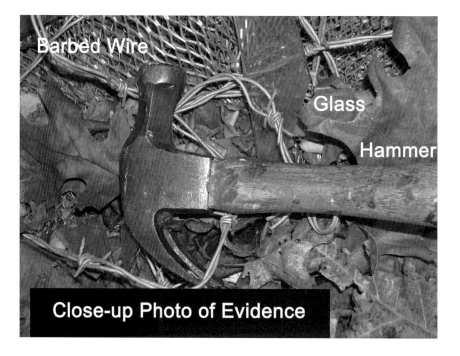

Figure 1.18 Take close-up photographs of all items of physical evidence found at the entry point, without and then with a scale.

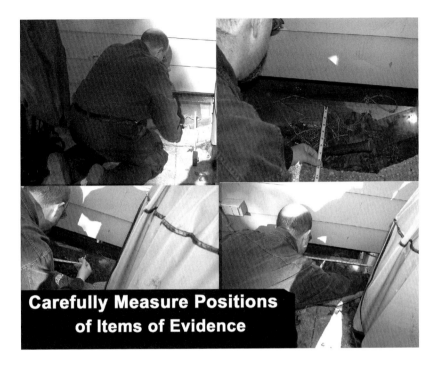

Figure 1.19 Document and measure the position of items of evidence. Document the suspected point(s) of entry and any physical evidence showing damage or entry. Look for tools, hairs, fibers, blood, or broken glass. Determine the direction of force used to break the glass. Remember: right–rear–radial (see section on glass evidence, pages 323–326).

Figure 1.20 Examine items for trace evidence. Photograph each item, and do not forget to use a ruler or scale.

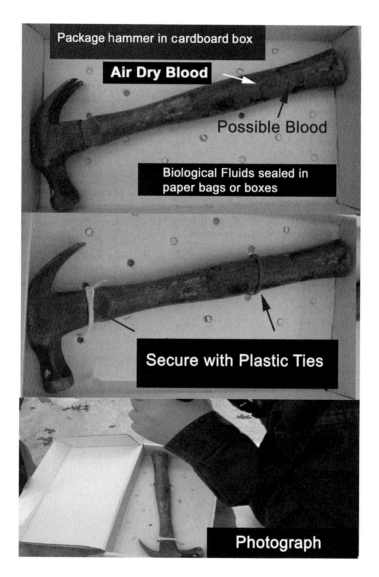

Figure 1.21 Package and secure the item in an appropriate container. A heavy hammer is best secured in a cardboard evidence box, held in with heavy plastic ties. Package the evidence, being mindful of future analysis possibilities.

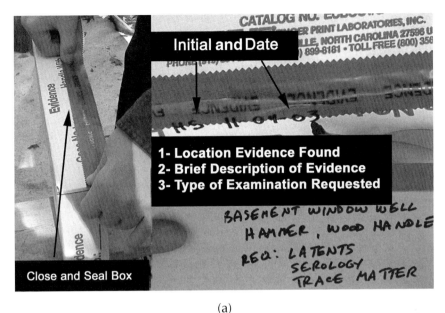

(a)

Figure 1.22a

(b)

Figure 1.22b   The box should be sealed with evidence tape, initialed, and marked for identi-fication. It is a good practice to identify the types of analyses being requested. An item such as the hammer containing possible blood should be stored in a climate-controlled cool environ-ment (always keep out of direct sunlight) immediately after packaging, and transported to the proper facility ASAP.

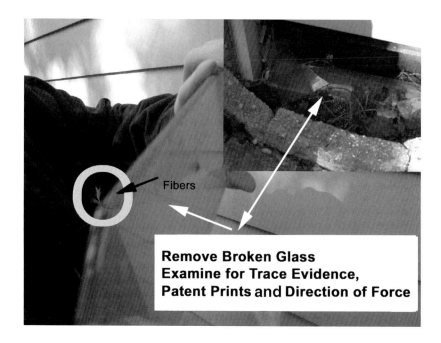

Figure 1.23   Remove broken glass and examine for trace evidence, blood, and patent finger-prints.

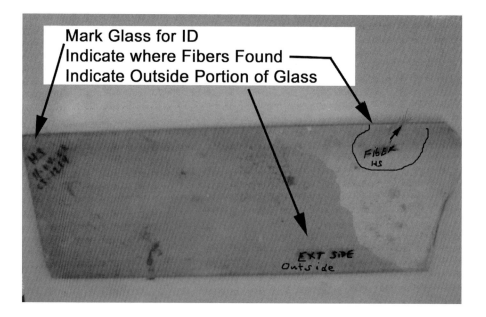

Figure 1.24   Mark the glass pane for identification. Indicate the interior and exterior sides of the glass pane.

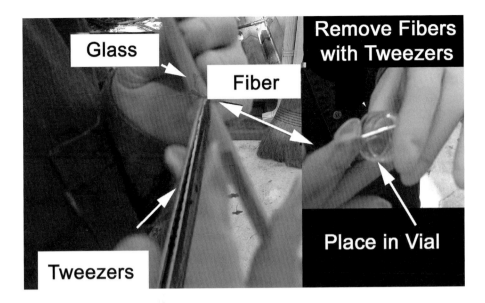

Figure 1.25   Carefully remove fibers from glass with tweezers, and package the fibers in a vial.

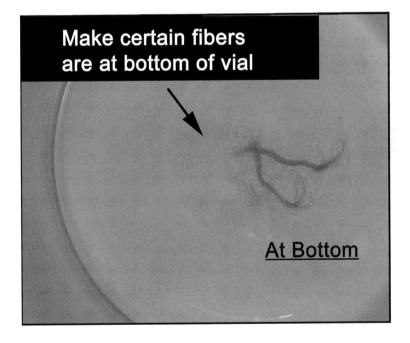

Figure 1.26   Gently place fibers in a vial or inside of a piece of weigh paper with a druggist fold. Double check that the trace evidence is inside packaging prior to sealing the package.

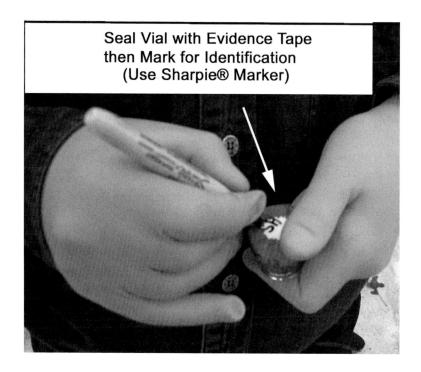

Figure 1.27   Seal vial with evidence tape, initial, date, and mark for identification.

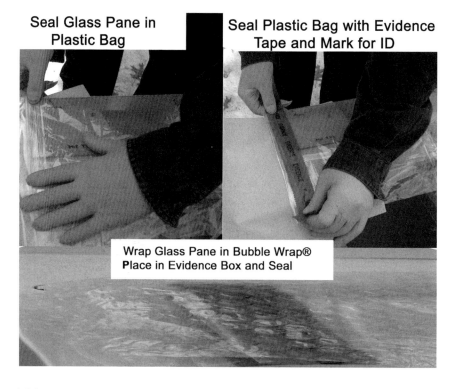

Figure 1.28   Seal glass pane in a plastic bag. Wrap the pane in bubble wrap, and seal in a box

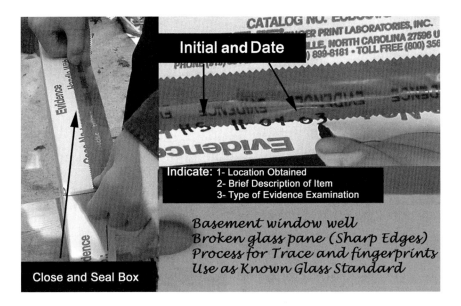

Figure 1.29 Seal glass pane in an evidence box, initial, and mark for identification.

Figure 1.30 Collect a glass stand for comparison (see section on standard collection, page 46).

Figure 1.31   Shown is a typical array of crime scene personal investigative protection equipment (PIPE).

Figure 1.32   Enter the premise through the rear so as to not disturb the front door exit point. Start the interior search.

Figure 1.33 Search the den and walk through to dining room.

Figure 1.34 Search the dining room and go into the living room.

Figure 1.35 Search the living room and continue walk-through. Continue looking for evidential clues.

Figure 1.36 Walk slowly down toward basement.

Figure 1.37a   Walk slowly towards basement.

Figure 1.37b   Walk slowly down into basement.

Figure 1.37c   Proceed towards basement.

Figure 1.37d   Walk slowly down into basement.

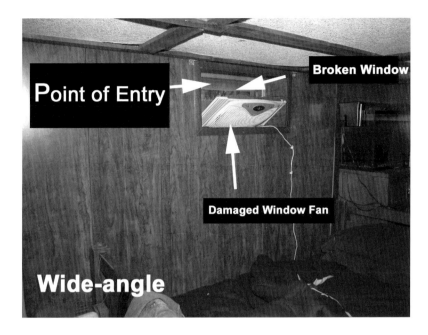

Figure 1.37e Walk slowly into basement room.

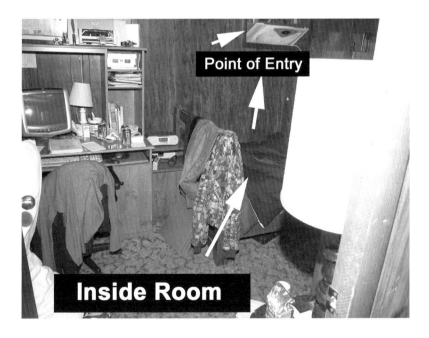

Figure 1.37f Walk slowly into basement room.

Basic Photographic Record of Crime Scene's Interior

After a walk-through of the interior is complete, make a plan to document, collect, package, and safeguard the following PE (see Figures 1.38 to 1.43):

Fingerprints (latent and patent)
Hairs and fibers (strands)
Pieces of textiles
Paint traces (smears, chips)
Glass (large and tiny fragments)
Soil (deposits or clumps)
Blood (wet or dry stains and stain patterns)
Tool marks
Tools
Damage and signs of forced entry
Footwear evidence

Figure 1.38 Take an overall photograph. Photograph the condition of the room and any physical evidence before collecting and packaging items of evidence. Be mindful to collect transient or fleeting evidence first.

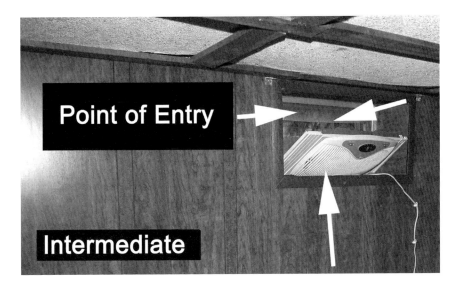

Figure 1.39a   Photograph the place of suspected entry into the premises.

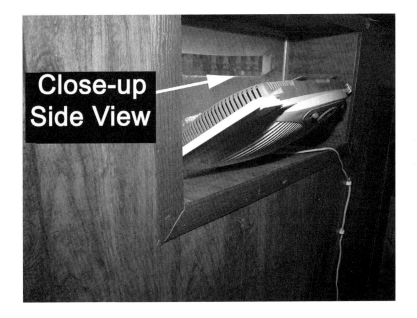

Figure 1.39b   Take close-up views.

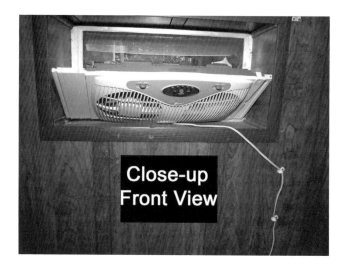

Figure 1.39c   Take close-up views.

Figure 1.40   Examine the place of entry for all types of physical evidence, e.g., blood, hair, fibers, glass.

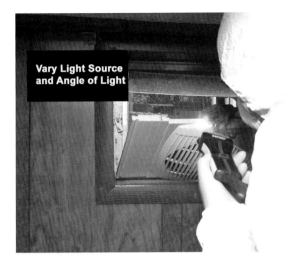

Figure 1.41   Use various light sources during search, e.g., an ultraviolet lamp, flashlight, blue light.

Figure 1.42   Document, remove, and package any items of physical evidence.

Figure 1.43 Process the point of entry for latent fingerprints.

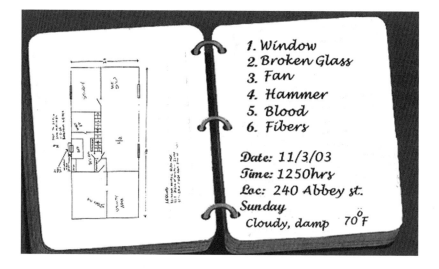

Figure 1.44 Keep a detailed notebook.

Keep in mind that the most fragile evidence should be collected first.

During this process, remember to make measurements, take notes, and draw rough diagrams (see Figure 1.44).

Process areas or items that may have been touched by the perpetrator, paying special attention to the points of entry and exit for latent fingerprints (see Figures 1.42 and 1.45a–m to 1.50).

Collection of Standards

Standard specimens of broken window glass from the window well, soil, and vegetation adjacent to footwear impression should be collected for use in future comparisons (see Figures 1.51 to 1.53).

Figure 1.45a   Process the point of exit.

Figure 1.45b   Choose the appropriate method based on the type of surface and process for latent prints.

Figure 1.45c Photograph the latent print *in situ* without scale.

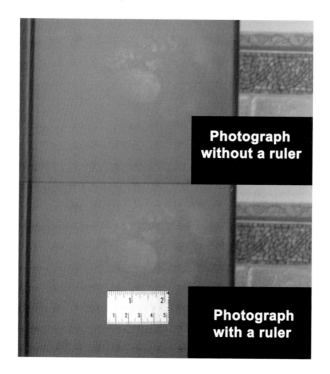

Figure 1.45d Photograph the latent print *in situ* with scale.

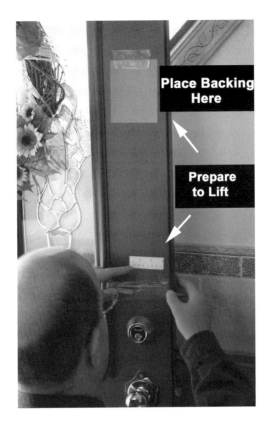

Figure 1.45e   Prepare to lift print. Place backing in proximity to the tape to avoid damaging the lift.

Figure 1.45f   Apply lifting tape to surface.

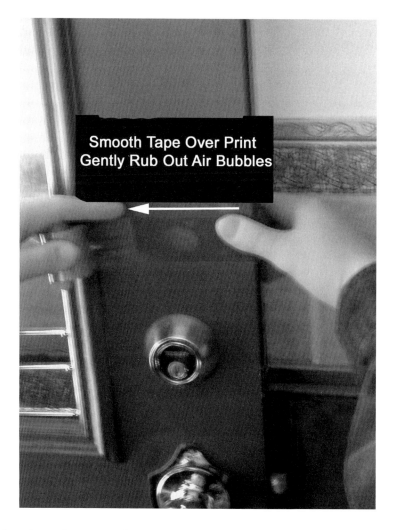

Figure 1.45g   Smooth tape evenly over print. Start at one side and proceed to the other side.

Figure 1.45h   Gently lift print from surface.

Figure 1.45i   Place print on contrasting color backing.

Figure 1.45j   Mark lift for identification.

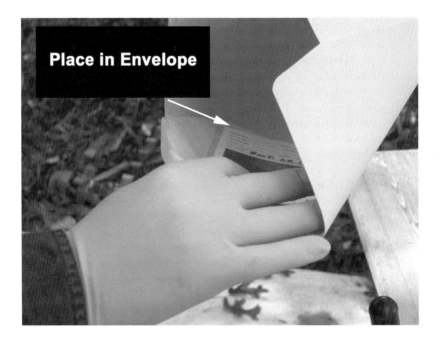

Figure 1.45k   Place lift into a manila envelope.

Figure 1.45l   Seal envelope with evidence tape.

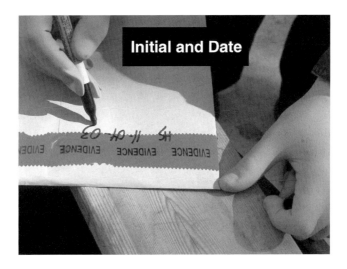

Figure 1.45m   Initial and date-seal with a Sharpie® marker.

Processing and Collection of a Footwear Impression

Figure 1.46a   Examine footwear impression.

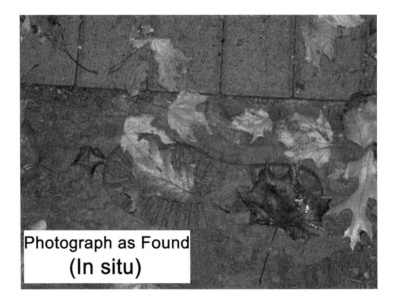

Figure 1.46b   Photograph as found.

Figure 1.47a Making measurements with the rectangular coordinate method.

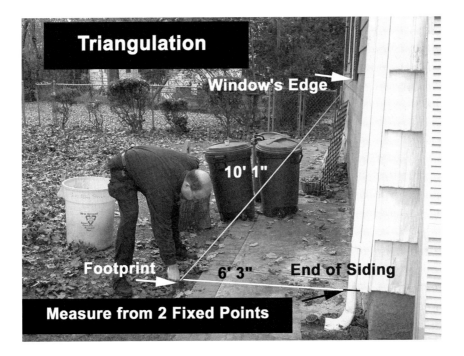

Figure 1.47b Making measurements with the triangulation method.

Figure 1.48a   Set up tripod.

Figure 1.48b   Level camera (make certain that the film plane is parallel to the surface being photographed). This will prevent distortion of the object being photographed.

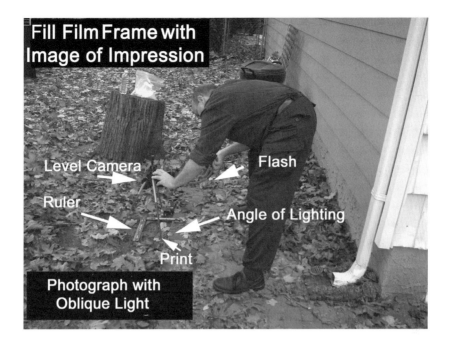

Figure 1.48c   Use oblique lighting to photograph footwear impression.

Figure 1.48d   Use oblique lighting.

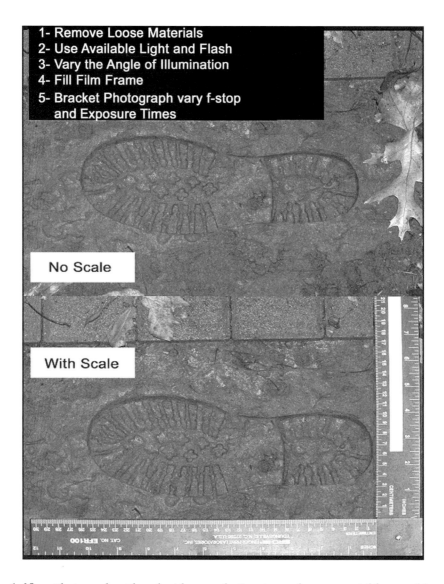

Figure 1.48e   Photograph with and without scale. Retain any loose material for possible analysis.

Casting the Impression

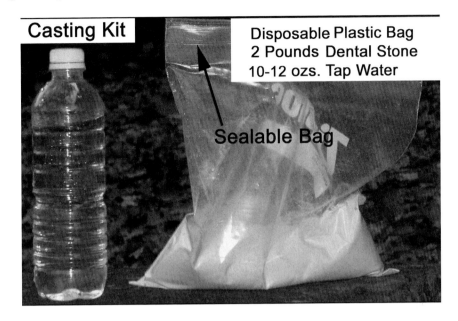

Figure 1.49a Casting kit.

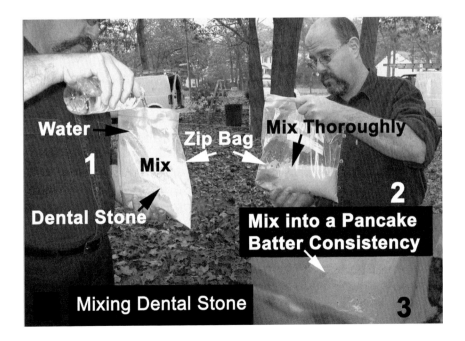

Figure 1.49b Dental stone mixing process.

Figure 1.49c   Pouring casting material into impression.

Figure 1.49d   Allow cast to harden.

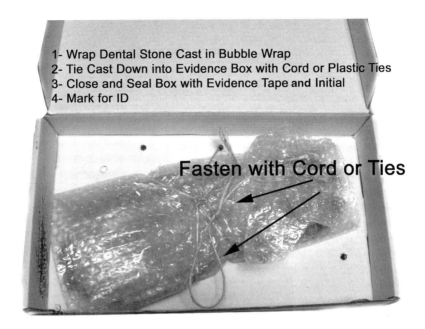

Figure 1.50a   After hardening, remove cast from impression site. Do not clean. Place bubble wrap or other packing material around cast, and tape. Secure in box to avoid breakage during transit.

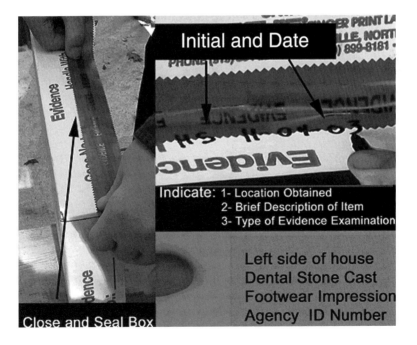

Figure 1.50b   Seal and mark box for identification.

Figure 1.51a Collect glass standard.

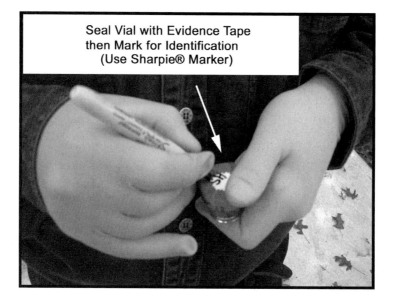

Figure 1.51b Seal glass standard in vial.

Figure 1.52 Collect botanical standards.

Figure 1.53a Collect soil specimens.

Releasing the Crime Scene

Prior to releasing the crime scene, review and complete notes.

Complete rough sketches of the location and of any relevant evidence (see Figures 154a–c). Keep a clear and concise notebook. Each sketch should have a key, a legend, and a notation of north. Note if to scale or not.

Figure 1.53b   Package soil specimens.

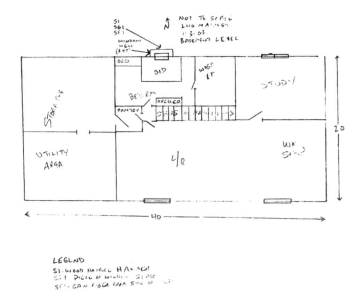

Figure 1.54a   Rough sketch of inside of basement.

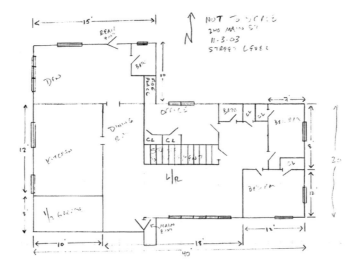

Figure 1.54b   Rough sketch of inside of top floor.

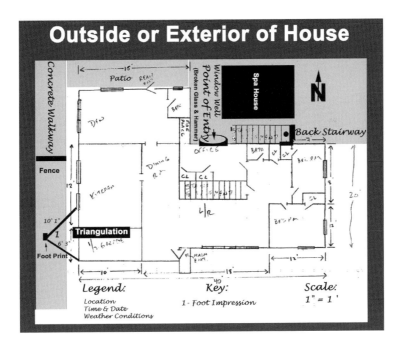

Figure 1.54c   Rough perspective drawing of inside and outside of premises.

Burglary Recap Sheet :Circle - Check - Write

Case No._____03-1234_____ Date__11/3/03__ Time__1230Hr Arrival__

Location_____240 Abbey St_____

Weather___Damp and Cloudy___

Reporting Party_____Mr. Smith_____ Owner Yes or No

Point of Entry____Basement window well rear____

Point of Exit_____Front Door_____

Security Devices Working_____N/a None present_____

Devices Defeated Yes or No / Explain:_____N/a_____

Damage to Property Yes or No   Description_____

__Broken Basement window_____

Fingerprints Recovered Yes or No Type: Latent □ Patent □ Plastic □
No. of Prints Recovered___1___ Process: Dusted Fumed Other_____
Items Sent to Laboratory for Fingerprint Processing (Yes) or No

Biological Evidence Recovered: Blood Salvia   Other_____
Description_Blood Possibly on Hammer_____

Trace Evidence Recovered: Hairs/Fibers___✓___   Paint_____
Glass_____   Soil_____   Other_____
Description_____On broken glass pane_____

Impression Evidence Recovered: Tool Marks Footwear Tire   Other

Description__Impression in mud photographed and cast__
_____with dental stone_____

Standartds or Knowns Collected Yes or No
_____Glass, Soil and Vegetation_____

Safeguarding Officer___P.O. Thamos Johnson, sh. 1278, 10 Pct.__
Crime Scene Examiner_____Det. H. Sherman, Det. , CSPU_____
Investigating Officer___Det. TB Johnson, Burglary Sqd.___

Figure 1.55 A prepared burglary worksheet.

In order to ascertain that all the necessary information has been recorded, prepare the appropriate worksheet before releasing the crime scene (see Appendix B for the appropriate blank form; Figure 1.55 is a completed example).

After conferring with the assigned investigator and prosecutor, release the crime scene and deliver all items of evidence to the laboratory. Remember: A search warrant may be needed to reenter and process a crime scene once the scene has been released.

Processing the Scene of a Homicide

2

The scene of a homicide is perhaps the most unnerving and challenging that a crime scene examiner (CSE) will be called upon to process. However, if one remembers that the well-established principles and procedures applicable to the processing of all crime scenes are also followed at the scenes of homicides, the task at hand will be less daunting.

In homicide cases, however, the following additional principles and conditions should be observed:

The body should not be touched or moved until examined by the medical examiner.

In appropriate cases, paper bags should be placed over the hands of the deceased to preserve trace evidence that may be on the deceased's hands or under the fingernails. Carefully note, document, and record:

Condition of the body
Degree of decomposition
Insect or animal activity
Blood and its proximity to the body
Blood spatter patterns
Type of wounds, e.g., stab wounds, bullet holes, lacerations, bruising, bullet entry and exit holes, or unusual wounds such as bite marks or tool marks
Position of ligatures
Knots tied with restraints or ligatures
Stage and degree of rigor mortis and lividity
Body temperature
Objects that may have been used to cause the wounds or death, or inserted into the body
Unusual or out of place objects in the area.

After the deceased is examined by the medical examiner and moved, inspect the area that is under the body for additional evidence.

It is important for the CSE to ascertain whether:

The body, weapons, or any other item was moved before the CSE's arrival;
Blood paths or trails or foot impressions were made after the crime was discovered;
Foreign or unusual objects were brought into the scene after its discovery; and,
Doors or windows were closed, open, locked, broken, or in operable condition.

Processing a Homicide

Discuss the crime scene and the status of the investigation with the first officer on the scene and the investigating officer(s) present at the scene.

Examine the general area; do a quick but careful and thorough walk-through of the suspected scene, making sure to not disturb anything prior to documentation of the scene and any potential physical evidence (PE) (see Figure 2.1).

After a walk-through of the interior is complete, make a plan to search and process the crime scene (CS) to find, document, collect, package, and safeguard all potential PE present (see Figures 2.2 to 2.24). Collect the most fragile evidence first:

Fingerprints (latent and patent)
Hairs and fibers (strands)
Pieces of textiles
Paint traces (smears, chips)
Glass (large and tiny fragments)
Soil (deposits or clumps)
Blood (wet or dry stains and stain patterns)
Tool marks
Tools
Damage and signs of forced entry
Footwear evidence

Photographing and Searching the Crime Scene

Photograph the overall exterior of the premises while looking for items of evidence and signs of damage to property and areas, e.g., broken windows, or bypassed or defeated alarms and security devices (see Figures 2.3 to 2.23).

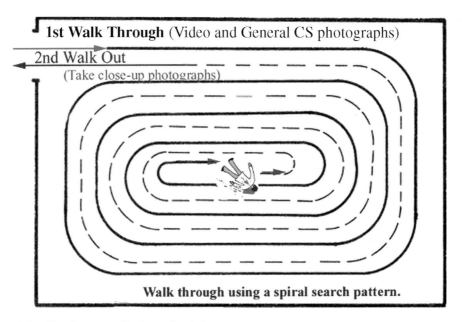

Figure 2.1   Conduct a walk-through of the crime scene.

Figure 2.2 Establish a search plan.

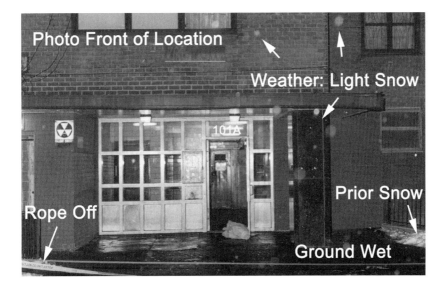

Figure 2.3 Photograph the front of the location, noting the time, date, address of location, lighting, and weather conditions. Establish the crime scene; secure it by roping off its area, and prevent unauthorized entry.

Figure 2.4 Before entering a crime scene, make certain to put on your personnel investigative protection equipment (PIPE).

Figure 2.5 Continue search.

Figure 2.6   Search the overall area.

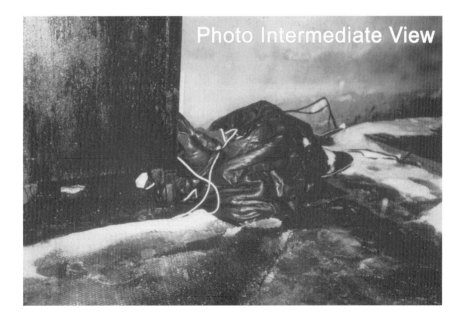

Figure 2.7   Carefully approach the suspected scene of crime.

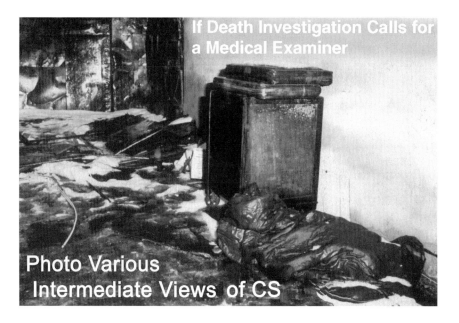

Figure 2.8 Document the scene of the crime. Take intermediate views of the crime scene. Too many photographs are better than too few.

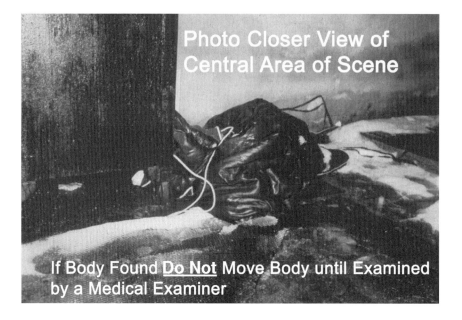

Figure 2.9 Take close-up views of the crime scene.

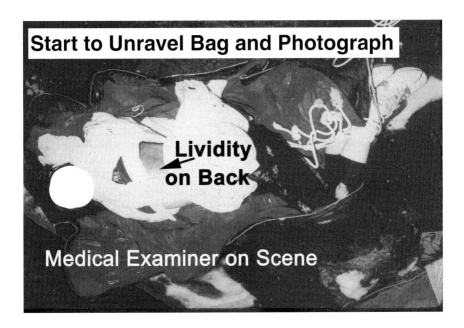

Figure 2.10 Document all aspects of the medical examiner's report of the victim.

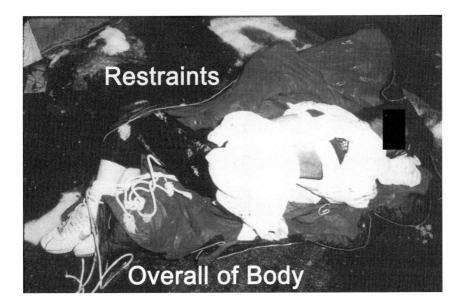

Figure 2.11 Note presence of lividity and decomposition, as well as the body's condition and position.

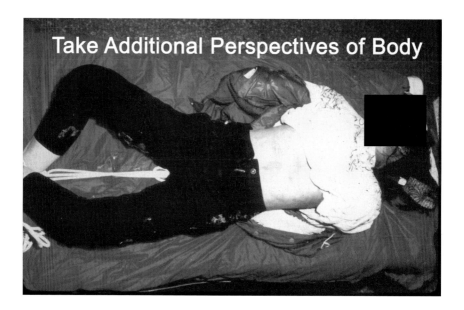

Figure 2.12 Document restraints, ligatures, wounds.

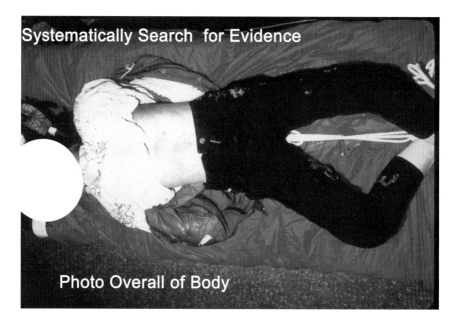

Figure 2.13 Search for any trace evidence methodically in conjunction with the medical examiner.

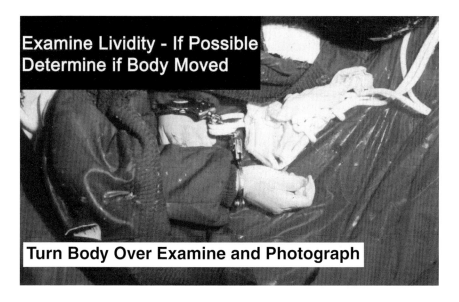

Figure 2.14 Turn the body over; photograph, examine, and rephotograph.

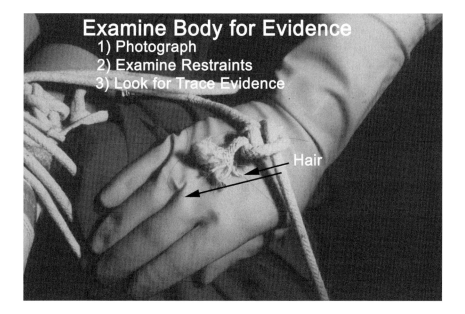

Figure 2.15 Document the presence of knots.

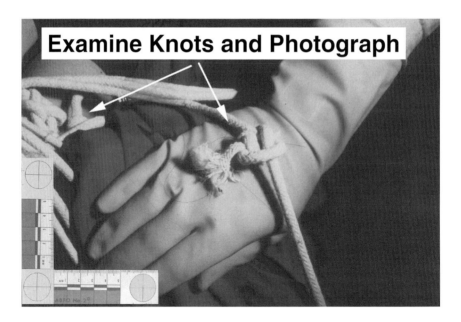

Figure 2.16   Examine knots, but do not untie them; keep them in their original configuration.

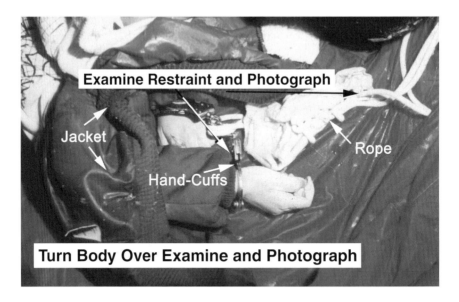

Figure 2.17   Carefully document and examine how the victim was restrained. Examine all ligatures and restraints for trace evidence.

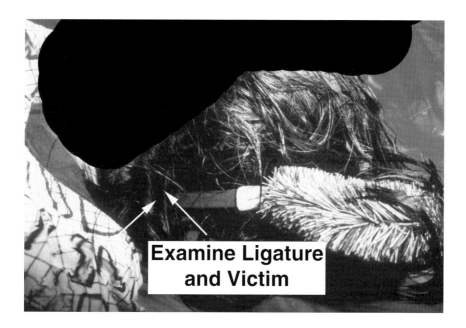

Figure 2.18   Examine and document ligature.

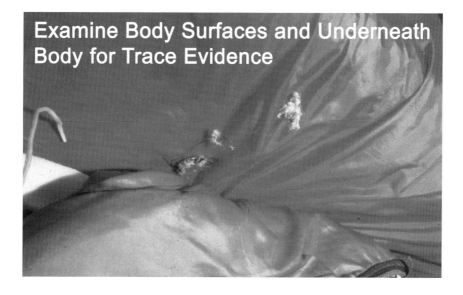

Figure 2.19   Examine all surfaces around and under the body.

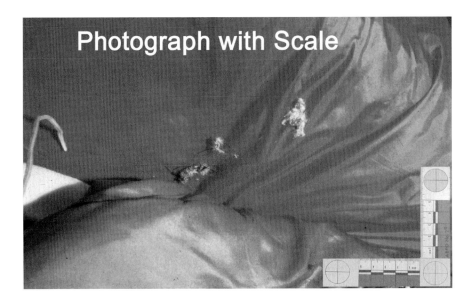

Figure 2.20 Take photographs with and without scales.

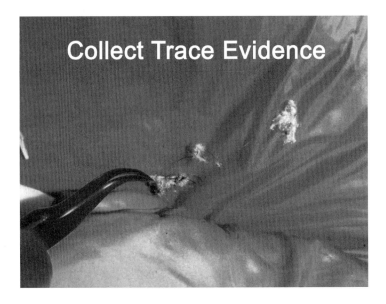

Figure 2.21 Document, collect, and package any trace evidence after a viewing and conference with the medical examiner.

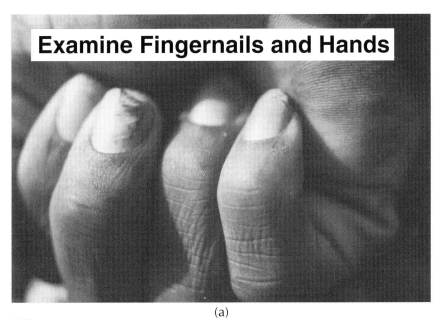

(a)

Figure 2.22a

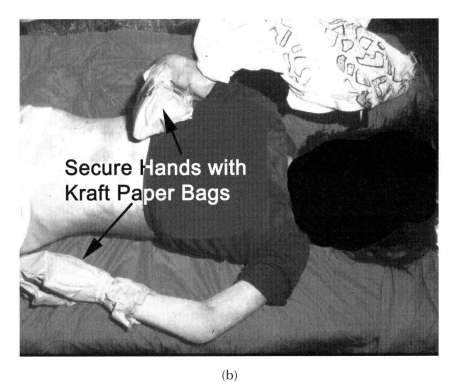

(b)

Figure 2.22b Secure any trace evidence on the victim's body; bag the hands.

Figure 2.23   Check all exits and entrances. Examine locks, doors, windows. Note their condition and whether mechanisms are engaged.

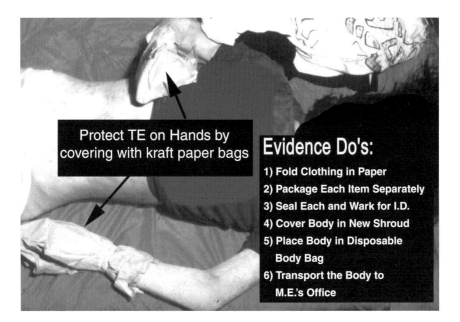

Figure 2.24   Collect all items of physical evidence and package and transport them to the appropriate facility. Always have an open dialogue with the medical examiner and learn the examiner's policies regarding packaging and transportation of the deceased.

Carefully search for and record any items of physical evidence. Look for misplaced items, such as clothing, e.g., hats, and impression evidence such as tool marks, footwear impressions, and fingerprints.

In homicide investigations it is particularly important to collect, document, record, and note all the information possible concerning the following conditions:

Degree of decomposition and overall condition of the body
Stage and degree of rigor mortis and lividity
Insect or animal activity (Figures 2.25 to 2.35)
Blood spatter patterns; blood and its distances from the body (Figures 2.36 to 2.53)
Position and type of ligatures
Type of restraints and knots tied with restraints (Figures 2.54 to 2.61)
Unusual wounds, e.g., bite marks, tool marks (Figures 2.62 to 2.64)
Gunshot residues (Figures 2.65 to 2.69)
Type of wounds, e.g., stab wounds, bullet holes, lacerations, bruising bullet entry, exit
    holes (Figures 2.70 to 2.74)
Body temperature
Unusual objects in the area that may have been used to cause the wounds or death
Drowning (Figure 2.87) or
Poisoning (Figure 2.88)

After the deceased is examined by the medical examiner and moved, inspect the area beneath the body for additional evidence (Figures 2.19 to 2.21).

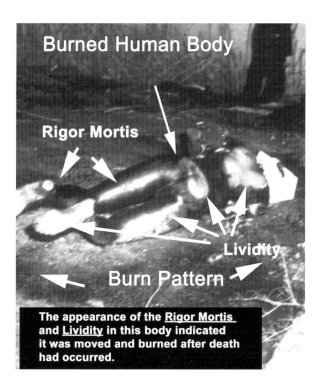

Figure 2.25

Figure 2.26

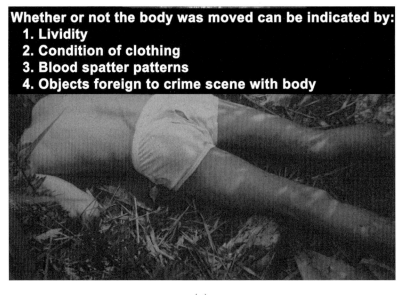

(a)

Figure 2.27a

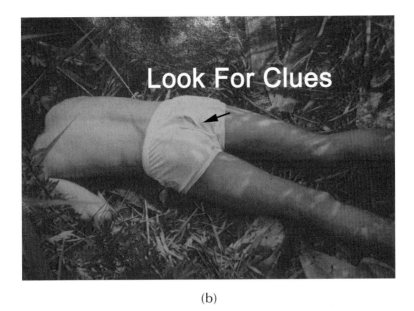

(b)

Figure 2.27b   Examine and document condition of stains or pattern evidence.

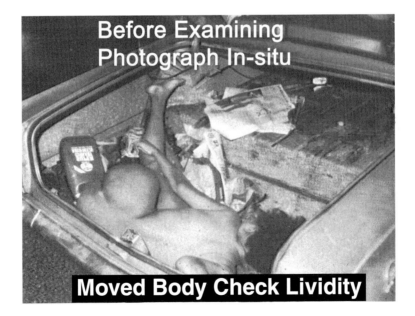

Figure 2.28   Always photograph the victim and surrounding area prior to handling or moving anything.

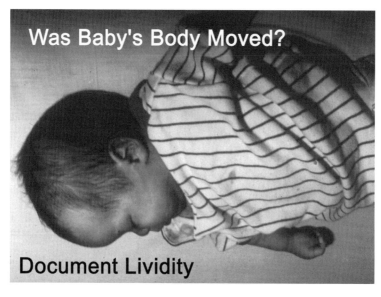

(a)

Figure 2.29a   Lividity (livor mortis) is the settling of solids in the blood to their lowest point. This occurs after death.

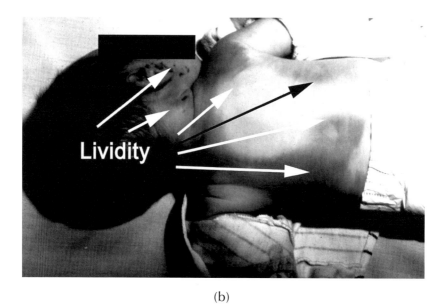

(b)

Figure 2.29b   Soon after death lividity sets in. After a period of time, it becomes "fixed" and cannot shift with movement of the body.

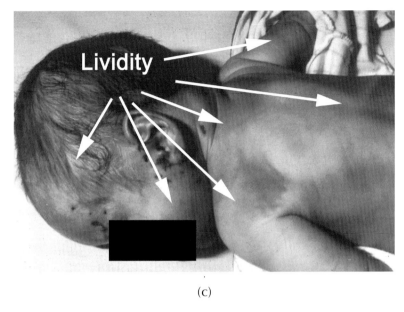

(c)

Figure 2.29c Clothing, sheets, and anything else beneath the deceased can affect the lividities' position and ultimate settling.

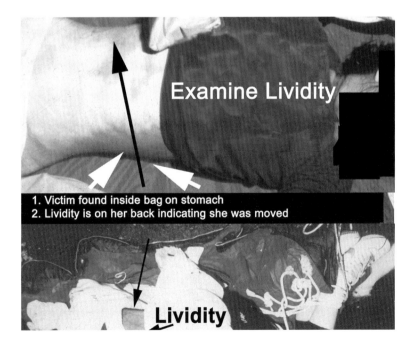

Figure 2.30 Examine lividity on the victim's back.

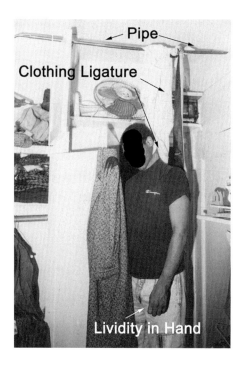

Figure 2.31   The hand shown is the lowest point of the deceased. Be sure not to untie ligatures, but cut far away from the knot(s).

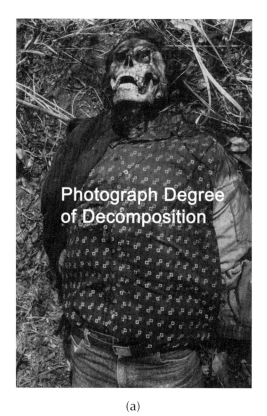

(a)

Figure 2.32a   Animals caused the postmortem damage to the deceased's face.

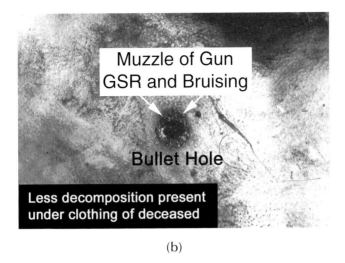

(b)

Figure 2.32b Same victim as Figure 2.32a, with clothing covering the bullet hole.

(a)

Figure 2.33a Collect flora samples and soil samples where appropriate.

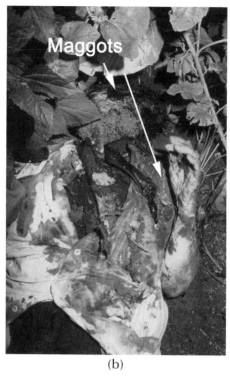

(b)

Figure 2.33b Bag the deceased's hands. Take multiple entomological samples. Cease life in some samples, but make sure you don't destroy the sample.

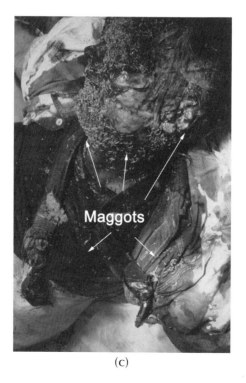

(c)

Figure 2.33c Flies lay eggs in eyes, ears, nose, mouth, and at trauma sites where blood is present.

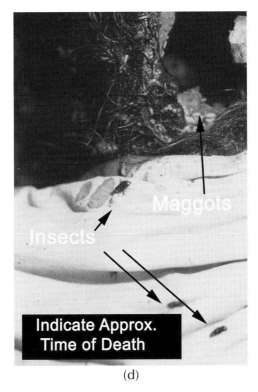

(d)

Figure 2.33d Sample type and size can often be an indicator of the time of death as well as the location. This information can provide a time range for when the incident occurred.

(e)

Figure 2.33e The interior of the skull allows for partial preservation from the elements.

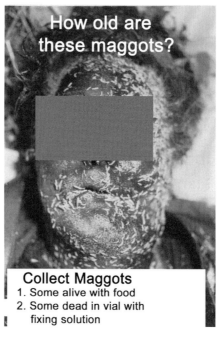

(a)

Figure 2.34a

1. Collect a few of each type of
   insect and insect larvae.
2. Save some alive in container
   with meat, or other growing medium.
3. Place some in a glass vial with
   fixing fluid.

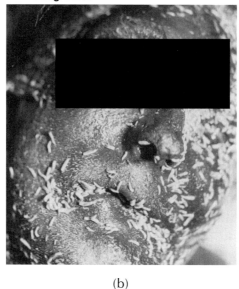

(b)

Figure 2.34b   Document the location of collection. Collect a variety of different sizes, shapes, and colors.

(c)

Figure 2.34c   Adult fly, after being allowed to mature from a maggot.

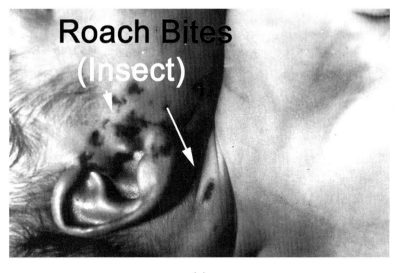

(a)

Figure 2.35a   Post Mortem Artifact (PMA) initially appeared to be wounds inflicted by a resident of the premise.

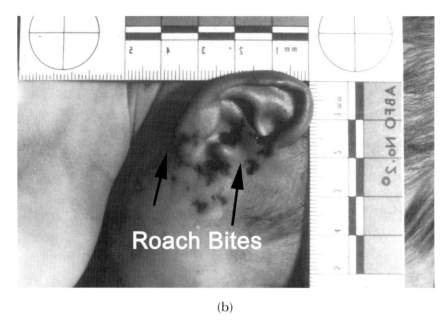

(b)

Figure 2.35b   Roach bites often are close to ears and the surrounding area.

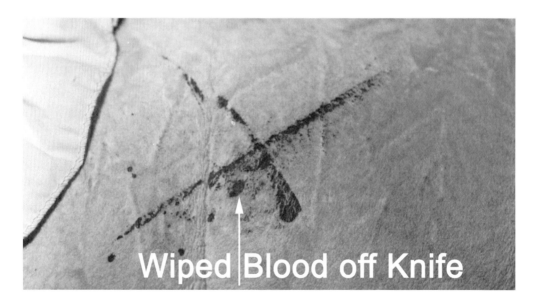

Figure 2.36   Look for a possible pattern left by the assailant or weapon.

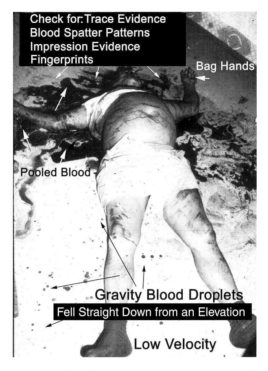

Figure 2.37 It is important to take photos showing the location of the evidence in addition to exclusively close-up photos.

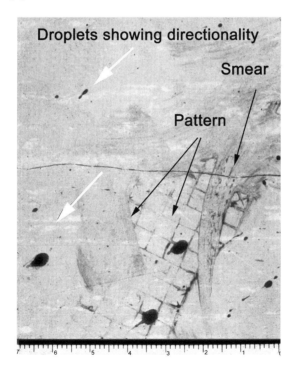

Figure 2.38 The morphology of the evidence is often as critical as the sample itself.

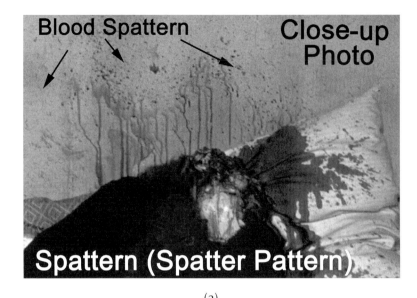

(a)

Figure 2.39a   Photograph the spattern with the plane of the film parallel to the object.

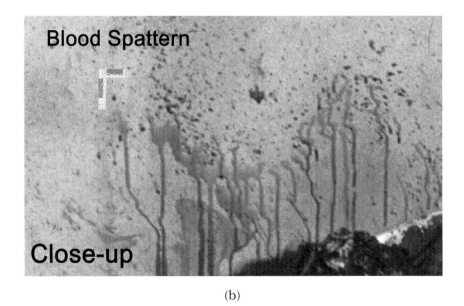

(b)

Figure 2.39b   Take close-up photographs with and without a readily reproducable scale.

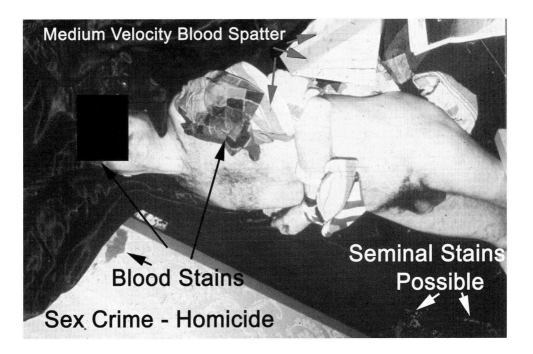

Figure 2.40 Several types of biological samples may be required. Samples may be cut from an object or swabbed. Allow wet samples to air dry to preserve their integrity.

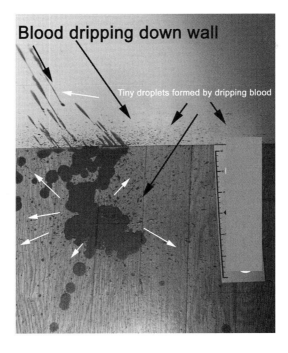

Figure 2.41 Secondary spatter pattern caused by dripping into pool of blood.

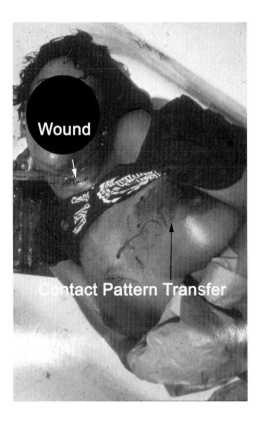

Figure 2.42 Bloody footwear impression on the deceased's chest.
Note: Hands are bagged.

Figure 2.43 Note the downward flow towards the mud made by the wound.

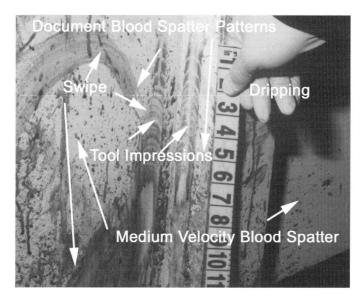

Figure 2.44   Multiple patterns in a small area show struggle and movement of the victim.

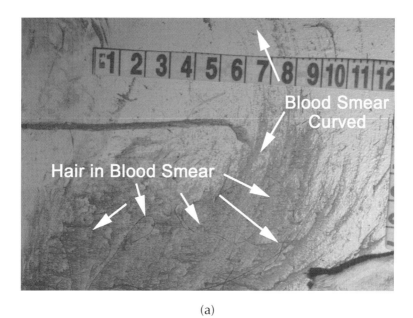

(a)

Figure 2.45a   Photograph, measure, and, if possible, remove the pattern on the piece of substrate.

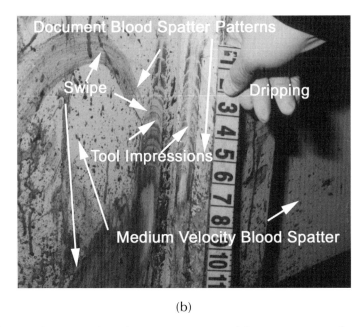

(b)

Figure 2.45b Much work and analysis can occur in a laboratory setting that is not possible at the scene.

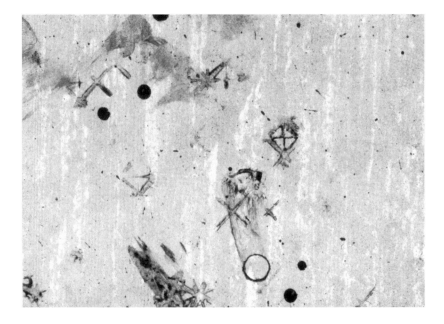

Figure 2.46 Chemicals, sprays, and an alternate light source can enhance the pattern seen here. Proper documentation and collection techniques allow the possibility of additional procedures.

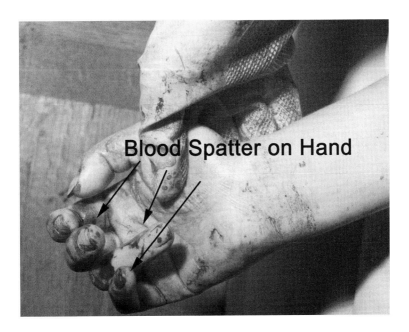

Figure 2.47 The spatter pattern on the deceased is preserved during examination by placing paper bags on the deceased's hands.

Figure 2.48 Floor tiles can be readily cut to retain samples' morphology. Substrate removal can be important during analysis.

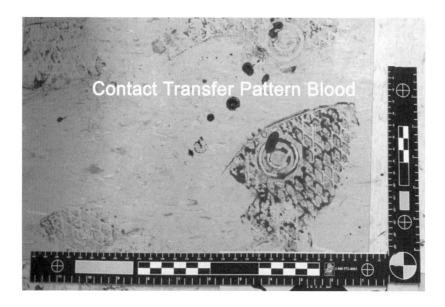

Figure 2.49   Fill film frame and place scale outside of pattern area.

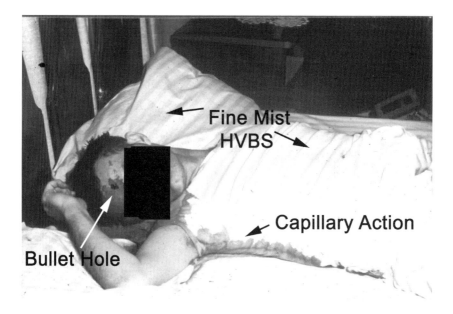

Figure 2.50   Document the stain size and type. Avoid commingling of samples on the same substrate or item.

Figure 2.51   Commonly referred to as "ghosting."

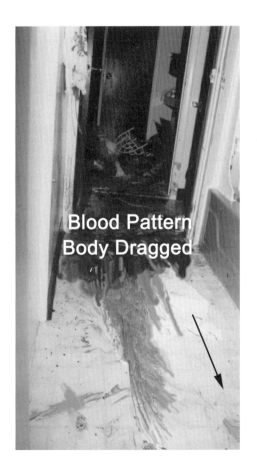

Figure 2.52

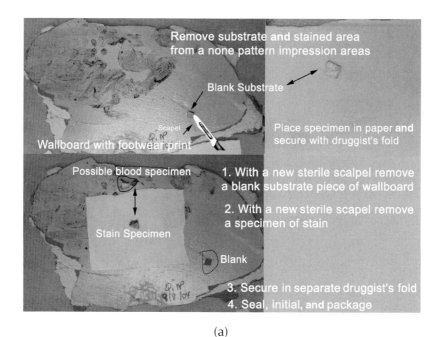

(a)

Figure 2.53a Remove blank substrate of wallboard and secure in a paper fold. Use a new sterile scalpel to remove specimen.

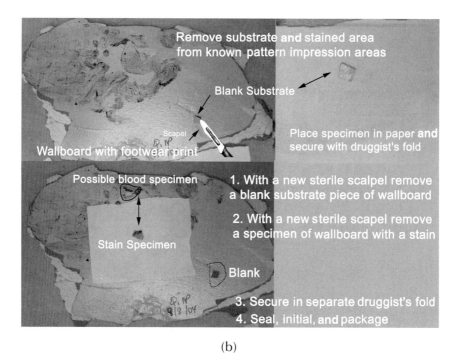

(b)

Figure 2.53b Remove a stained area of wallboard with a new sterile scalpel and secure in a paper fold. Store blank and stain specimens in a cool environment.

(a)

Figure 2.54a   Cut ligature away from knots. Do not untie ligatures.

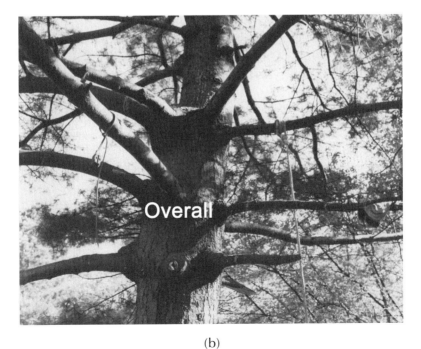

(b)

Figure 2.54b   Remove the tree limb to maintain the integrity of the knots.

(c)

Figure 2.54c

(d)

Figure 2.54d   This close-up shows the apex of the knot's location.

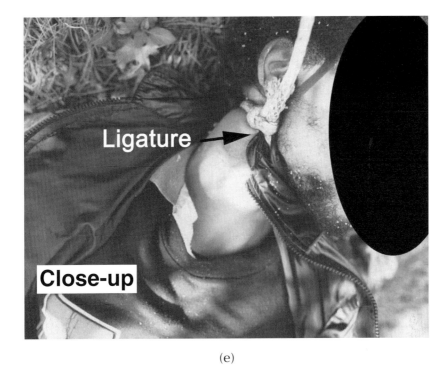

(e)

Figure 2.54e   Note the jacket placed beneath the knot.

(f)

Figure 2.54f

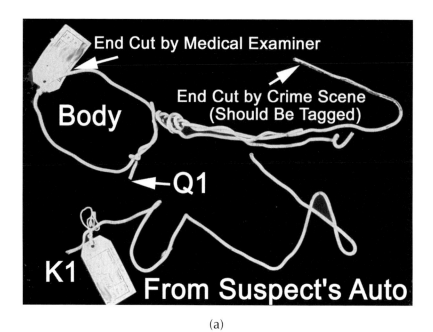

(a)

Figure 2.55a   Q-Questioned rope from scene.
K-Known sample from suspect's auto.

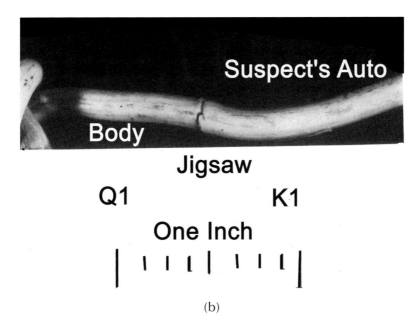

(b)

Figure 2.55b Do not place Questioned and Known samples in close proximity at the scene. Cross contamination is possible.

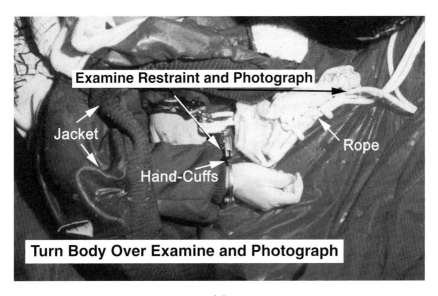

(a)

Figure 2.56a

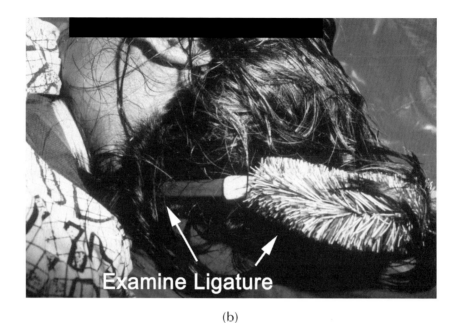

(b)

Figure 2.56b Examine ligature for trace, knots, and type of material, e.g. wire, rope.

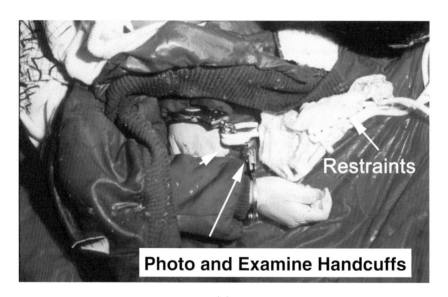

(c)

Figure 2.56c Be sure to examine restraints for possible trace evidence.

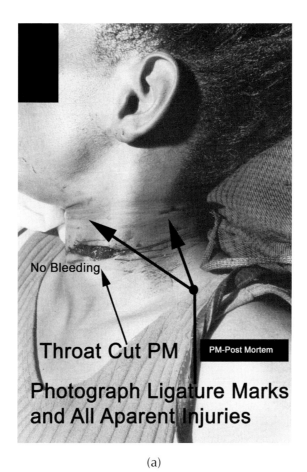

(a)

Figure 2.57a

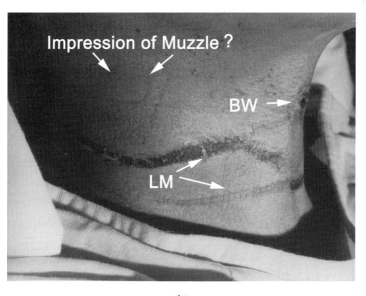

(b)

Figure 2.57b

Figure 2.58 Ligature cuts and ends are secured for future analysis—only by the medical examiner.

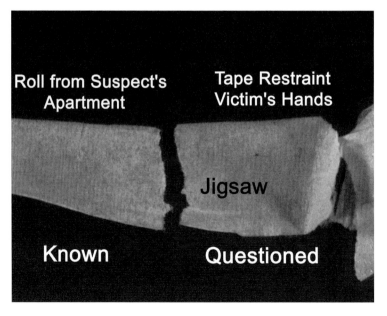

Figure 2.59 Document and be careful to not damage ends. Do not attempt to perform a jigsaw match without sufficient macro photography.

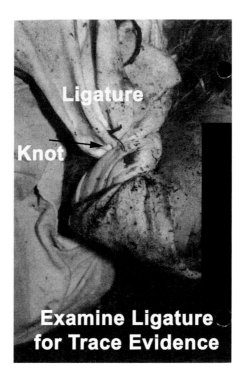

Figure 2.60

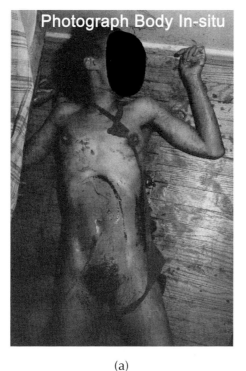

(a)

Figure 2.61a Mechanical ligature around neck. Leave it in place unless otherwise advised by the medical examiner.

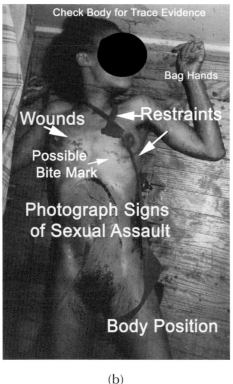

(b)

Figure 2.61b

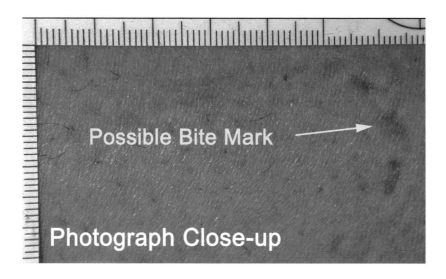

Figure 2.62 Vary lighting techniques. Remember to fill film frame, use a scale, and keep the camera plane parallel to the object to prevent distortion.

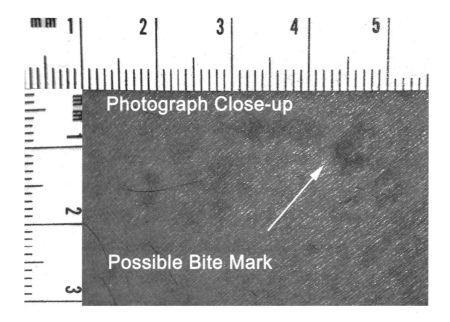

Figure 2.63 Secure the area of possible bite to be swabbed for DNA. Confer with the medical examiner for possibly swabbing the area prior to transporting deceased to the morgue.

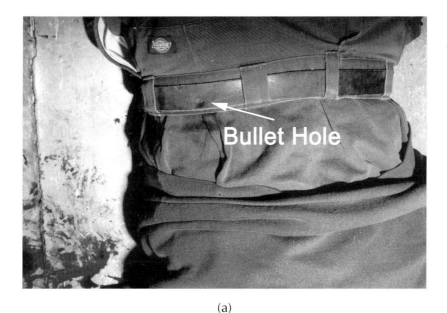

(a)

Figure 2.64a Positionality of the bullet hole and the object need to be documented prior to disturbing the evidence.

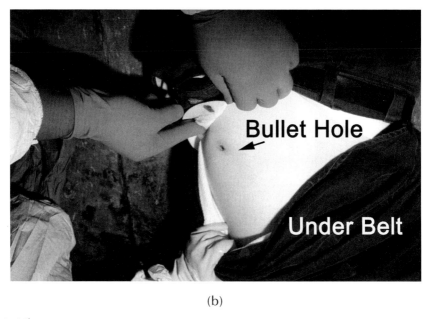

(b)

Figure 2.64b   The bullet hole in the clothing will be compared to the bullet hole in the body to determine if clothing positionality is consistent with other information.

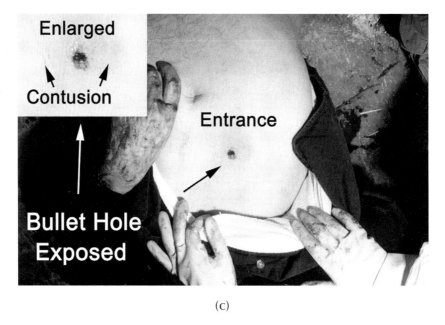

(c)

Figure 2.64c   Note if contusions or stippling is present adjacent to the bullet hole.

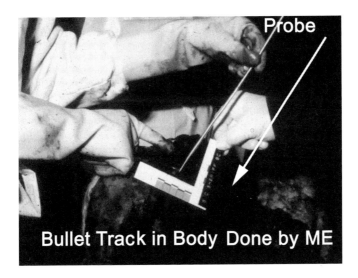

Figure 2.65 Determine the angle between the deceased and the shooter.

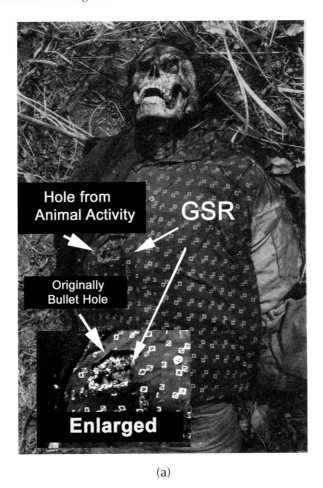

(a)

Figure 2.66a Be aware of potential post mortem artifact (PMA) changes between the time of occurrence and the discovery of the victim.

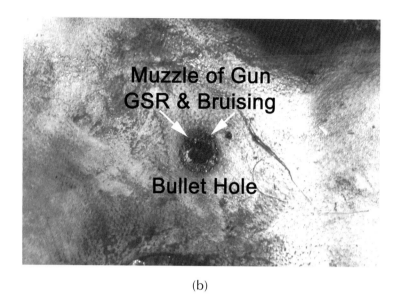

(b)

Figure 2.66b

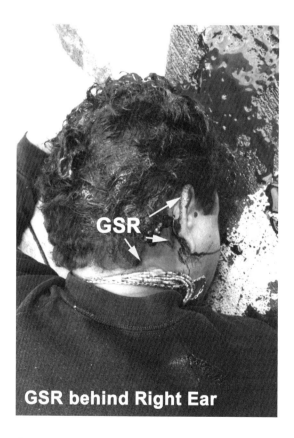

Figure 2.67 GSR on the surrounding area shows the proximity of the shooter to the deceased. The actual weapon and ammunition are required to establish an accurate distance range.

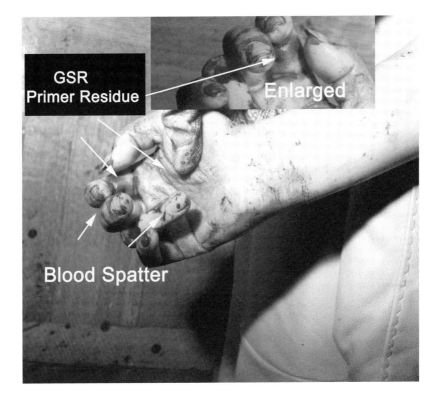

Figure 2.68   Ensure hands are bagged to preserve valuable trace evidence (TE).

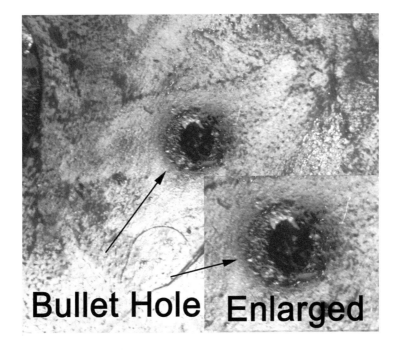

Figure 2.69   Stippling and muzzle impression show proximity of muzzle-to-wound range.

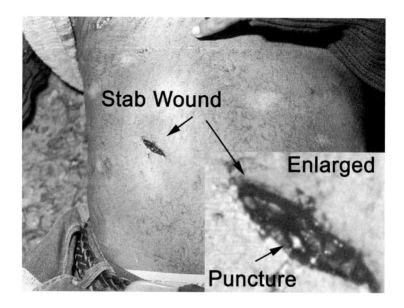

Figure 2.70   Lack of blood shows potential post mortem infliction of wound.

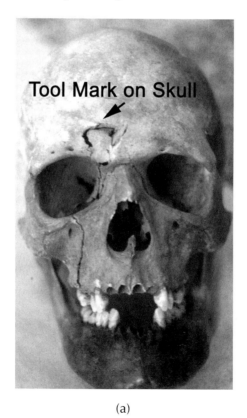

(a)

Figure 2.71a   Blunt object struck the victim above the eye.

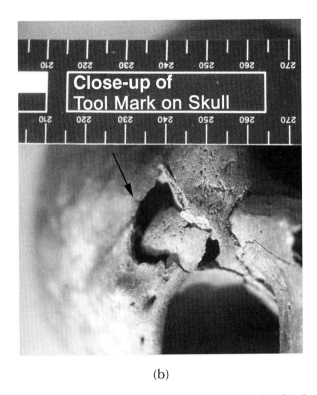

(b)

Figure 2.71b Be sure to adjust the aperture setting to allow for depth of field changes of close-up photos.

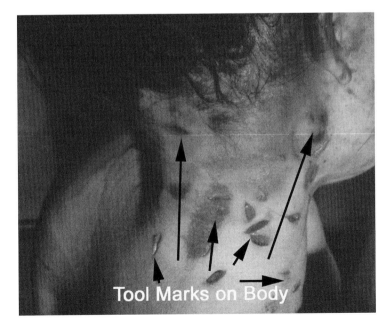

Figure 2.72 Skin possesses elasticity. Usually one can include or exclude an object that may have caused the injury. Never place a suspected weapon or object close to the wound. Avoid possible transference of trace evidence between the object and the wound.

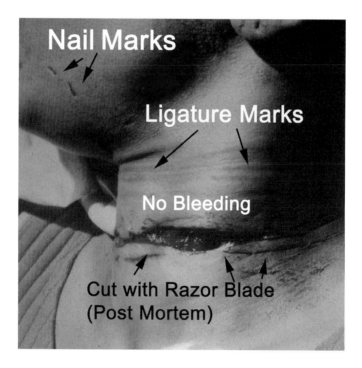

Figure 2.73 Be cognizant of a staged crime scene, especially involving multiple types of wounds sustained by the deceased.

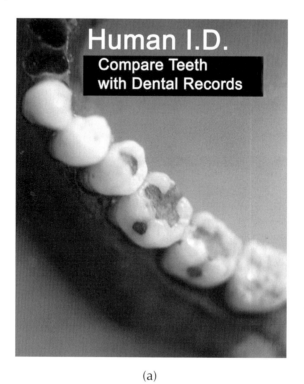

(a)

Figure 2.74a A forensic odontologist can compare X-rays (known Information) to the deceased's (Questioned Object) to confirm identity.

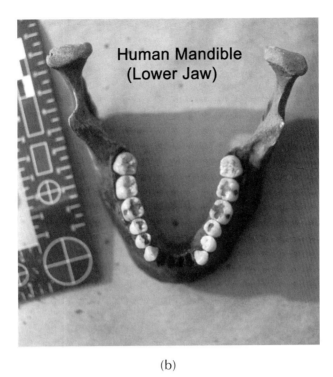

(b)

Figure 2.74b The object being photographed must be in focus for comparison rather than the ruler or readily reproducible scale.

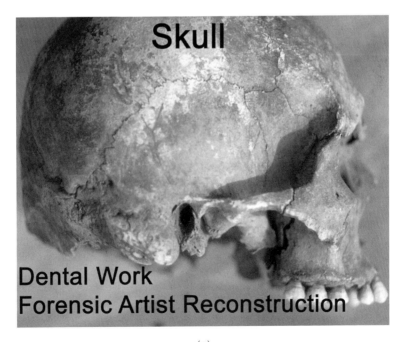

(c)

Figure 2.74c The side view of the skull is used for dental identification and artist reconstruction.

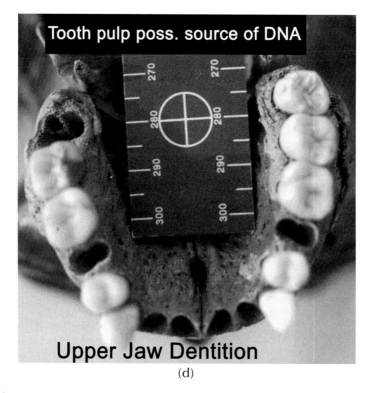

(d)

Figure 2.74d The areas beneath the toothline are also useful if teeth are not present. X-rays taken by the dentist also show the area beneath the teeth.

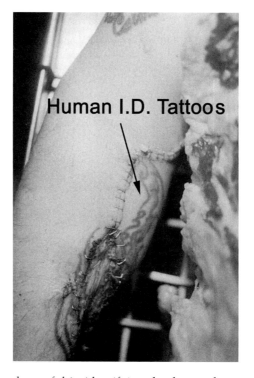

Figure 2.75 Tattoos can be useful in identifying the deceased.

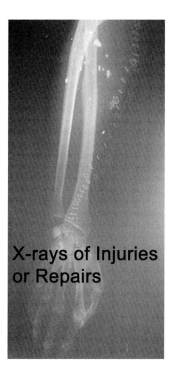

Figure 2.76 Be aware of medical intervention when interpreting objects observed in X-rays.

Figure 2.77 A site safety plan and search plan must be discussed before exhuming a victim.

In cases where human remains have been buried, the area should be processed as an archaeological site under the supervision of a forensic archaeologist (see Figures 2.78 to 2.86).

In order to ascertain that all the necessary information has been recorded, prepare the appropriate review worksheets and forms before releasing the crime scene (see Appendix E and the Crime Scene Review Sheet for appropriate blank forms and for a homicide review form, page 396).

Figure 2.78 Grid lines must be established and documented prior to starting the search.

Figure 2.79 The utmost caution must be used to search to prevent damaging an underground object.

Figure 2.80 Hand tools will prevent damaging the object and also minimizes the chance of overlooking any small items.

Figure 2.81 Measure the items from two fixed points (the vertical and horizontal grid lines).

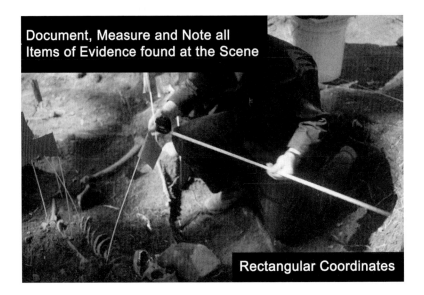

Document, Measure and Note all Items of Evidence found at the Scene

Rectangular Coordinates

Figure 2.82

1. Sieve all soil placed in buckets
2. Start with course sieves working down to fine mesh sieves
3. Remove any physical evidence

Sieve

Figure 2.83

Figure 2.84 Insect larvae recovered during the exhumation.

Figure 2.85

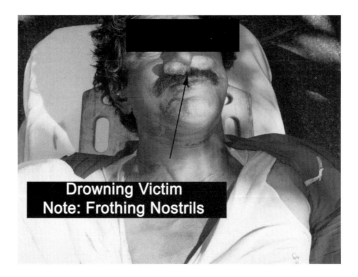

Figure 2.86 Frothing is common in drownings and asphyxiation deaths.

Figure 2.87 The deceased's mouth and lips were burnt by caustic fluid.

Homicide Recap Sheet :*Circle - Check - Write*

Case No.___03-1234___ Date___11/3/03___ Time___1230Hr Arrival___
Location_____240 Abbey St_____
Weather___Damp and Cloudy_____
Reporting Party_____Mr. Smith_____ Owner Yes or No
Point of Entry____Basement window well rear_____
Point of Exit_____Front Door_____
Security Devices Working_____N/a None present_____
Devices Defeated Yes or No / Explain:_____N/a_____
Damage to Property Yes or No   Description_____

___Broken Basement window_____

Fingerprints Recovered Yes or No Type: Latent □ Patent □ Plastic □
No. of Prints Recovered___1___ Process: Dusted Fumed Other_____
Items Sent to Laboratory for Fingerprint Processing   Yes   or   No

Biological Evidence Recovered: Blood Salvia   Other_____
Description Blood Possibly on Hammer

Trace Evidence Recovered: Hairs/Fibers ✓   Paint_____
Glass_____ Soil_____ Other_____
Description _____On broken glass pane_____

Impression Evidence Recovered: Tool Marks Footwear Tire   Other
Description Impression in mud photographed and cast
                with dental stone

Standartds or Knowns Collected Yes or No
                Glass, Soil and Vegetation

Safeguarding Officer____P.O. Thamos Johnson, sh. 1278, 10 Pct.__
Crime Scene Examiner_____Det. H. Sherman, Det. , CSPU_____
Investigating Officer____Det. TB Johnson, Burglary Sqd._____

Figure 2.88   Completed recap sheet

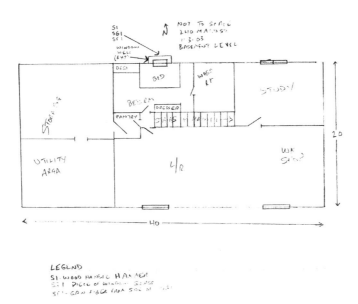

Figure 2.89   Rough sketch note "not to scale," compass points, measurements and legend utilized.

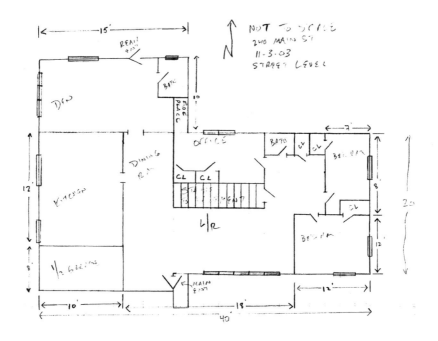

Figure 2.90 Be sure to include preparer's name, date, address, and if to scale or not.

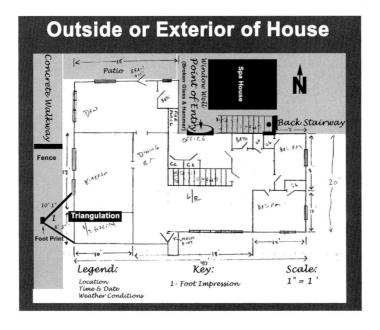

Figure 2.91 Exterior of premise, with evidence included, drawn to scale.

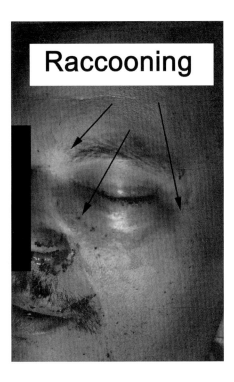

Figure 2.92 Basal skull fracture caused by bullet passing behind deceased's eyes. Resembles a black eye or a "shiner."

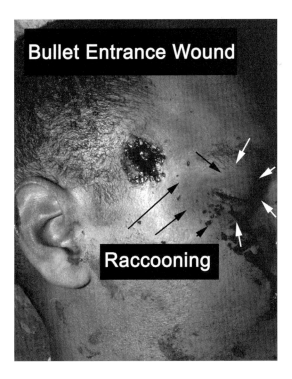

Figure 2.93 Note the proximity of the entry wound to the deceased's eye.

Crime Scene Review Sheet

Homicide Investigation

Date _____ Time _____

Case #_____

CSE _____

Assistant _____

Investigator

Assigned _____

First   Officer   at   the

Scene_____

Occurrence

Location_____

Points   of

Entry/Exit_____

Date _____ Time _____

Weather Condition _____

Date   and   Time   of

Occurrence_____

Victim

No._____

Address

_____

Male   Female   Age _____   Race _____   Eye Color _____   Hair Color _____

Height _____

Weight _____

Body at Scene or Removed To _____

Weapon Used?   Yes   No   If yes,

Type?_____

Ballistics Evidence/Weapon

Weapon: Handgun   Knife   Rifle   Shotgun   Other _____

Discharged Bullets _____   Discharged Shells _____

Cartridges_____

Weapon Safeguarded _____

Processed for Fingerprints _____

Fingerprint Evidence

Latent _____ Patent _____

Plastic_____

Process: Dusted _____   Fumed _____   Chemical _____

Elimination Prints_____Yes   No

Location/Item

Obtained

_____

DNA/Serology Evidence

Blood _____ Semen _____ Other _____

Trace Evidence

Hair/Fibers _____ Glass _____ Paint _____ Soil _____
Other_____
Tape Lifts _____ Vacuum Sweepings _____
Other_____

Physical Evidence

Footprints _____ Tire Treads _____ Arson/Explosive _____ Tool Marks _____
Documents _____
Textile _____
Other

_____

Photographic/Video Evidence

No. _____
Description or Comment

_____
_____
_____
_____
_____
_____

Processing a Robbery Scene

3

The crime of robbery can be defined as the taking of property from a person under the threat of force. The force can be either real, such as pointing a gun at someone, or implied, as in the threat "If you don't give me all your money, I'll shoot you!" A weapon may or may not be involved. There are five categories of robbery:

Commercial premises, e.g., banks, stores, hotels
Private residences, i.e., home invasions
Hijacking of cargo
Carjacking, i.e., forcibly taking an automobile from an individual;
Individuals, e.g., purse snatchings, muggings

Remembering that each crime is unique, the crime scene examiner (CSE) must, for each incident of robbery:

Discuss the crime scene with the first officer on the scene.
Review the status of the investigation with the investigating officer(s) present at the scene.
Elicit available information about the number of perpetrators and their actions, including their methods and routes;
Learn everything possible about each assailant's action(s).
Find out whether a weapon or weapons were used.
Acquire all known facts concerning the way in which the robbery occurred (modus operandi and attempt to determine whether this is part of a pattern).
Ascertain whether anyone was injured during the commission of the robbery.
Determine whether any items of potential evidence were found or collected prior to your arrival.

The CSE must be open minded, objective, and alert to discover minute details:

Survey the general area; do a quick, careful walk-through of the suspected scene making sure to not disturb anything prior to documentation of the scene and any potential physical evidence (PE).
Note pertinent data, e.g., time, date, location.

Figure 3.1

Establish a crime scene. Larger is better. The scene can always be made smaller once it is determined not to contain any evidence.

Carefully search the suspected crime scene and vehicle(s).

Photograph the overall outside location, while looking for items of evidence and signs of damage to property and areas, e.g., broken windows; or bypassed or defeated alarms and security devices (see Figures 3.1 to 3.20).

Be sure not to include any equipment brought into the scene. Also, do not photograph responders inside the scene.

Figure 3.2

Figure 3.3   Photograph address of premise, or adjacent structure.

Figure 3.4   Show areas to which potential witnesses may have access.

Figure 3.5   Different views and perspectives should be captured.

Figure 3.6

Figure 3.7   Premise with adjacent place of business (potential witnesses or video surveillance should be sought).

Figure 3.8   Midrange photo of adjacent commercial establishment.

Figure 3.9   A "from-to" description can also be helpful (Camera facing east. Along south side of premise).

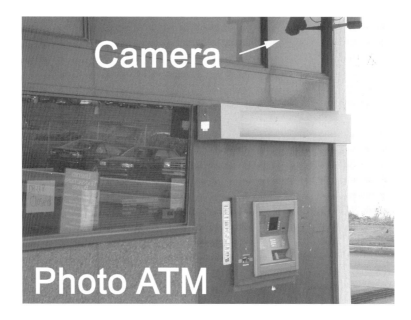

Figure 3.10   Document camera locations and, if possible, what views the cameras capture.

Figure 3.11   Security cameras, photographed showing a fixed-point perspective.

Figure 3.12   Show vehicle (or any other piece of evidence) juxtaposition to another fixed point.

Figure 3.13   Overall view of suspect vehicle, shown in proximity to the bank.

Figure 3.14   Document anomalies or other points of interest that appear out of place.

Figure 3.15 Vehicle and evidence shown in proximity to utility pole. Pole number is obtained and documented.

Figure 3.16 Car location documented (From:to description, with fixed point documented).

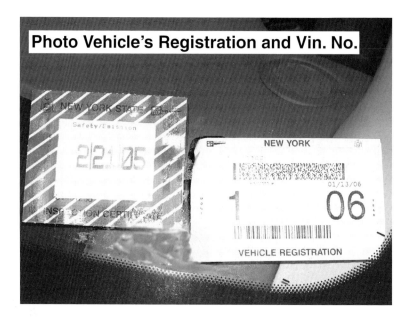

Figure 3.17 Registration and inspection stickers need to be documented and recorded.

Figure 3.18

Figure 3.19 Multiple views of the vehicle, showing premise involved.

Measure, note, and sketch any potential items of PE.
Look for items of PE such as clothing, ballistics evidence, trace evidence, impression
    evidence, and fingerprints (see Figures 3.22 to 3.34).
Photograph all items of evidence found at the crime scene before moving them.
Prepare a detailed photo log.
If appropriate, determine the points of entry and exit.
Attempt to establish a modus operandi.
Make rough sketches of the crime scene (see Figure 3.21).
Take detailed notes.
Note the time, date, weather, and all circumstances of the crime.

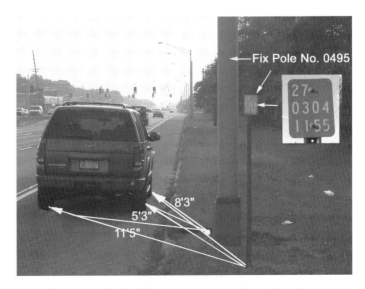

Figure 3.20 Triangulation method of documenting evidence location.

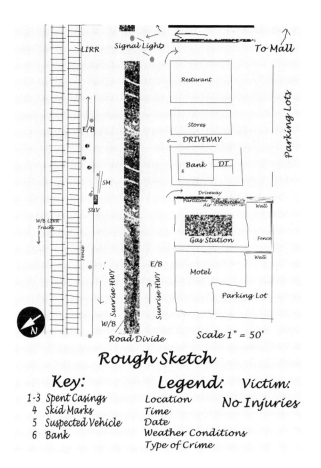

Rough Sketch

Key: Legend: Victim:
1-3 Spent Casings   Location   No Injuries
 4   Skid Marks   Time
 5   Suspected Vehicle Date
 6   Bank   Weather Conditions
                        Type of Crime

Figure 3.21

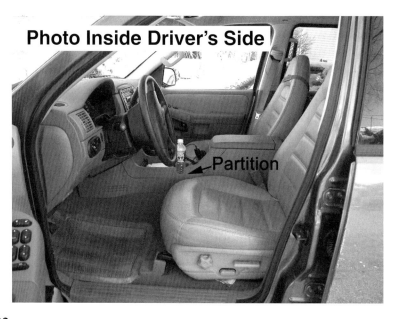

Figure 3.22

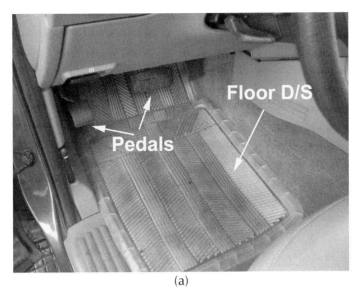

(a)

Figure 3.23a   Overall view of evidence recovery location.

Make certain to photograph and/or videotape:

The area where the crime occurred.
The time and date on which the crime occurred
The escape route
All evidence recovered
Signs of forcible entries
Recovered vehicles

Sketch and measure the position of relevant evidence. Collect, label, and package all evidence, such as:

Bank robbery notes
Impression evidence
Tire standards (see Figure 3.35)
Shoe impressions

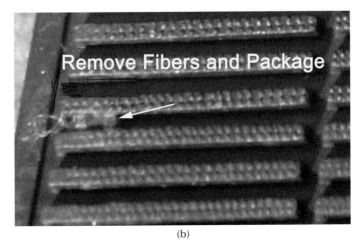

(b)

Figure 3.23b   Macro view of evidence, prior to the evidence recovery.

(c)

Figure 3.23c Midrange photo.

(d)

Figure 3.23d Photograph showing absence of evidence.

(a)

Figure 3.24a   A midrange or establishing photograph assists in putting evidence location in perspective.

(b)

Figure 3.24b   Photograph shows greater detail than the midrange photo.

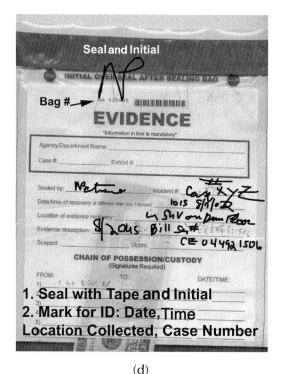

(c)

Figure 3.24c   Collection process, minimizing contamination of evidence.

(d)

Figure 3.24d   Put sufficient information on the exterior of the package to ensure individual-ization of evidence submitted.

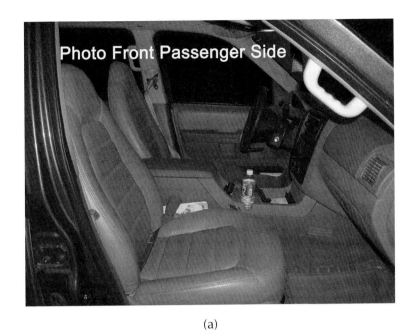

(a)

Figure 3.25a Multiple views can either prove or disprove statements of witnesses or the involved party.

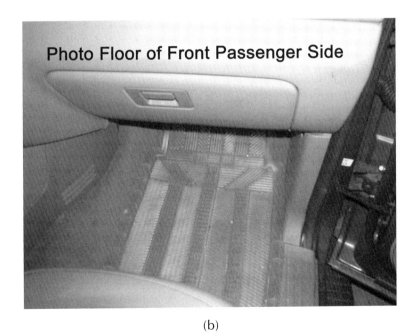

(b)

Figure 3.25b

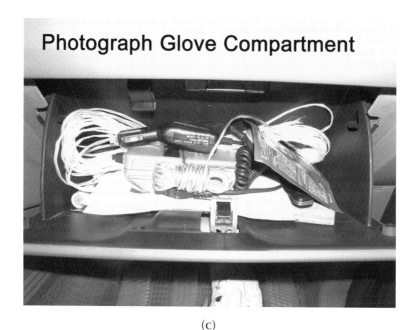

(c)

Figure 3.25c Document areas that may or may not contain evidence. Objects within a "lunging reach" should always be documented.

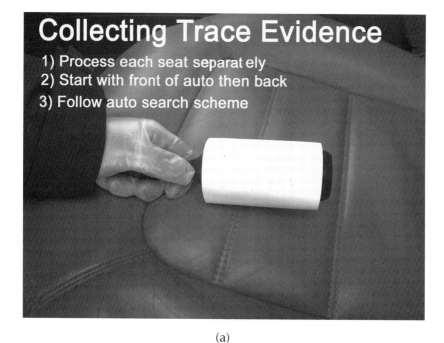

(a)

Figure 3.26a Document the location of the tape lift's recovery. Remember: once the tape is no longer tacky, it will not allow items to stick to it. A large area may require several different tape lifts be used.

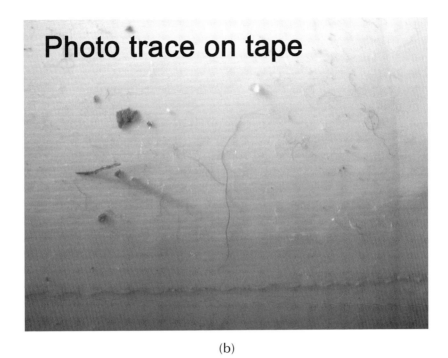

(b)

Figure 3.26b Affix the tape to a sheet of acetate or a piece of plastic bag. Prevent the tape from adhering to itself and possibly damaging the trace evidence (TE).

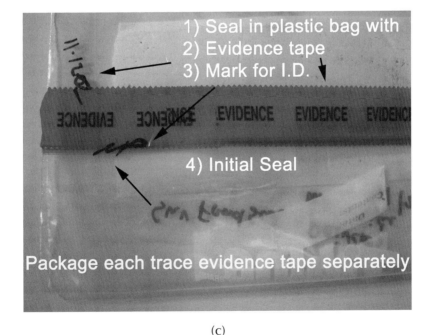

(c)

Figure 3.26c Place each tape lift into its own plastic bag. Be mindful to avoid cross-contamination. Package each tape lift separately.

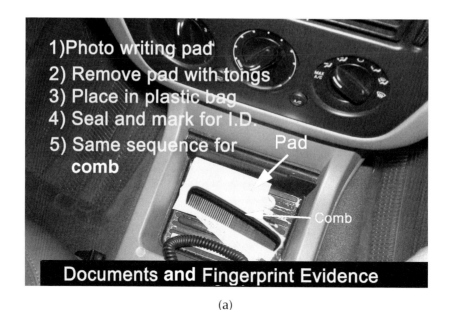

(a)

Figure 3.27a

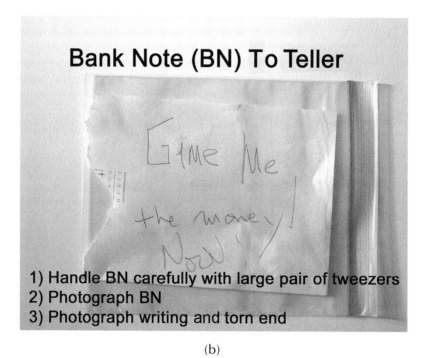

(b)

Figure 3.27b Place note into bag. Be sure that the note's contents are visible to the outside.

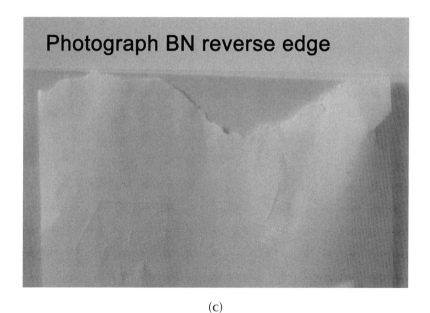

(c)

Figure 3.27c   Packaging should be premarked to avoid adding any indented writing.

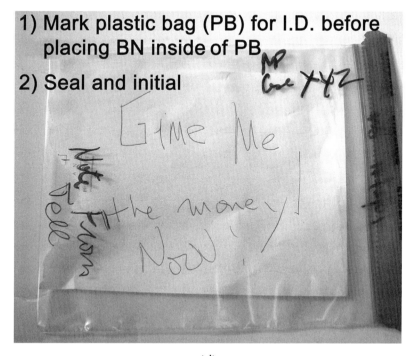

(d)

Figure 3.27d

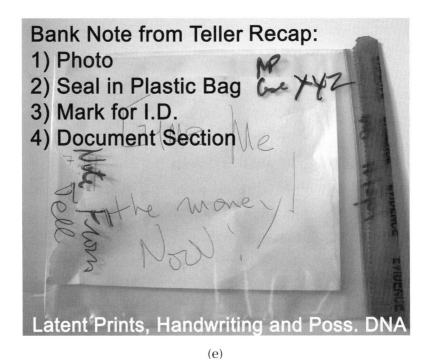

(e)

Figure 3.27e   Write on packaging the type(s) of analysis being requested of the laboratory.

(a)

Figure 3.28a   Evidence location prior to recovery.

(b)

Figure 3.28b   Be mindful of additional possible tests that can be performed, such as DNA on a bottle mouth area.

(c)

Figure 3.28c   Alternate views of evidence can be helpful.

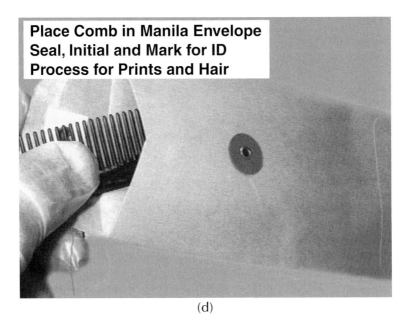

(d)

Figure 3.28d　Avoid excessive handling of items that may contain TE or to avoid obliterating any latent prints.

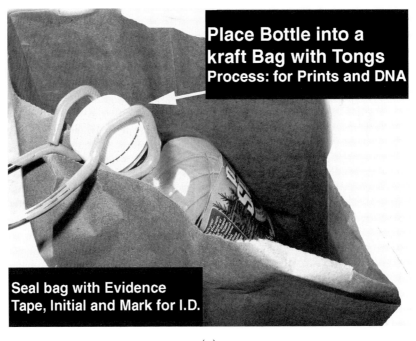

(e)

Figure 3.28e

(a)

Figure 3.29a

(b)

Figure 3.29b   Always attempt to locate and document any "unique identifiers" on the PE.

(a)

Figure 3.30a   Midrange or establishing view of evidence.

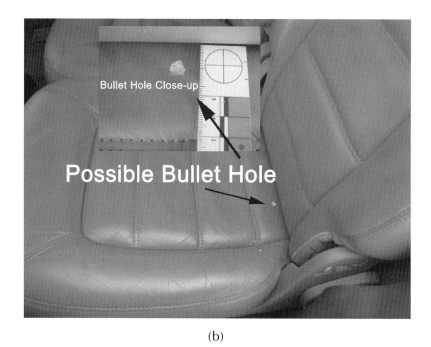

(b)

Figure 3.30b   Until tested at the laboratory and confirmed, use terms such as "suspected," "possible," or "alleged" for describing certain anomalies.

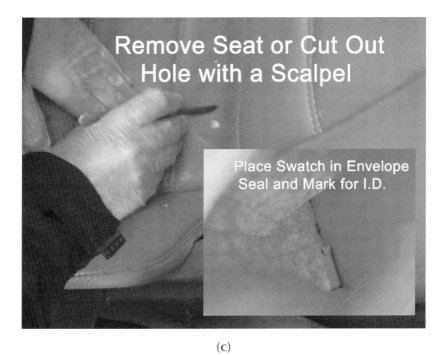

(c)

Figure 3.30c Hole and substrate collected for analysis.

(a)

Figure 3.31a   Midrange or establishing view of evidence.

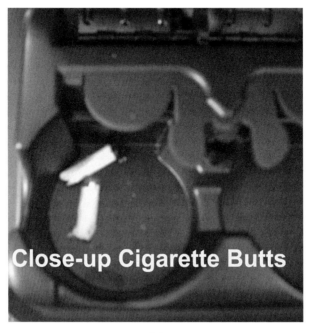

(b)

Figure 3.31b

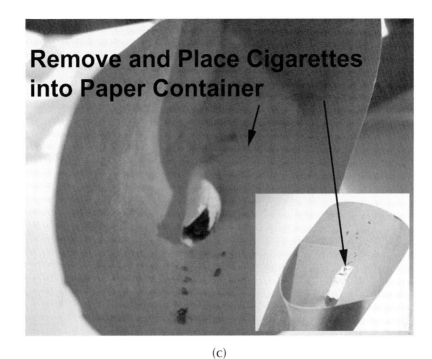

(c)

Figure 3.31c   Package individually. Avoid cross-contamination.

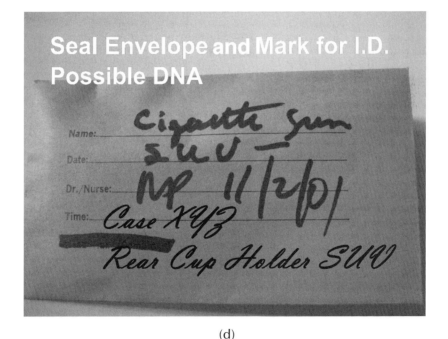

(d)

Figure 3.31d   Place tape on envelope flap, sign, and seal across the tape.

Figure 3.32 Vacuuming commingles the top layer of evidence with the "deep down" TE.

Figure 3.33 Document all information from the head stamp on the ammunition or discharged shell casings.

(a)

Figure 3.34a Midrange or establishing view of ballistic evidence, in proximity to a fixed object.

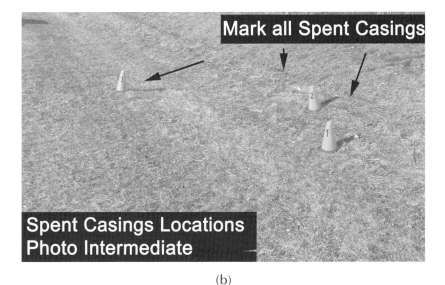

(b)

Figure 3.34b After initial photographs, use cones or placards to better establish the evidence location.

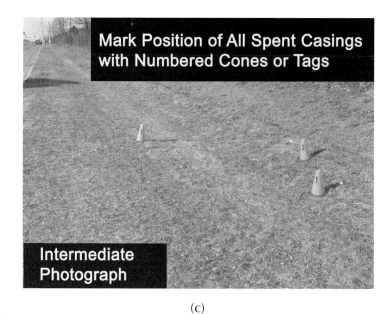

(c)

Figure 3.34c

(d)

Figure 3.34d

(e)

Figure 3.34e   Close-up photos should be taken without and then with markers.

(f)

Figure 3.34f   Discharged shells or spent shell casings should be marked on an area not used for comparison or analysis—inside the opening or as close to the front as possible.

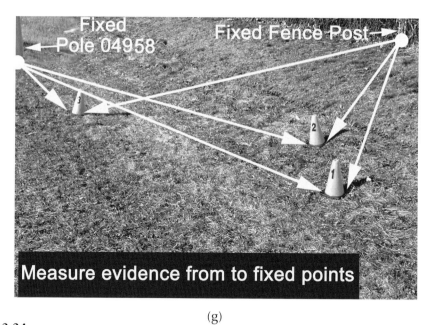

(g)

Figure 3.34g

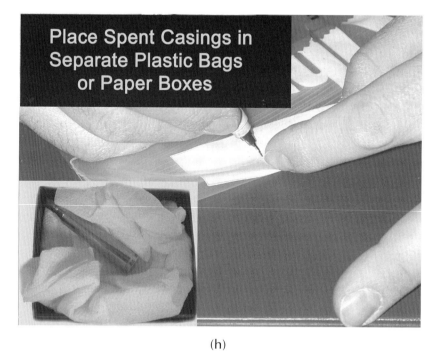

(h)

Figure 3.34h   Avoid adding minutiae on evidence. Package items separately.

(i)

Figure 3.34i Place initials and date across the evidence tape.

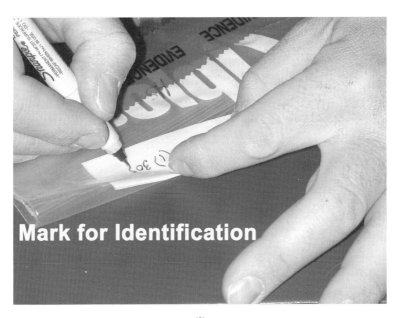

(j)

Figure 3.34j

(k)

Figure 3.34k List all writings on head stamp. Include color of casing, plastic or otherwise.

(a)

Figure 3.35a

(b)

Figure 3.35b   Multiple views of evidence showing different perspectives is useful.

(c)

Figure 3.35c   Evidence shown juxtaposition to area of interest.

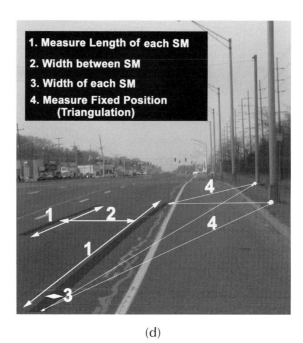

(d)

Figure 3.35d

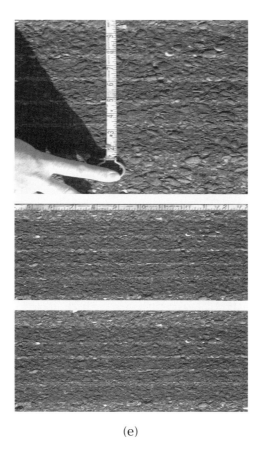

(e)

Figure 3.35e Photograph without and then with a readily reproducable scale. Adjust settings to capture the evidence.

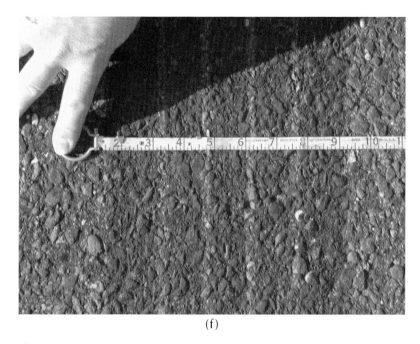

(f)

Figure 3.35f   Fill film frame completely, scale included.

(g)

Figure 3.35g   Placing the camera on a tripod ensures clarity and consistency of photos.

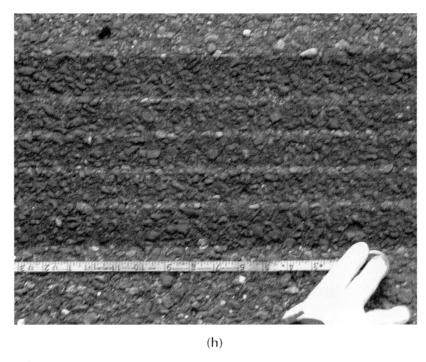

(h)

Figure 3.35h Aperture changes highlight certain anomalies of the tire impression.

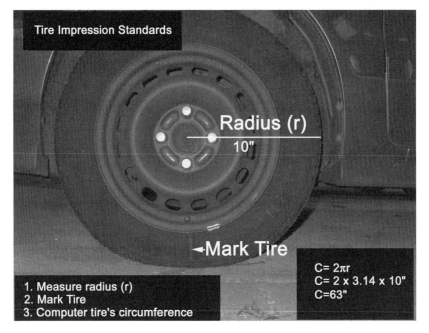

(a)

Figure 3.36a

(b)

Figure 3.36b Use the tire wheel stem as a point of reference to the tire's circumference.

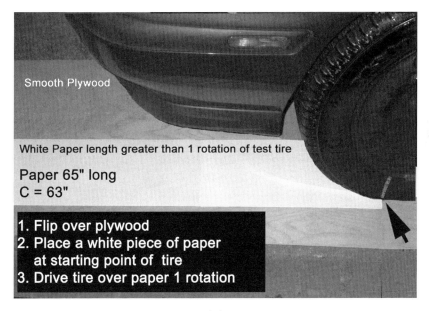

(c)

Figure 3.36c

(b)

Figure 3.36b   The tire print is embossed with digital photography.

Trace materials, e.g.: Hair, fibers, glass, soil, botanical, etc.
Blood
Hair and fibers
Ballistic evidence
Adhesive tape, rope, or any other binding materials

Where there was physical contact between a victim and an assailant, a close examination of the suspect, the victim, and their clothing should be conducted for the presence of:

Hair and fibers
Serological stains
Known samples of hair and fibers
Fingernail scrapings when appropriate

Deliver any such evidence to the crime laboratory.

After removal of all potential evidence, process for latent prints. Concentrate on surfaces and objects that may have been touched by the perpetrator, e.g., areas inside the vehicle(s), such as the dashboard, radio knobs, and steering wheel.
Document, collect, package, and transport ASAP all items of PE to the appropriate facility for examination and evaluation.
Be guided by laboratory personnel regarding special packaging requirements.
Prepare necessary forms, review sheet, and crime scene sketches.

Processing of a Sexual Assault Scene

4

In crimes involving sexual acts, there is normally personal contact between victim and perpetrator, with possible exchange of evidentiary substances such as blood, body fluids, hairs, and clothing fibers. Sex crimes are very devastating and traumatic events. Extreme tact, sympathy, and understanding must be used when dealing with victims of sex crimes.

Sex crimes often occur in conjunction with other crimes, such as burglary, robbery, and homicide. Therefore, it is important that the crime scene examiner (CSE) take steps to conduct a comprehensive crime scene search, assessment, documentation, and collection of the potential physical evidence (PE) present at the scene, as explained in previous chapters and as depicted in Figures 4.1 to 4.21.

In all crime scenes, it is important for the CSE to:

Discuss the crime scene with the first officer on the scene.

Review the status of the investigation with the investigating officer(s) present at the scene.

Elicit available information about the number of perpetrators and their actions, including their methods and routes.

Ascertain the condition of the victim.

Learn everything possible about the each assailant's action(s).

Find out whether a weapon or weapon(s) were used.

Acquire as many known facts concerning the way in which the sex assault occurred (modus operandi). Try to determine if the act was part of a pattern both to victim and assailant.

Ascertain the type of sexual encounter.

Inquire about any injuries during the commission of the crime.

Determine whether any items of potential evidence were found or collected prior to your arrival.

Be open-minded, objective, and alert to discover minute details. Do not hesitate to change your theory or hypothesis as the investigation continues. Avoid being rigid in your thought process.

Survey the general area; do a quick, careful walk-through of the suspected scene making sure to not disturb anything prior to documentation of the scene and any potential PE.

Note pertinent data.

Secure the crime scene.

Carefully search the crime scene and vehicle(s).

Figure 4.1

Record the crime scene by photographing the:

Type of wounds, bruising, bite marks, cigarette burns;
Ligatures or restraints;
Knots;
Objects that may have been used to cause the injuries;
Writing notes of observations; and,
Sketching the scene.

Figure 4.2 Show proximity to other premises.

Figure 4.3 Obtain numerous perspectives of scene and surroundings.

Figure 4.4

Figure 4.5 Look for discarded items along path traveled.

Figure 4.6

1. Walk towards backyard and photograph location and any P.E.

Figure 4.7

Entry Point

Chair with footwear print

Figure 4.8 Note additional interior crime scene established around chair with footwear print.

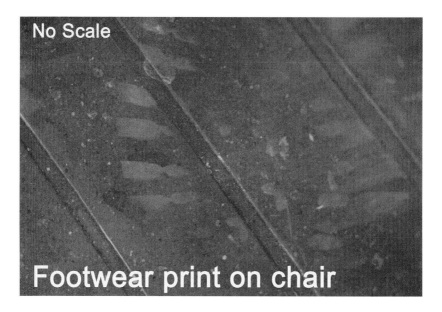

Figure 4.9

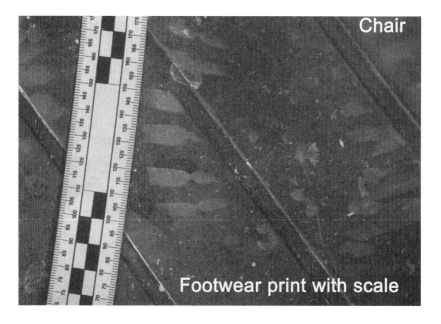

Figure 4.10

Figure 4.11   Overall or establishing view of assault location.

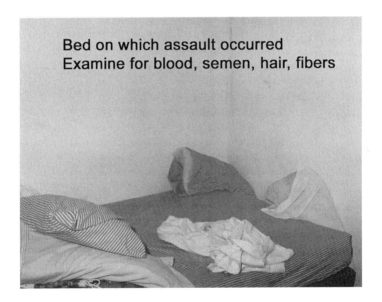

Figure 4.12   Pluck any visible hairs or fibers from sheet. Then tape lift the substrate. After complete of the trace search (TE), mark and package the sheet for serological examination.

Figure 4.13   Overall or establishing photo towards the seat of the crime, with blood evidence in the doorway.

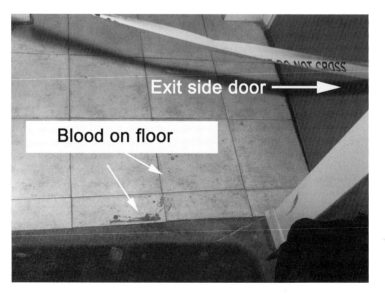

Figure 4.14   Blood evidence on the floor. Note the presence of additional crime scene tape cordoning off additional crucial evidence.

Figure 4.15 Area of egress used by assailant.

Figure 4.16 The assailant was injured during the incident. He removed most of his outer garments to change the description that was initially given to police. Clothing was processed for TE at the scene.

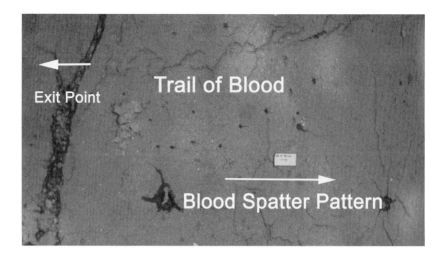

Figure 4.17   Spatter pattern shows directionality of travel. Assailant was bleeding and trail shows movement.

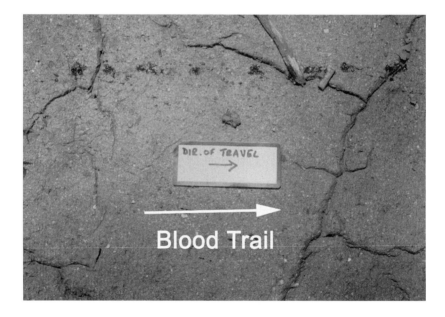

Figure 4.18   Remember to fill film frame with evidence. Also, be sure to have the plane of the film parallel with the object to prevent distortion. Photos with and without scales have to be taken.

Figure 4.19 Macro view of blood droplets show directionality. Be aware that different substrates will produce different spatter patterns.

Figure 4.20 Bloody hand print photographed with and without scale. Entire impression was cut from asphalt to preserve the evidence.

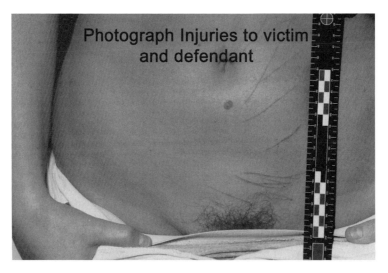

Figure 4.21   Wounds on the victim were self-inflicted.

In crimes involving sexual assault, the following procedures should be performed.
Search, document, collect, and package any biological or fragile evidence (see Figures 4.22
to 4.28) such as:

Vaginal, oral, and anal swabs (transport and refrigerate ASAP)
Semen stains (transport and refrigerate ASAP)
Used condoms
Condom packaging
Saliva (transport and refrigerate ASAP)
Blood (transport and refrigerate ASAP)
Bruises, bite marks, injuries
Fibers or hairs
Fingernail scrapings
Clothing items
Samples of the victim's head and pubic hair

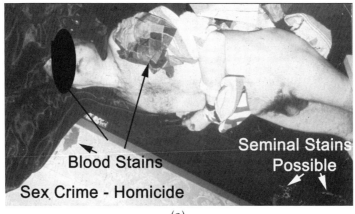

(a)

Figure 4.22a

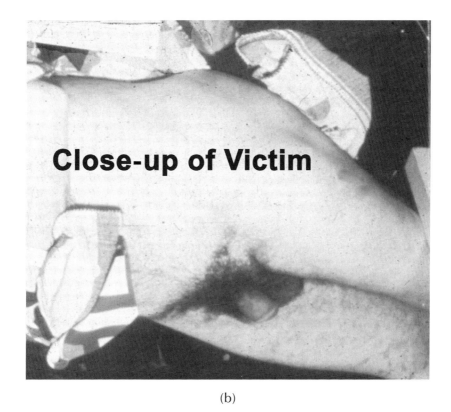

(b)

Figure 4.22b

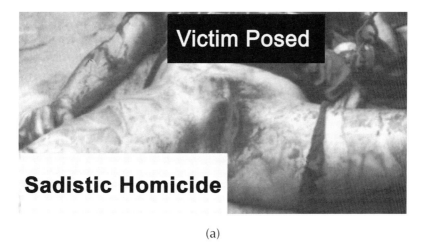

(a)

Figure 4.23a Victim staged or positioned for shock effect.

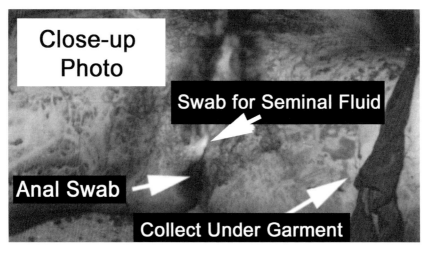

(b)

Figure 4.23b   Areas to collect specimens for DNA analysis. Done by the medical examiner.

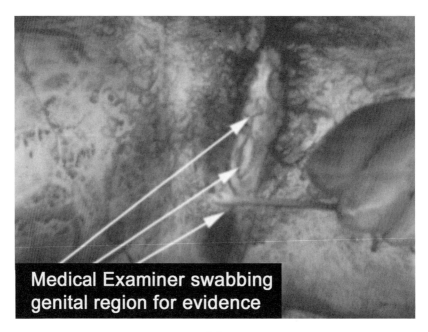

(a)

Figure 4.24a   Evidence collected or removed from a deceased victim must be done with prior approval of the medical examiner.

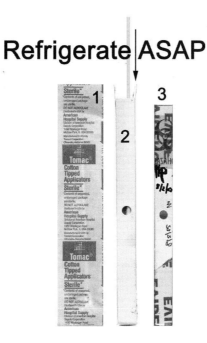

Refrigerate ASAP

1. Remove sterile swab just prior to use.
2. Swab suspected stain or area.
3. Air dry and place in a swab box
4. Seal, initial and mark for ID.
5. Transport and refrigerate ASAP.

(b)

Figure 4.24b

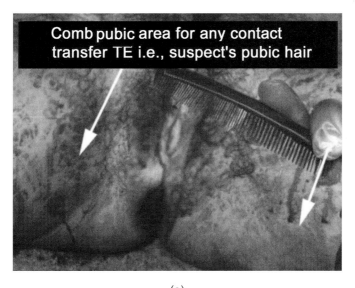

Comb pubic area for any contact transfer TE i.e., suspect's pubic hair

(a)

Figure 4.25a

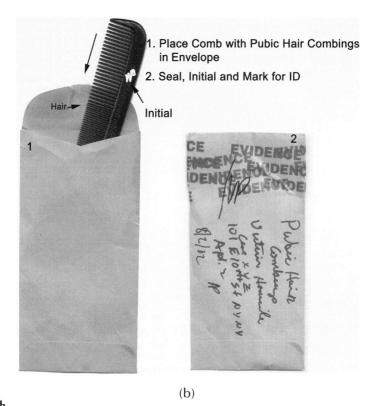

1. Place Comb with Pubic Hair Combings in Envelope
2. Seal, Initial and Mark for ID

(b)

Figure 4.25b

Collection of Hair Standards

1. Pubic: Comb or pull at least 25 hairs from all over pubic region.

2. Head: Comb or pull at least 100 hairs from all over scalp.

3. Place in an envelope, seal and mark for ID.

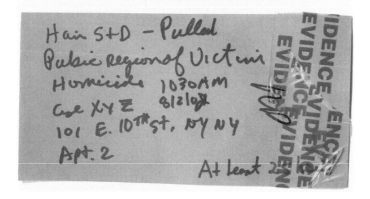

(c)

Figure 4.25c

(a)

Figure 4.26a Prior to collecting evidence from the victim, you must get permission and approval from the medical examiner.

(b)

Figure 4.26b

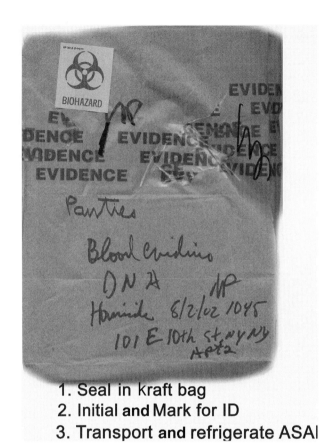

1. Seal in kraft bag
2. Initial **and** Mark for ID
3. Transport **and** refrigerate ASAI

(c)

Figure 4.26c

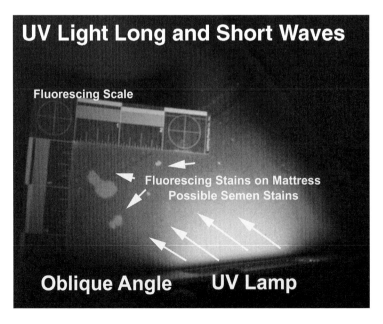

Figure 4.27

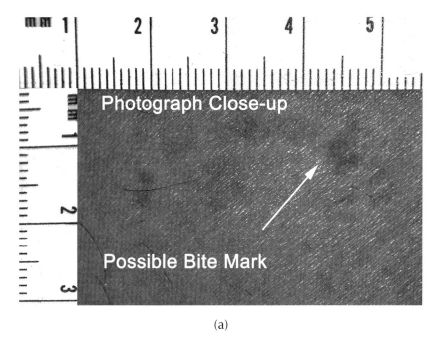

(a)

Figure 4.28a Safeguard area for DNA swab. Maintain an open dialogue with the health care professional on collection. Because of a bite mark, the health care worker may want to clean the wound. Wound cleaning should be done after the swabbing is performed.

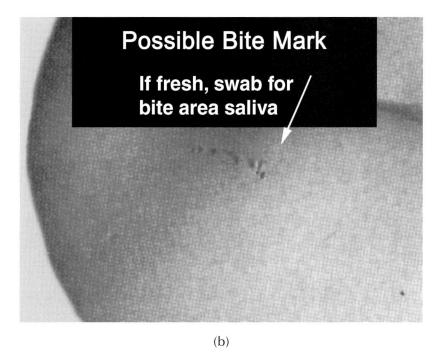

(b)

Figure 4.28b Confer with the medical examiner prior to obtaining the sample and follow his instructions.

Note: Evidence from the victim will be documented and collected at the hospital by the attending physician or certified forensic nurse. However, the CSE is usually called upon to properly package, safeguard, and transport these items of evidence to the forensic laboratory. The CSE is also required to:

Collect and package clothing and articles left or dropped by the perpetrator(s).
Process the scene for fingerprints.
If the suspect is in custody:
Collect and package his/her clothing for trace material, while standing over clean paper.
Collect samples of suspect's head and pubic hair for comparison purposes. Confer with legal authorities to determine whether a search warrant is required.
Photograph recent physical marks such as bruises, scratches, cuts, etc.
If the crime was committed in an outside location:
Recover unusual debris, such as buttons, handkerchiefs, discarded paper or rags, etc.
Collect representative samples of soil, vegetation, etc.

Complete the documentation, collection, packaging, and labeling of all evidence for transportation to the appropriate laboratory for further examination. Prepare all necessary forms and review sheet before releasing the crime scene.

Processing Scenes of Arson or Explosion 5

Arson is the illegal, intentional incineration, or attempted incineration of property. Arsons are also perpetrated in order to cause the injury or death of individuals, and to terrorize people. Motives for arson may include greed, jealousy, fraud, and/or terrorism. Often, the crime of arson is committed as a ploy to hide or cover up other crimes, such as homicides.

Typically, the crime of arson involves the use of flammable liquids, such as gasoline, lighter fluid, or some other easily available volatile organic liquid. In addition, explosive also materials and incendiary devices are also used in the commission of these types of crimes. The use of these types of destructive materials, and the subsequent extinguishing of the fire, inherently results in the loss of much of the physical evidence. The crime scene examiner (CSE) should actively look for evidence of the use of such materials, paying close attention to the damage present at the crime scene.

The CSE should conduct a comprehensive search and assessment of the crime scene and document, collect, package, and transport, in a timely manner, all of the potential physical evidence present at the scene, as explained in previous chapters.

Procedures.   Photograph the following (see Figures 5.1 to 5.25):

Point of origin of the fire
Burn patterns
Seat of explosion
Forced entries or exits
The overall crime scene and specific damage
Items of evidence

Examine the following (see Figures 5.26 to 5.46):

Forced doors and windows
Burned people
Containers
Burn patterns
Soot deposits
Stained areas
Odors of flammable materials, e.g., gasoline, lighter fluid
Fire trails
Charred documents

Figure 5.1   Exit from the interior of the train station.

Figure 5.2   Establishing the midrange view of the train platform.

Figure 5.3 Photograph showing the train station and train number (in lieu of the premise's address).

Figure 5.4 Station location and exit area.

Figure 5.5   Secondary interior crime scene established.

Figure 5.6   Take an overall left intermediate photograph of the crime scene.

Figure 5.7 Multiple angles show possible views of witnesses.

Figure 5.8 Additional evidence recovered outside of the initial seat of the crime.

Continue to Search and Document CS

Figure 5.9

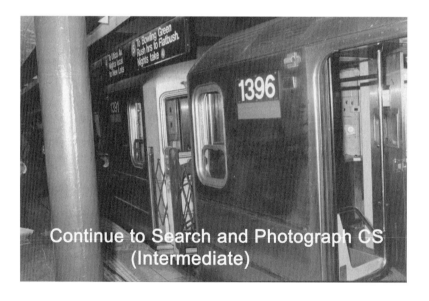

Continue to Search and Photograph CS
(Intermediate)

Figure 5.10

Figure 5.11 Exterior of the train showing residue.

Figure 5.12 More residue on the train's exterior.

Figure 5.13   Always perform a "walk through" to ascertain what types of evidence will be document and recovered.

Figure 5.14

Figure 5.15

Figure 5.16

Figure 5.17   Photograph in "as in" condition. Take additional photos after additional evidence is discovered (prior to collection).

Figure 5.18   Generally burned areas absorb more light than bright areas. Be sure to lower the F-stop by one or two stops when the area that is burned is photographed. As always, bracket your photos.

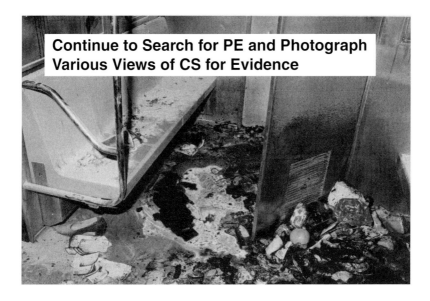

Figure 5.19   Change or adjust lighting and lighting angles to highlight certain details.

Figure 5.20

Figure 5.21

Figure 5.22

Figure 5.23   Be sure to package components separately.

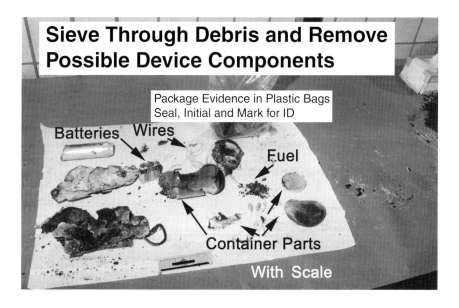

Figure 5.24   Avoid commingling of evidence. Package components separately.

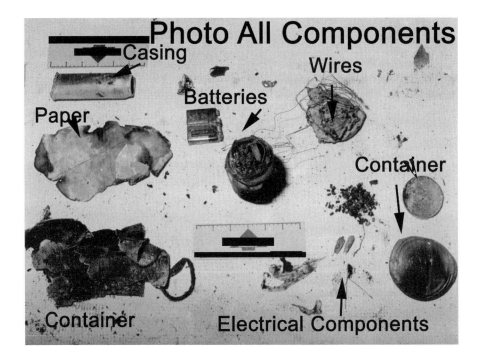

Figure 5.25

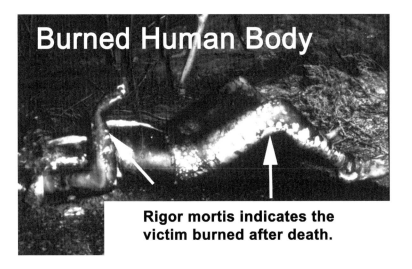

Figure 5.26   Deceased was in the car for a period of time before rigor mortis set in.

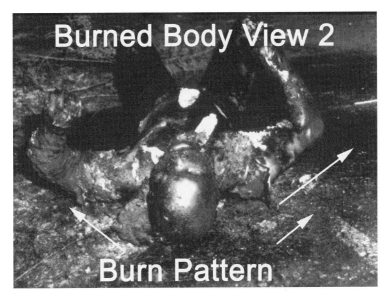

Figure 5.27   Look for pooling of accelerant and pattern evidence.

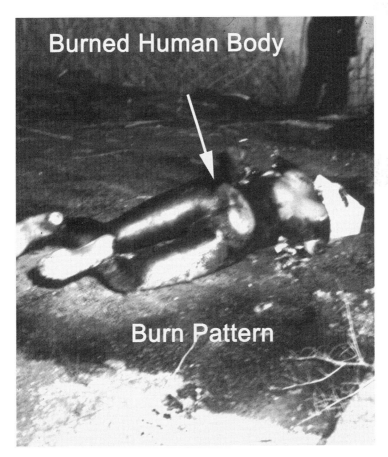

Figure 5.28   A portion of the body that wasn't burned is where the accelerant did not come in contact with the deceased (the pattern on the rear resembles livor mortis because it's the lowest area in contact with the ground).

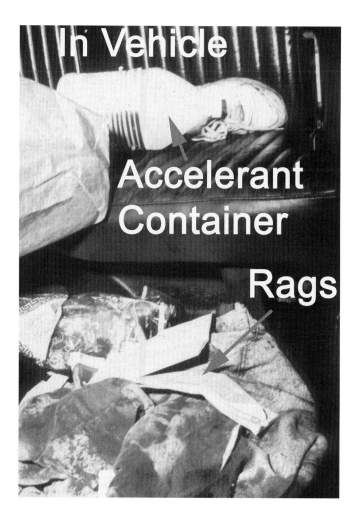

Figure 5.29 Package items separately, possibly to compare to items at the initial fire scene.

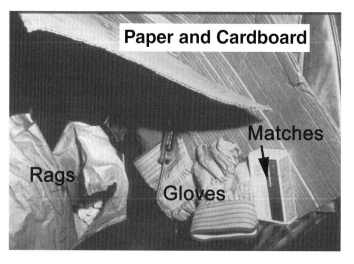

Figure 5.30 Matches at the scene were compared to matches at the initial fire scene.

Figure 5.31

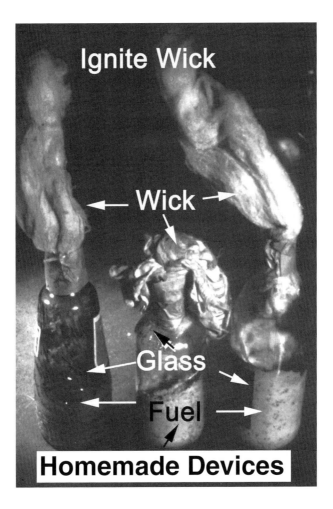

Figure 5.32   Mark the container to show the quantity of accelerant inside the container. Wicks may be compared to additional material from the person constructing the device.

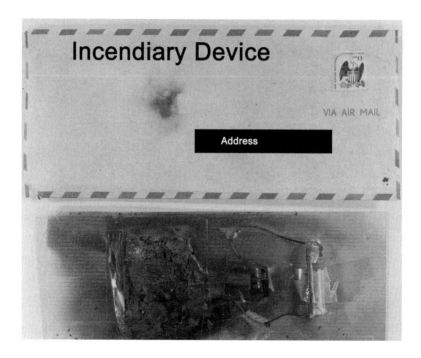

Figure 5.33 Always note the address, postage, and postmark.

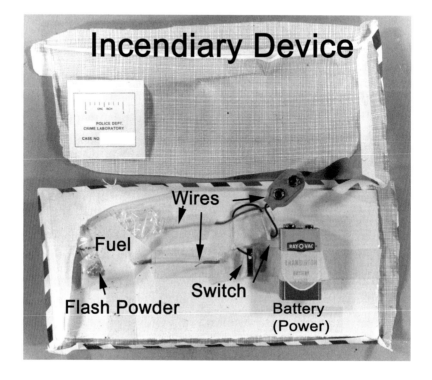

Figure 5.34

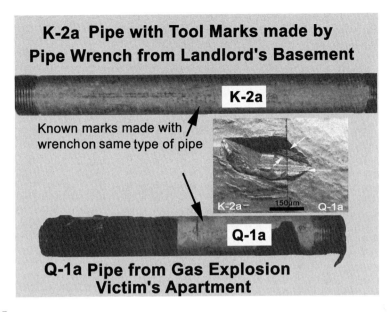

Figure 5.35

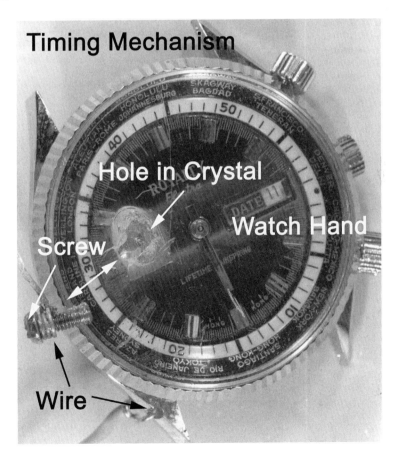

Figure 5.36   A crude timing mechanism was manufactured for an improvised explosive device (IED).

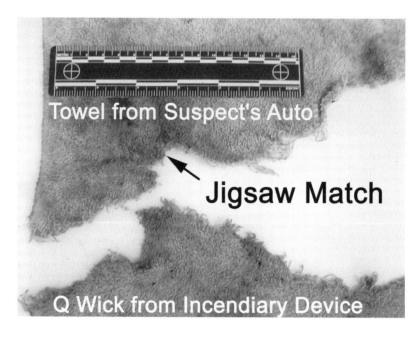

Figure 5.37

(a)

Figure 5.38a Look for unique identifiers, such as lot numbers or the manufacturing date, on the container. Save a paper product. There may be a match with a newspaper from the initial scene.

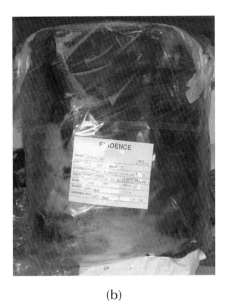

(b)

Figure 5.38b A plastic container from inside the vehicle contains gasoline.

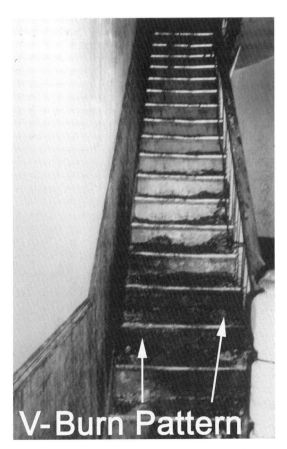

Figure 5.39 Charring or alligatoring of the stairs shows where the accelerant was poured and lit on fire.

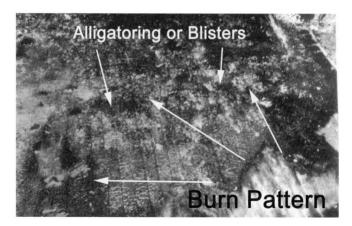

Figure 5.40 Cut out a piece of substrate with burn and also a control sample from an unburned piece of flooring.

Figure 5.41 Adjust the aperture for highlights of burned areas.

Figure 5.42

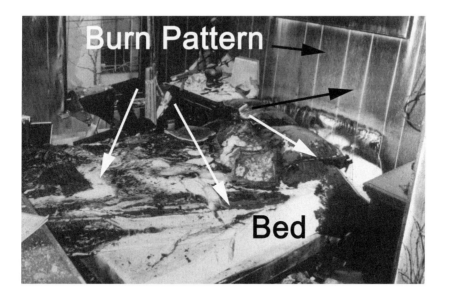

Figure 5.43 An outline of the body on the bedding.

Figure 5.44

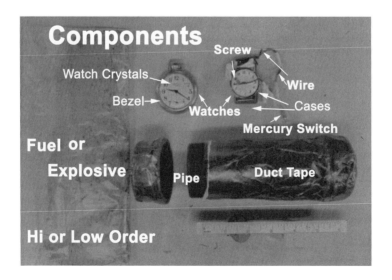

Figure 5.45

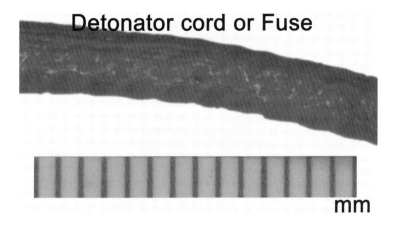

Figure 5.46   Overall, close-ups of length and width.

Collect and package evidence, such as:

Igniting instruments
Electrical components
• Wires
• Batteries
• Lightbulbs
• All types of switches
• Fuses
Watches and parts
Textiles
Rags
Pipe parts
Glass bottles and parts
Materials of explosives residues and flammables
Upholstery
Wood
Carpeting
Soil
Volatiles in containers or puddles of water
Debris from the fire's or explosion's origin
Vapor samples trapped in capillary tubes

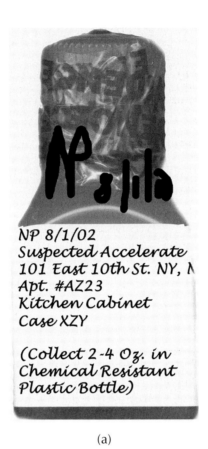

NP 8/1/02
Suspected Accelerate
101 East 10th St. NY, N
Apt. #AZ23
Kitchen Cabinet
Case XZY

(Collect 2-4 Oz. in
Chemical Resistant
Plastic Bottle)

(a)

Figure 5.47a

Arson debris and burned
accelerant container

Figure 5.47b

(a)

Figure 5.48a

(b)

Figure 5.48b Seal the container with tape. Initial and date the container.

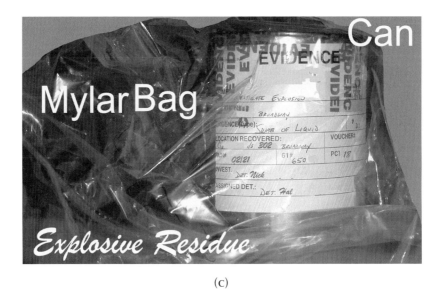

(c)

Figure 5.48c

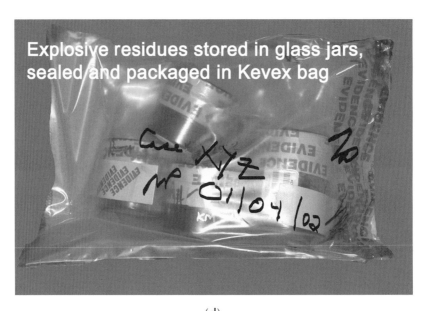

(d)

Figure 5.48d

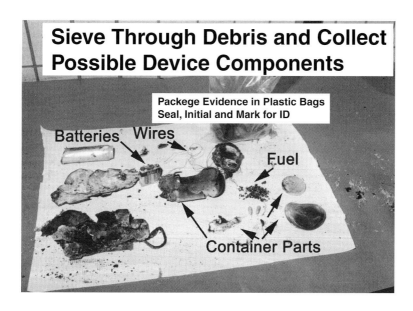

Figure 5.49

All volatile evidence must be packaged in airtight containers, sealed, and then delivered to the crime laboratory for analysis (see Figures 5.47 to 5.50). Examples of such containers are:

Paint cans
Glass jars
Mylar® bags

Note that since arson is often committed in connection with other crimes, it is essential that the CSE take steps to do a comprehensive processing of the original crime scene.

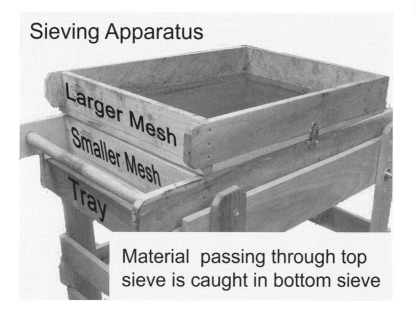

Figure 5.50

Investigation of Leaving the Scene of an Auto Accident

A leaving-the-scene-of-an-accident investigation often involves injury or death of individuals, damage to vehicles, and damage to property. In these types of cases, the careful search for transfer trace evidence exchanged between the principals of the accident is crucial to identifying the vehicle that left the scene. Often the ability to solve these crimes, and reconstruct the accidents, is based solely on the trace evidence collected.

As in all crime scene inquiries, the crime scene examiner (CSE) should conduct a comprehensive search of the accident scene; and the documentation, collection, packaging, and transportation of all physical evidence should be carried out in a timely manner, as explained and demonstrated in previous chapters.

The scene should be methodically photographed. As in all crime scene investigations, the photographs should include overall, intermediate, and close-up shots of the accident scene, vehicles, and people involved. In particular, photographs of the following conditions and evidence should be taken (don't forget scales in the photos) for documentation:

Injuries to the people involved
Any injury patterns present on victim(s)
Exact location of damage to vehicle(s)
Damage patterns present on vehicle(s)
Exact location of trace evidence found on vehicle(s)
Damage to tires
Tire pressure of all four tires
Trace evidence at scene
Trace evidence on victim(s)
Trace evidence on vehicle(s)

Measurements should be made on vehicles from the ground up or from the roof down; not from the tire(s) up, because heights of tires can change. The pressure of each tire should also be recorded.

The scene of the accident should be examined for the following types of physical evidence:

Trace evidence
Skid marks

Tire impressions

Parts of vehicles, e.g., broken headlights, broken grilles, pieces of taillights, moldings

The vehicles (if and when available) and individuals should be examined for the following types of evidence:

Paint chips
Paint smears
Glass fragments
Hairs
Fibers
Blood
Human tissue
Pieces of textile(s)
Impressions or imprint patterns

Close attention should be paid to the undercarriage of the vehicle. Often pieces of the victim's clothing as well as his/her hair and tissue are discovered attached to parts of the undercarriage. Figures 6.1 to 6.9 depict common types of physical evidence documented and collected in accidents and leaving-the-scene investigations.

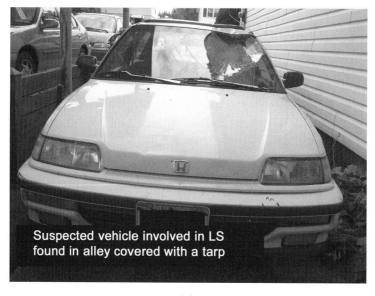

(a)

Figure 6.1a

(b)

Figure 6.1b

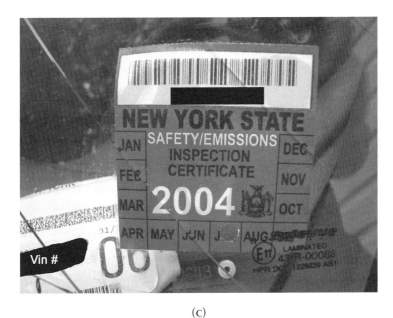

(c)

Figure 6.1c Inspection sticker examined and documented. Inspection station may have a history of the vehicle prior to the incident under investigation.

(d)

Figure 6.1d   Photograph vehicle prior to processing.

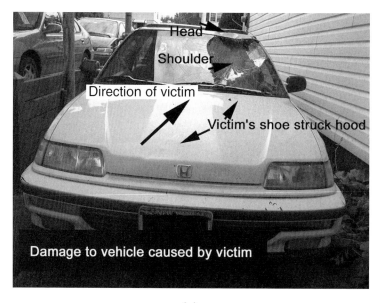

(e)

Figure 6.1e   Latent print processing with black powder made some damage more visible.

(f)

Figure 6.1f

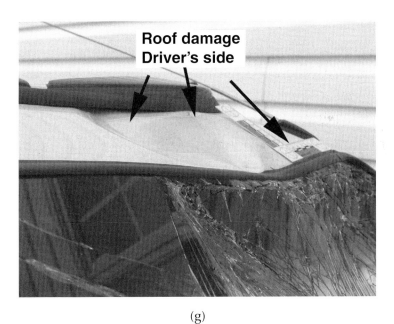

(g)

Figure 6.1g   Different perspectives of auto reveal damage as unseen by different angle views. Alternate views show alternate damage.

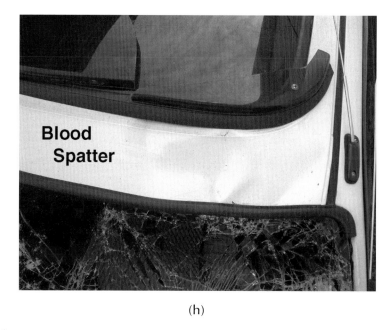

(h)

Figure 6.1h   Area between windshield and the sunroof was damaged by the victim's head.

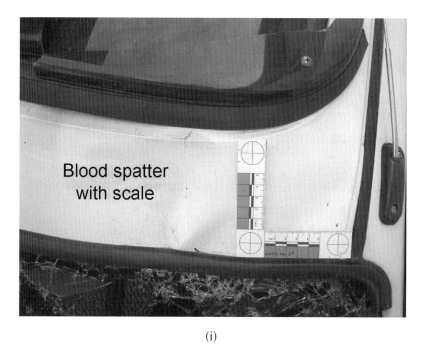

(i)

Figure 6.1i

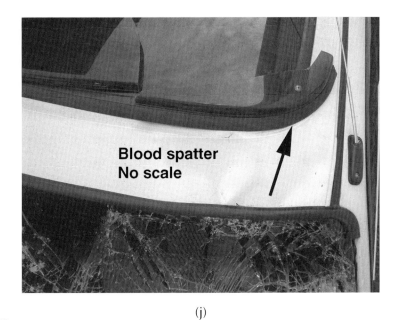

(j)

Figure 6.1j

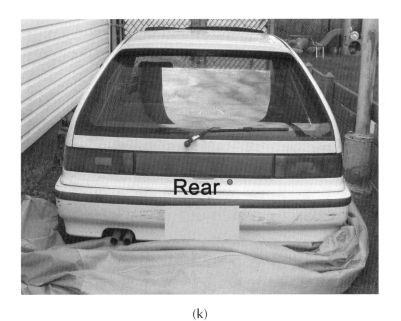

(k)

Figure 6.1k   Examine the vehicle's rear for any sign of damage.

(l)

Figure 6.1l   Driver's side front towards the rear.

(m)

Figure 6.1m   Passenger's side front towards the rear.

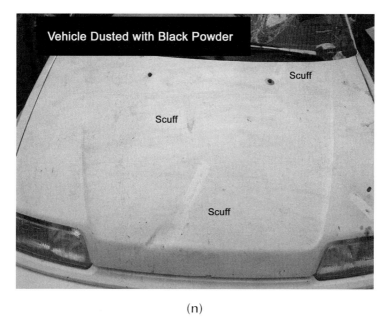

(n)

Figure 6.1n   Damage documented and photographed.

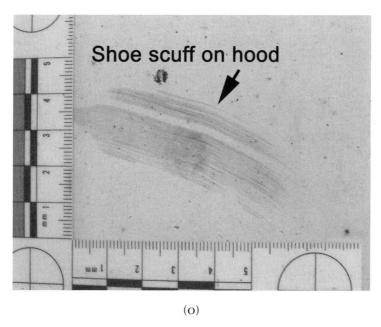

(o)

Figure 6.1o   Scuff measured from two fixed points, photographed and tape lifted.

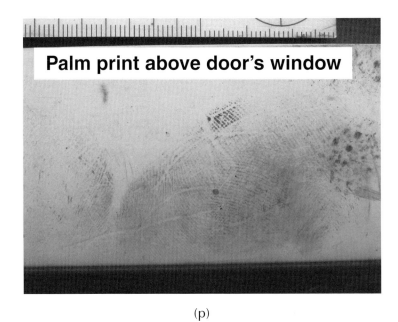

(p)

Figure 6.1p Photographed with and without scale, and lifted.

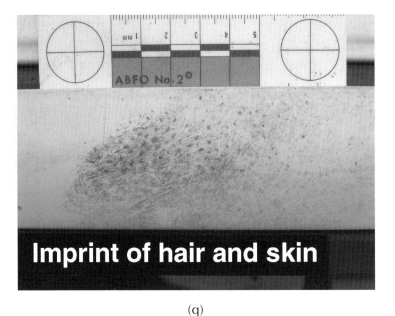

(q)

Figure 6.1q Imprint located and documented. The location of the impression evidence was difficult to explain absent the accident.

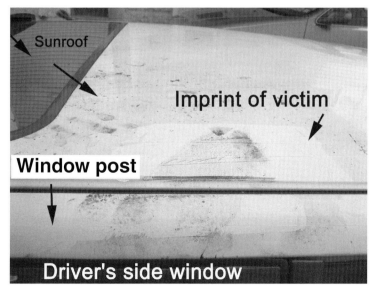

(r)

Figure 6.1r   Positionality and morphology of the evidence is as important as the actual piece of evidence.

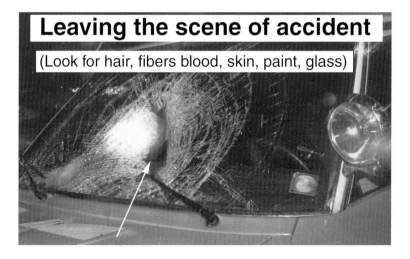

Figure 6.2

Figure 6.3

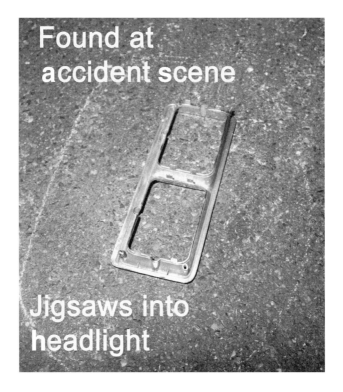

Figure 6.4 Do not attempt a jigsaw match by placing two different items together in the field. Trace evidence can inadvertently be transferred and give a false finding.

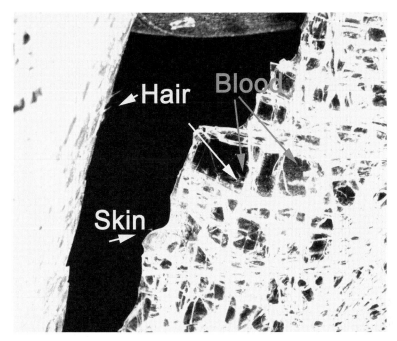

Figure 6.5   Whenever practical, the vehicle should be brought into a climate-controlled garage. Use different lighting equipment and search methodically.

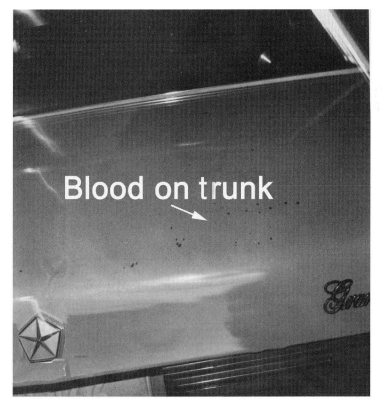

Figure 6.6   Be sure to search all areas of the vehicle. Even a front end striking of a person can have evidence adhere to the trunk area.

Figure 6.7　This wheelchair was struck by a vehicle that fled the scene.

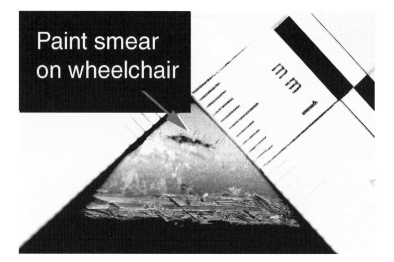

Figure 6.8　Microscopic examination of the frame of the wheelchair revealed paint from the auto. Proper safeguarding, packaging, and handling of the evidence preserved the sample.

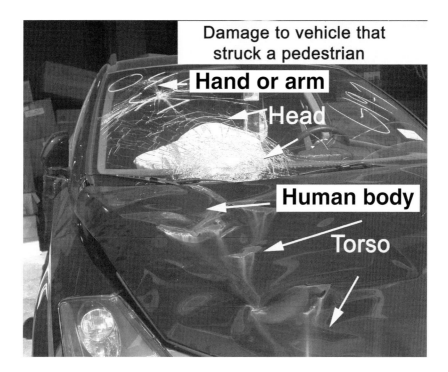

Figure 6.9

Appendix A: Essential Crime Scene Equipment

Stationery

- Pens and pencils
- Chalk
- Wax pencils
- Sharpie® markers
- Coin envelopes
- Laser pen
- Level and angle finders
- Tape measures, rulers
- Protractors
- Crime scene worksheets
- Recap forms
- Notebooks
- Evidence receipts
- Photography record forms
- Paper clips
- Scotch™ tape
- Rubber bands
- Scissors
- Graph paper

Evidence Marker and Tapes

- Small pre-numbered or -lettered cones
- Numbered marking tags
- Wire evidence tags
- Evidence tape

Protective Clothing (PIPE)

- Disposable footwear covers
- Disposable protective suits of various sizes
- Disposable leg covers
- Latex gloves of different sizes
- Heavy vinyl gloves of various sizes
- Disposable head caps
- Assorted face masks
- Assorted sizes of rubber gloves
- Disposable masks
- Safety goggles
- Disposable booties
- Shrouds

Evidence Collection Containers

- Assorted sizes of kraft paper evidence bags
- Assorted sizes of white envelopes
- Whitman® filter paper 6 × 6 sheets
- Evidence bags with serial numbers
- Red plastic bags
- Manila envelopes
- Various sizes of Ziploc® plastic bags
- Small paper boxes
- Evidence boxes in assorted sizes
- Assorted heavy plastic jars
- Assorted glass vials
- Safety, hazard, and biohazard labels
- Heavy duty plastic ties

Impression Evidence Collection

- Magnifiers
- Fingerprint brushes
- Fiberglass powder brushes
- Feather dusters
- Magna-powder brush
- Lift cards
- Clear lifts and overlays
- White and black powder
- Assorted colors of fingerprint powder
- Redwop® powder
- Magnetic powder

- Brushes, squeegee, roller
- Mikrosil, various colors
- Fingerprint lift tape and covers
- Footwear print lifts (clear, black, and white)
- Clear lifting tape and lift cards
- Spray lacquer

Camera Equipment

- Portable video camera
- Camera power unit and batteries
- 35-mm cameras, film and digital
- Assorted rolls of camera film
- Memory cards
- Lenses: 24–120 mm, 16–18 mm fisheye, 105 mm macro, 100–300 mm telephoto
- Illumination sources for camera and video equipment
- Portable floodlights
- Camera flash units and batteries
- Assorted photographic scales

Ballistic Collection Equipment

- Poles and connectors of different sizes
- Fine string
- Laser trajectory scope
- Metal detector

Biology and Trace Equipment

- Disposable pipettes
- Sterile swabs
- Sterile containers
- Sterile swab containers
- Collection tubes and envelopes
- Test tubes of different sizes
- Plastic tubes of different sizes
- Assorted kraft paper bags
- Multichamber kraft evidence bags
- Coin envelopes
- Scalpel and surgical blades
- Alcohol swabs
- Gauze
- pH paper

- Tweezers
- Tongs
- Filter paper
- Weigh paper
- Scribes
- Microscope slide holders
- Ultraviolet (UV) lamp, long and short wave
- UV markers
- UV rulers
- Filter paper
- Tongue depressors
- Biohazard stickers
- Gel lifts
- Evidence tape
- 3M tape for removing hairs and fibers
- Double-coated tape
- Small magnifier
- Turbo vacuum and filters (150-mm Whitman® filter paper)
- Trace evidence lifting tape and covers
- Mag-Lite® with blue filter

Specialized Team Evidence Collection Equipment

- Electrostatic dust lifting device and lifting film
- Omnichrome® or Crimescope® alternative light source with safety glasses
- Blue-Light®
- Cyanovac® fuming chamber systems
- Luminol application equipment and reagents
- Hemadent presumptive blood reagents

Miscellaneous

- Assorted screwdrivers, pliers, pry bars, saws, hammers
- Box of first-aid supplies
- Tire pressure gauge
- Thermometer
- Portable electrical generator(s)
- Electrical extension cords
- Electrical power outlet strips
- Laptop computer with crime scene software
- Large tackle box

Appendix B: Photographic Review of Evidence Collection and Packaging Techniques

This appendix is a photographic review of the collection, packaging, and safeguarding of various types of physical evidence frequently encountered at scenes of crimes. It is intended to serve as a quick guide and reference for the collection, packaging, and safeguarding of common types of physical evidence.

(a)

Figure B.1a Try to put the items of interest as close to the center as possible.

(b)

Figure B.1b   Record all information from the head stamp.

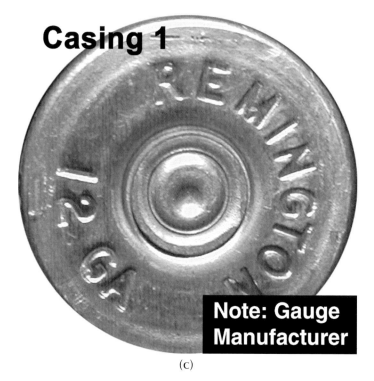

(c)

Figure B.1c   Note all information from the head stamp and color and composition of the casing.

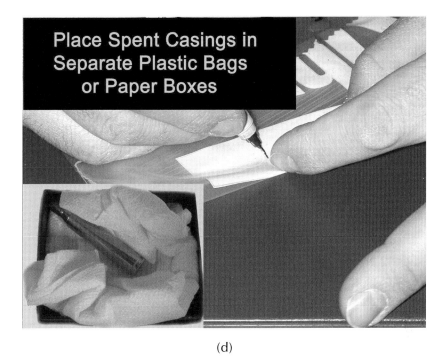

(d)

Figure B.1d   Do not allow the discharged shell casings to rub or scratch against other items of evidence.

(e)

Figure B.1e   Mark the discharged shells inside the throat or as close to the front opening as possible.

Figure B.2 Indicate the type of analysis requested, such as blood, latent prints, and trace, on the box's exterior.

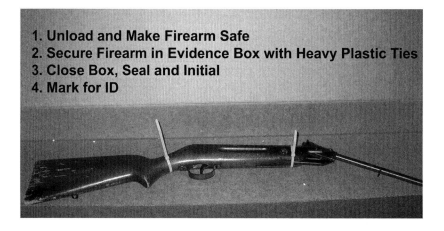

Figure B.3 Note the serial number, barrel length, stock type, and also the type of analysis being requested, such as blood, hairs, fibers.

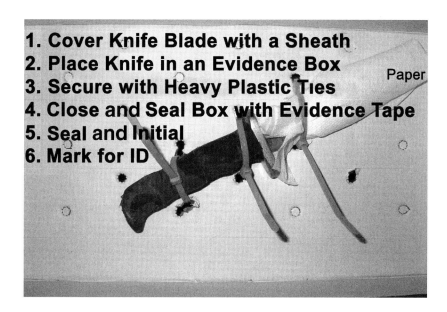

Figure B.4

(a)

Figure B.5a Only mark the base of the bullet. Do not mark any areas with lands or grooves. Do not remove any trace evidence from the projectiles. Allow the bullets to be photographed at the laboratory and removed under controlled conditions at the lab.

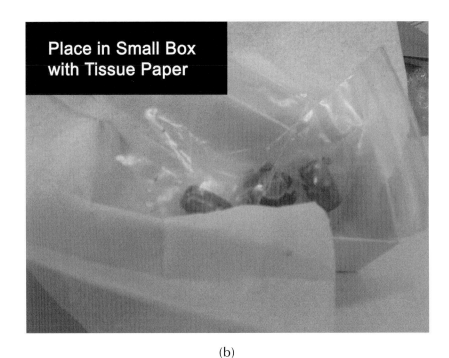

(b)

Figure B.5b   Package to ensure preservation of minutiae and possible trace matter.

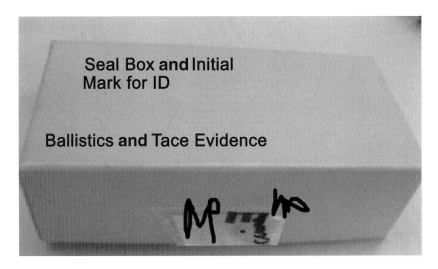

(c)

Figure B.5c

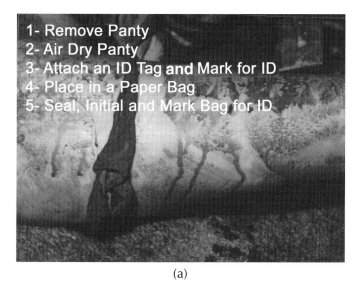

(a)

Figure B.6a   Remove only at the direction of the medical examiner.

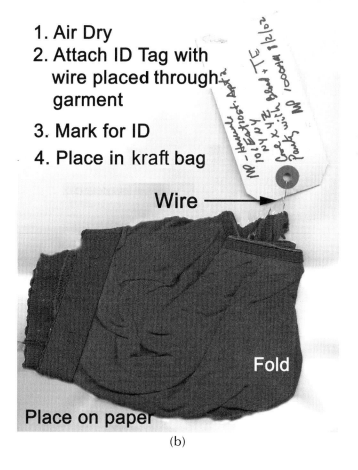

(b)

Figure B.6b

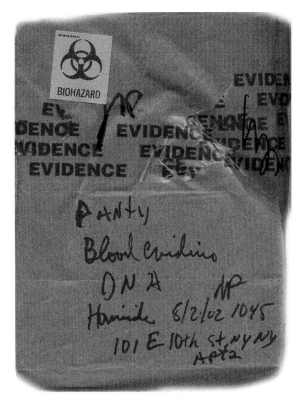

1. Seal in kraft bag
2. Initial and mark for ID
3. Maintain in a cool, dry
   climate-controlled environment,
   always out of direct sunlight.

(c)

Figure B.6c

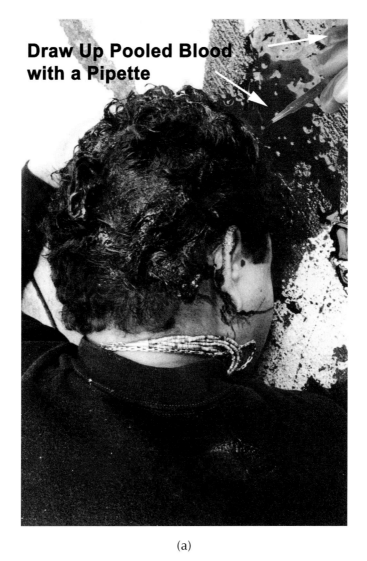

Draw Up Pooled Blood with a Pipette

(a)

Figure B.7a   Take a blood specimen from the suspected area by swabbing with a sterile cotton swab. Allow to air dry. A larger volume of liquid blood can be taken with a pipette as shown.

Pipette blood specimen into specimen tube.

(b)

Figure B.7b

1. Seal tube with screw cap and evidence tape
2. Initial, seal and mark for ID

3. Refrigerate ASAP   Bio-Hazard Label

(c)

Figure B.7c

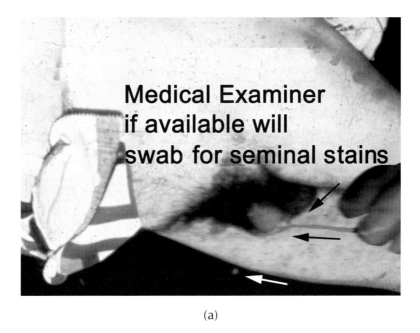

(a)

Figure B.8a Do not perform without knowledge and permission of the medical examiner.

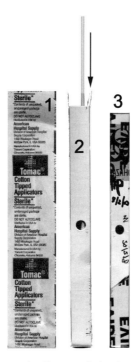

1. Remove sterile swab just prior to use.
2. Swab suspected stain or area.
3. Place in paper box, seal and mark
   for ID.

(b)

Figure B.8b

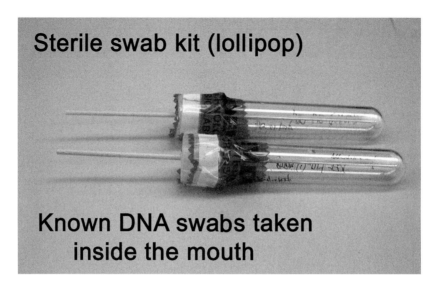

Figure B.9

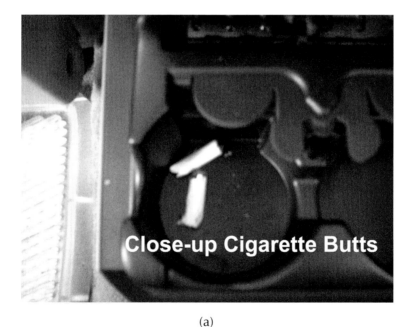

(a)

Figure B.10a   Package separately. Do not commingle with other items.

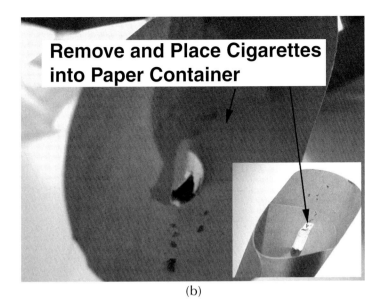

(b)

Figure B.10b

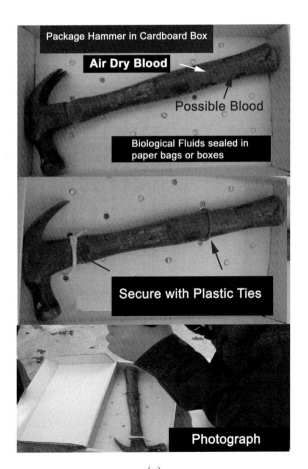

(a)

Figure B.11a

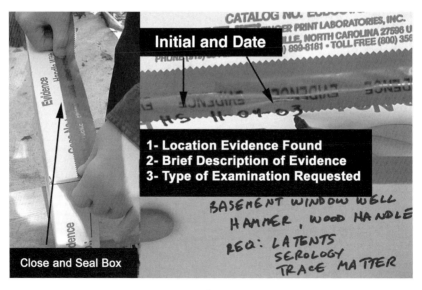

(b)

Figure B.11b

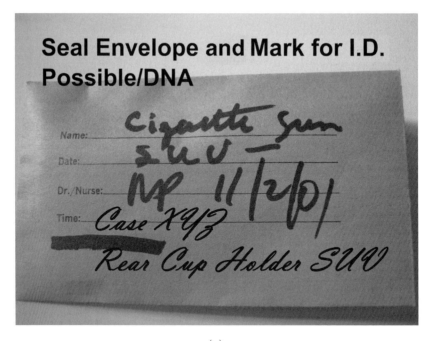

(a)

Figure B.12a

(b)

Figure B.12b

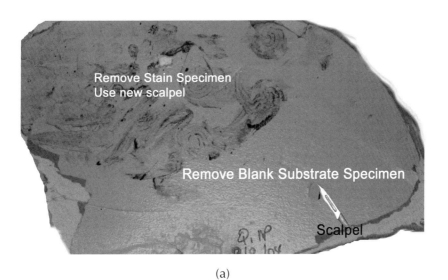

(a)

Figure B.13a

(b)

Figure B.13b

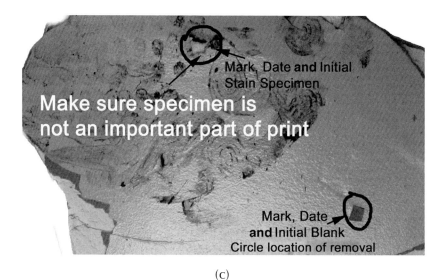

(c)

Figure B.13c Samples affixed to the substrate are more reliable than those removed and submitted.

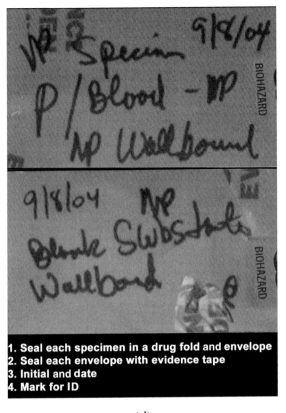

1. **Seal each specimen in a drug fold and envelope**
2. **Seal each envelope with evidence tape**
3. **Initial and date**
4. **Mark for ID**

(d)

Figure B.13d

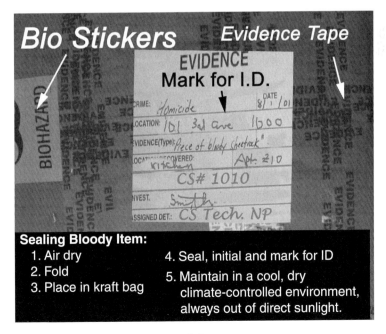

Bio Stickers   *Evidence Tape*

EVIDENCE
Mark for I.D.

BIOHAZARD

CRIME: Homicide   DATE 8/1/01
LOCATION: 101 3rd ave   1600
EVIDENCE(Type): Piece of bloody Sheetrak"
LOCATION RECOVERED: Kitchen   Apt. #10
CS# 1010
INVEST. Smith
ASSIGNED DET: CS Tech. NP

Sealing Bloody Item:
1. Air dry
2. Fold
3. Place in kraft bag
4. Seal, initial and mark for ID
5. Maintain in a cool, dry climate-controlled environment, always out of direct sunlight.

(e)

Figure B.13e

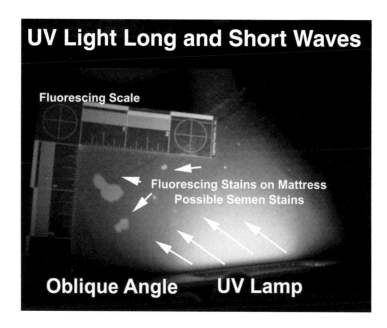

Figure B.14   Use of an alternate light source can often reveal the location of the specimen.

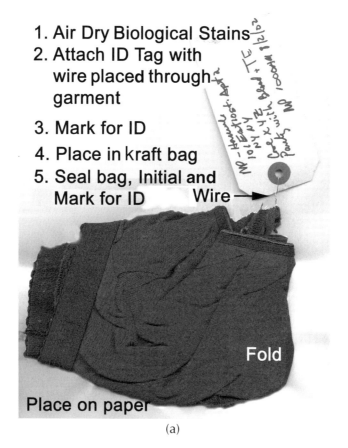

1. Air Dry Biological Stains
2. Attach ID Tag with wire placed through garment
3. Mark for ID
4. Place in kraft bag
5. Seal bag, Initial and Mark for ID

Wire →

Fold

Place on paper

(a)

Figure B.15a

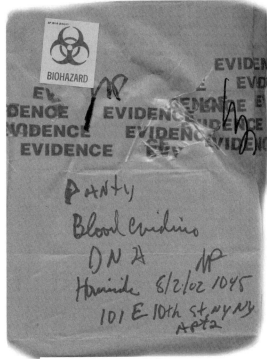

1. Seal in kraft bag
2. Initial and mark for ID
3. Refrigerate ASAP

(b)

Figure B.15b

Figure B.16

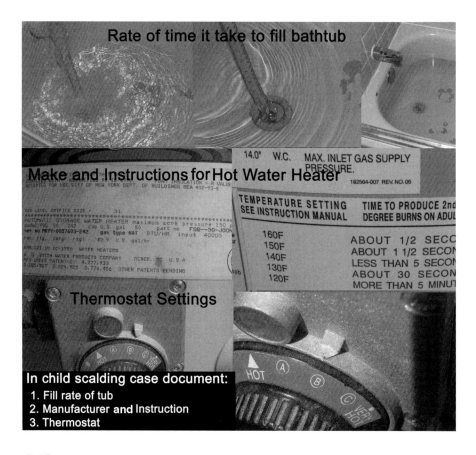

Figure B.17

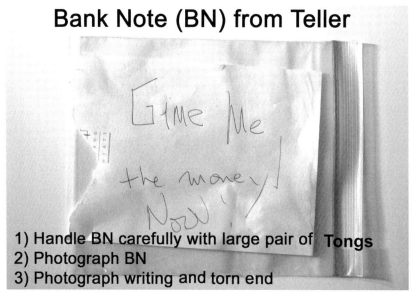

(a)

Figure B.18a

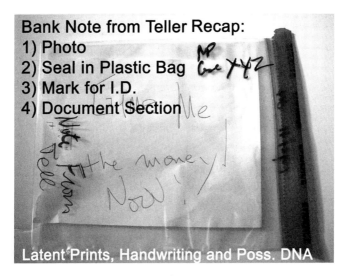

(b)

Figure B.18b

(a)

Figure B.19a

Seal and Initial

NP

INITIAL OVER SEAL AFTER SEALING BAG

8/11/04

Bag # → HA 020845

EVIDENCE

Information in box is mandatory

Agency/Department Name: _____

Case #: _____ Exhibit #: _____

Sealed by: *Metro* _____ Incident #: *Case XYZ*

Date/time of recovery (if different than line 1 below): *1015 8/11/04*

Location of evidence recovery: *in SUV on Pass Floor*

Evidence description: *$2 US Bill Ser # CE 04492 1506*

Suspect: _____ Victim: *CE 04492 1506*

CHAIN OF POSSESSION/CUSTODY
(Signatures Required)

FROM: TO: DATE/TIME:
1) *1 us Bill NP*
2)
3)
4)
5)

1. Seal with Tape and Initial
2. Mark for ID: Date, Time,
Location Collected, Case Number

(b)

Figure B.19b

(a)

Figure B.20a

(b)

Figure B.20b

Box with Tissue

1. Place charred document in a box
2. Gently wrap with tissue paper
3. Place cover on box, seal, initial and mark for I.D.

(c)

Figure B.20c

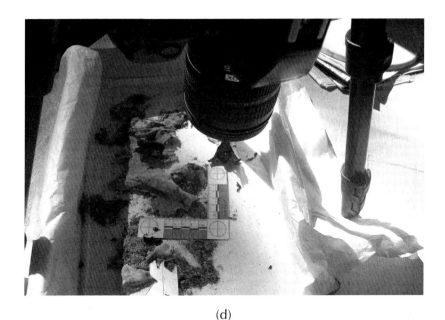

(d)

Figure B.20d

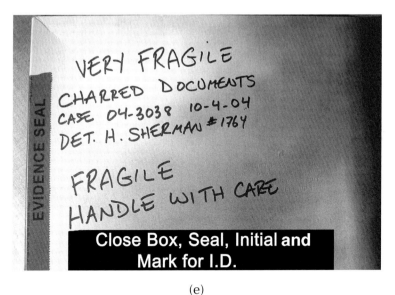

(e)

Figure B.20e

(f)

Figure B.20f Photograph once inside of box, with and without a scale. A tripod will allow for the camera to remain parallel to the object being photographed and minimize distortion.

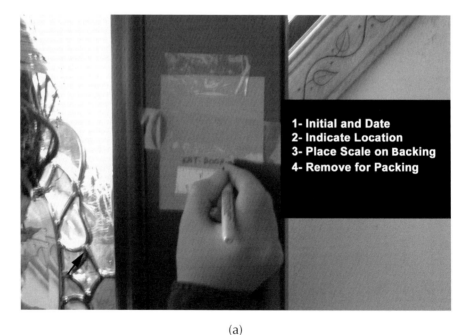

(a)

Figure B.21a Place any special handling instructions on the outside of the container's packaging.

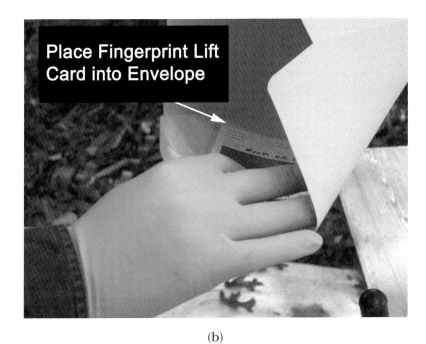

(b)

Figure B.21d

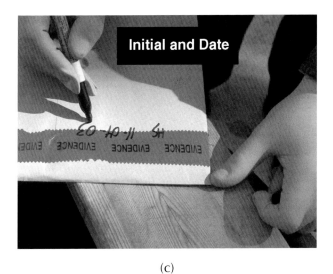

(c)

Figure B.21c

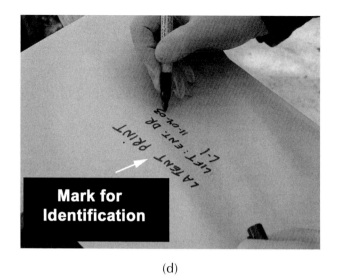

(d)

Figure B.21d

(a)

Figure B.22a　Glass samples must be packaged and secured to minimize breakage potential.

(b)

Figure B.22b Wallboard must be packaged properly. Consider placing a rigid object to hold secure the evidence.

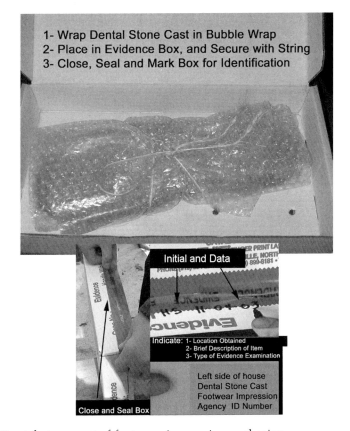

Figure B.23 Dental stone cast of footwear impression packaging.

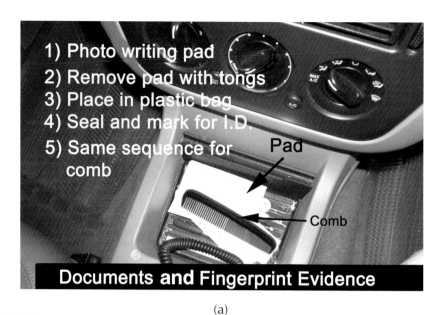

(a)

Figure B.24a

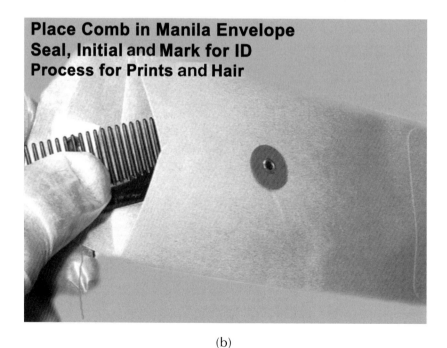

(b)

Figure B.24b

(a)

Figure B.25a Always consider additional test possibilities when choosing packaging methods.

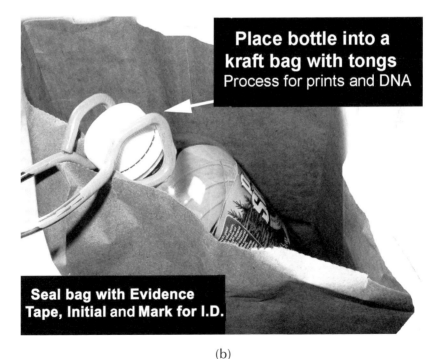

(b)

Figure B.25b Handle evidence as little as possible to ensure integrity of the samples and avoid possibly losing TE or obliterating latent points.

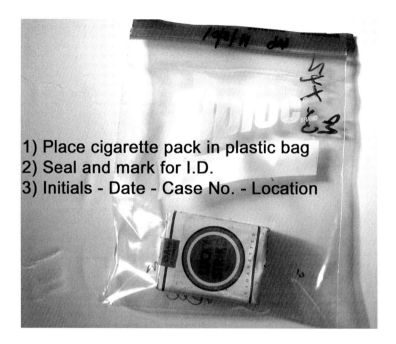

1) Place cigarette pack in plastic bag
2) Seal and mark for I.D.
3) Initials - Date - Case No. - Location

Figure B.26

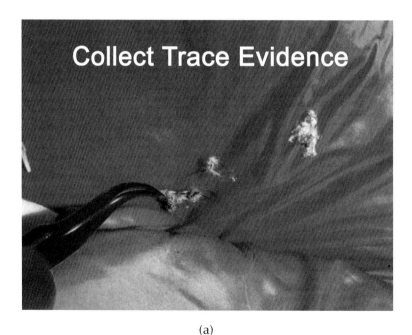

Collect Trace Evidence

(a)

Figure B.27a   Use tweezers for large items initially, then tape lift for smaller items.

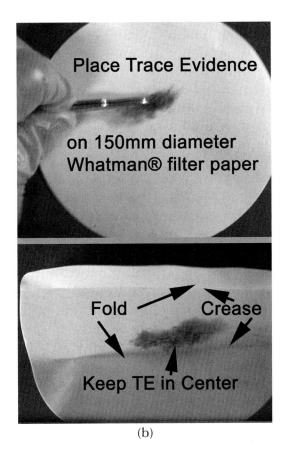

(b)

Figure B.27b

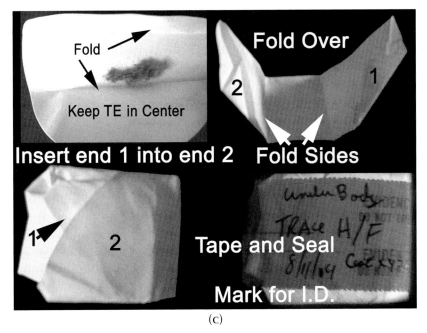

(c)

Figure B.27c Consider fashioning the filter paper into the druggist fold prior to placing the TE inside.

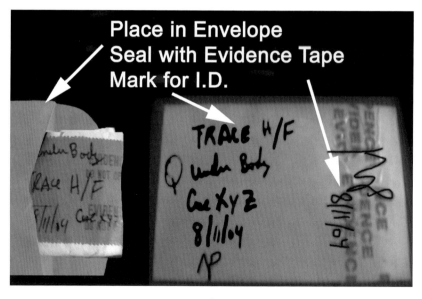

(d)

Figure B.27d   A hair and fiber druggist fold containing TE.

Figure B.28   Perform only after conferring with the medical examiner. Photograph evidence in place. Bag the hands afterwards.

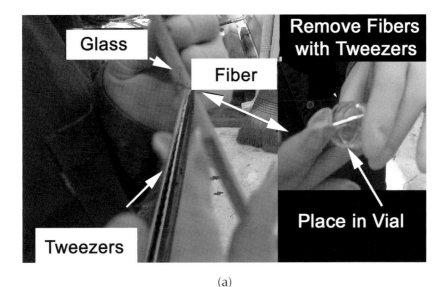

(a)

Figure B.29a

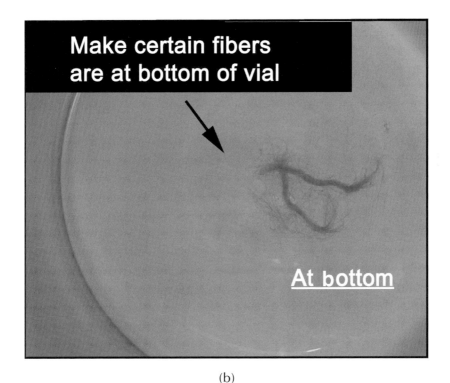

(b)

Figure B.29b   Always be sure the item is inside the packaging container before sealing.

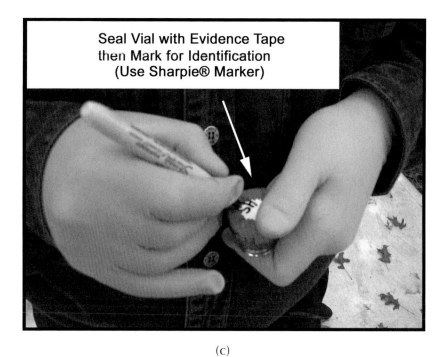

(c)

Figure B.29c

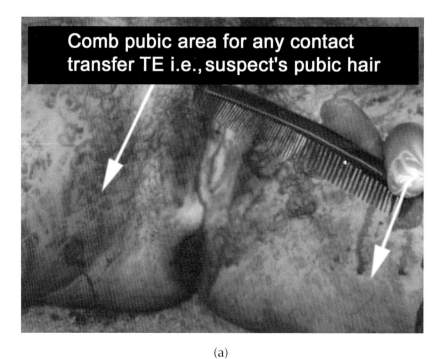

(a)

Figure B.30a Comb only with the knowledge and permission of the medical examiner. Package the comb and submit it along with the rest of the evidence.

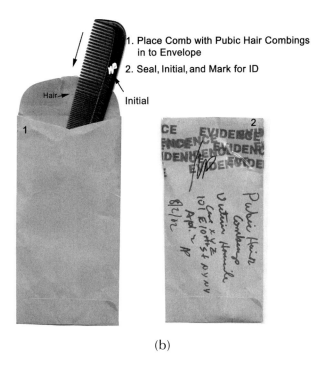

1. Place Comb with Pubic Hair Combings in to Envelope
2. Seal, Initial, and Mark for ID

Hair→

Initial

(b)

Figure B.30b

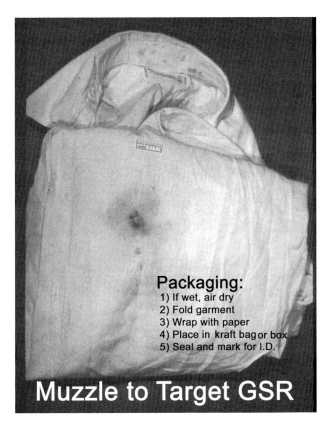

Packaging:
1) If wet, air dry
2) Fold garment
3) Wrap with paper
4) Place in kraft bag or box
5) Seal and mark for I.D.

Muzzle to Target GSR

Figure B.31 Photograph with and without a scale to document the condition at the time of recovery.

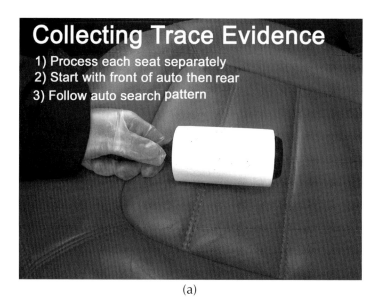

(a)

Figure B.32a Once the tape is no longer tacky, TE will not adhere to the tape and might fall off the tape.

(b)

Figure B.32b Package each area collected separately. Do not commingle different areas of collection on the same piece of tape or inside the same packaging container.

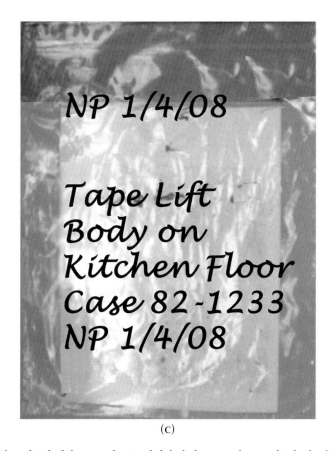

(c)

Figure B.32c If multiple lifts are obtained, label the area from which the lift was recovered.

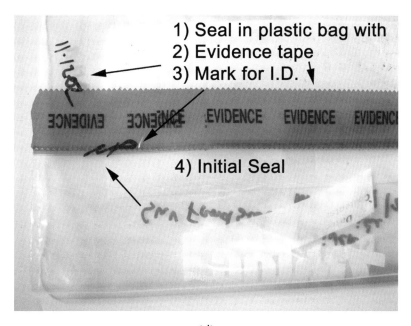

(d)

Figure B.32d

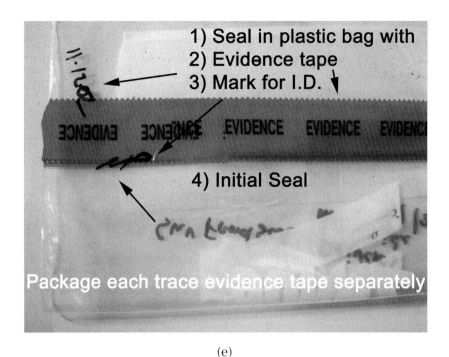

(e)

Figure B.32e

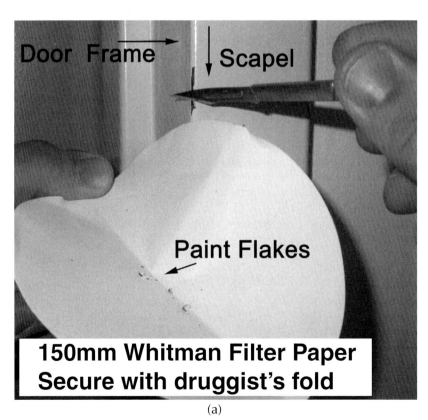

(a)

Figure B.33a   A piece of tape affixing the paper to the wall will minimize the loss of small flecks.

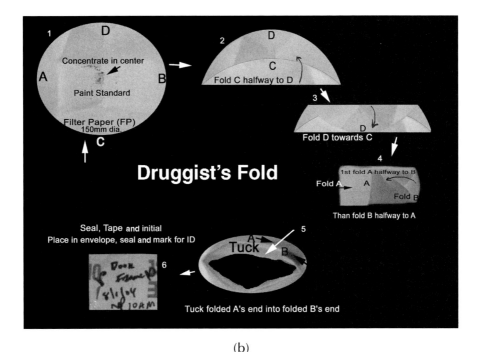

(b)

Figure B.33b Consider fashioning the druggist's fold prior to the sample collection.

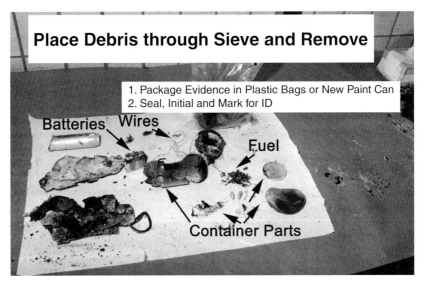

(a)

Figure B.34a

(b)

Figure B.34b   Seal tightly to prevent vapor loss.

(c)

Figure B.34c

NP 8/1/02
Suspected Accelerant
101 East 10th St. NY, N
Apt. #AZ23
Kitchen Cabinet
Case XZY

(Collect 2-4 Oz. in
Chemical Resistant
Plastic Bottle)

(d)

Figure B.34d

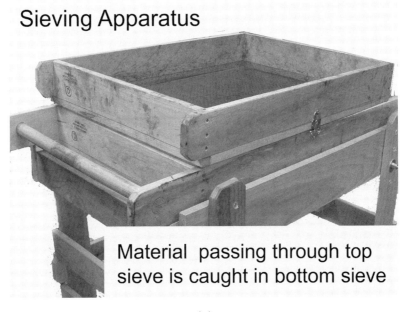

Sieving Apparatus

Material passing through top
sieve is caught in bottom sieve

(e)

Figure B.34e

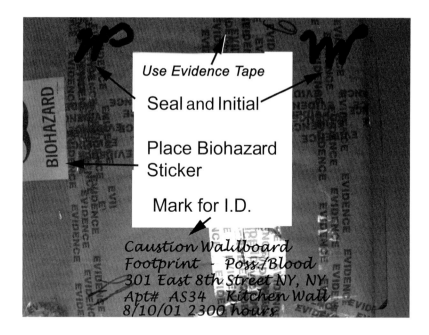

Figure B.35 Consider placing fragile items with a support to prevent breakage. Mark the packaging "Fragile" to ensure proper precautions are taken.

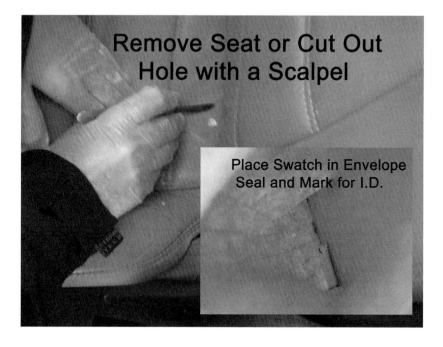

Figure B.36 Remove a section large enough to include the questioned area/sample along with an area sufficient in size to contain a control sample of the substrate that the questioned substance is deposited on.

Figure B.37   Gunshot residue (GSR) collection kit with the stubs. Kit was collected at the scene and analyzed at the lab. Make sure to collect a blank background.

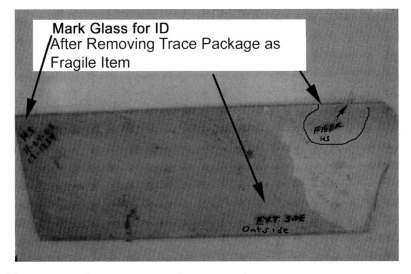

Figure B.38   Note on object interior and exterior sides.

Appendix C: Photographing a Crime Scene

Accurate and timely documentation is of fundamental importance when processing scenes of crime. A photographic record of the pristine crime scene is essential to the investigation, and ultimately to the presentation of the physical evidence in a court of law.

When photographing a crime scene, the crime scene examiner (CSE) must document all of the elements of the scene that will help the investigator understand when, where, and how the crime was committed. Consequently, intermediate and close-up views of the crime scene containing any perceived important aspects of the event should complement photographs of the general area. Each piece of physical evidence and the area in which it is located should be photographed so that the observer can locate it easily in relation to other objects in the crime scene.

Crime scene photographs should provide prospective views of the crime scene as it appeared to the CSE. The crime scene photographer should take enough photographs to show an area of the crime scene, an aspect of the crime, and an item of physical evidence satisfactorily. Normally, five photographs are required to meet these requirements. Overall views, intermediate views, close views, close-up views, and macro views are made of important objects and areas. Normally, three lenses and an array of photographic equipment are needed to adequately document a crime scene (see Figures C.1 to C.9). A detailed photographic record and log of each photograph should be maintained. An example of a blank form is shown.

The remaining illustrations depict important aspects of photographing and documenting a crime scene (see Figures C.10 to C.22).

Figure C.1   Focusing ring and F-stop aperture adjustment mechanism located on barrel of lens.

Figure C.2   Front view of Nikon D 100 camera body with 24-120mm lens attached.

Figure C.3   Lens sizes may vary and information specification of lens are written on top.

Figure C.4   Lens and area where lens is attached to a body of the camera.

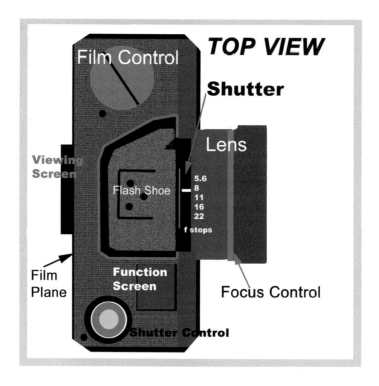

Figure C.5

Figure C.6   Camera with flash attached to hot shoe on top of body.

Figure C.7   Ensures no distortion of subject or item being photographed.

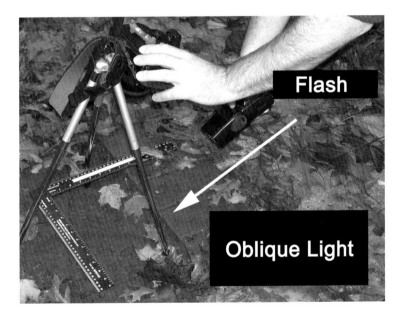

Figure C.8   Tripod allows for consistent photographs, especially useful when bracketing close-up objects.

Photographic Record Sheet

Page #___

Case No._____ Date Arrived_____ Time_____
Location of Crime:_____
Classification_____
Camera Model_____ Lens_____Film_____

Photo#	Subject	Date/Time	f-Stop/Exp.

Figure C.9

Figure C.10   Midrange or establish photo of the two victims.

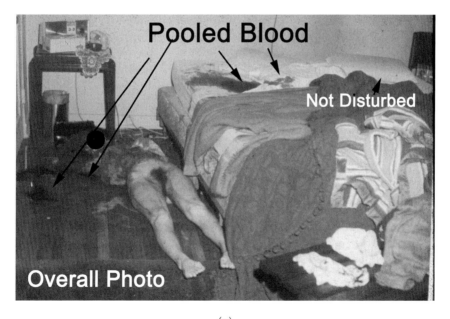

(a)

Figure C.11a

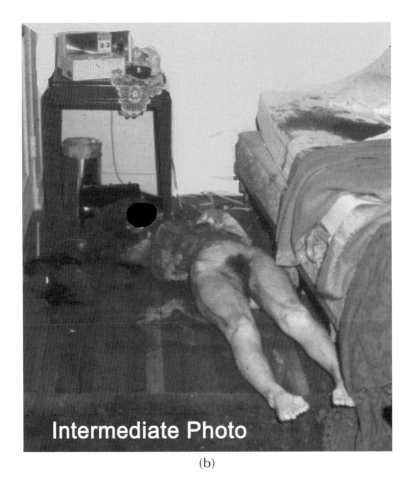

(b)

Figure C.11b   Photographs with a logical progression from overall to close-up.

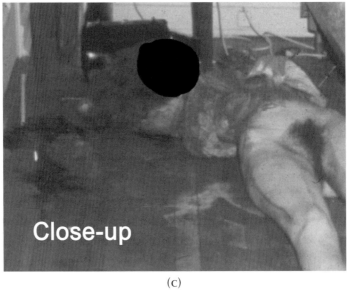

(c)

Figure C.11c

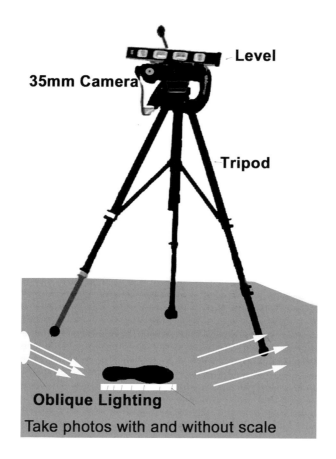

Figure C.12 Fill film frame, minimizing extraneous items in the photo.

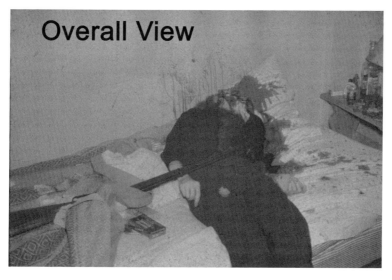

(a)

Figure C.13a Deceased with weapon and spatter on the wall.

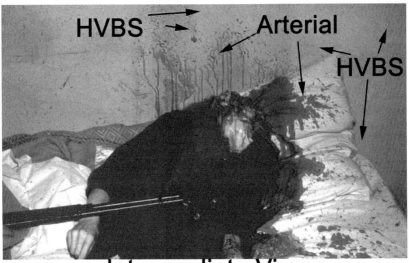

(b)

Figure C.13b

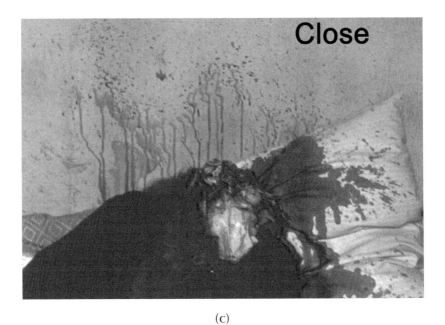

(c)

Figure C.13c

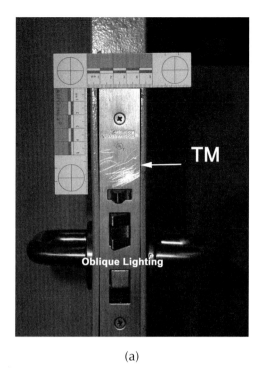

(a)

Figure C.14a   Midrange photo. Close-up to be taken filling film frame with the TM anomaly.

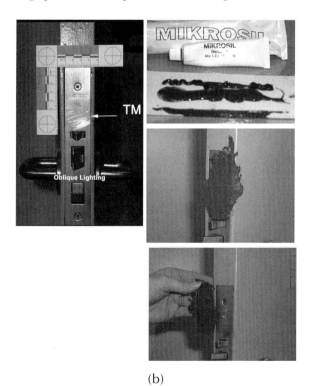

(b)

Figure C.14b   Mikrosi® Toolmark Recovery Substance.

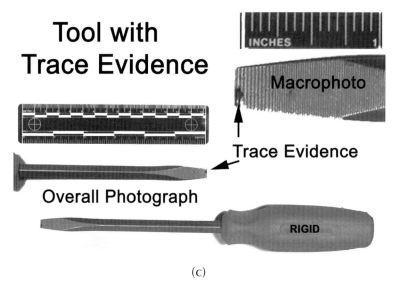

(c)

Figure C.14c   Do not attempt to remove the trace evidence from the tool at the scene, but do package it securely to prevent loss or damage.

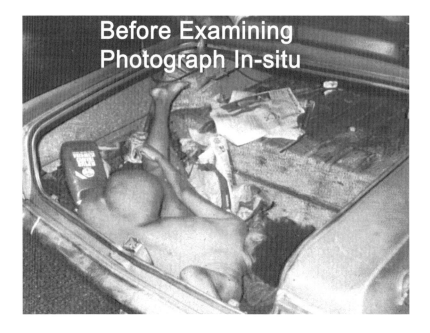

Figure C.15   Show each angle of the trunk and its contents and condition.

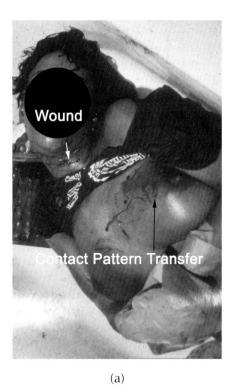

(a)

Figure C.16a Overall view of the footwear impression on the deceased's chest.

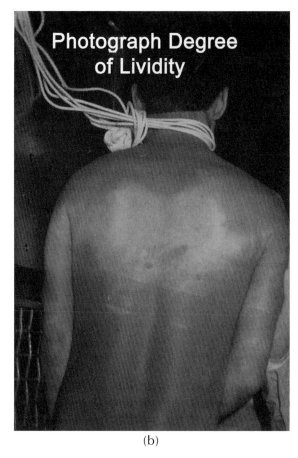

(b)

Figure C.16b   Lividity of livor mortis starts at the time of death. It becomes "fixed" after a period of time.

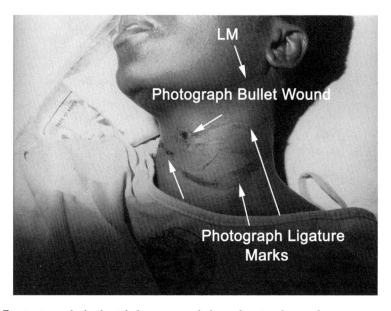

Figure C.17   Patient choked with ligature and then shot in the neck.

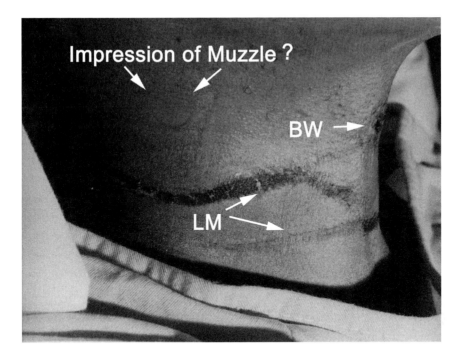

Figure C.18 Close-up view of the ligature marks without scale.

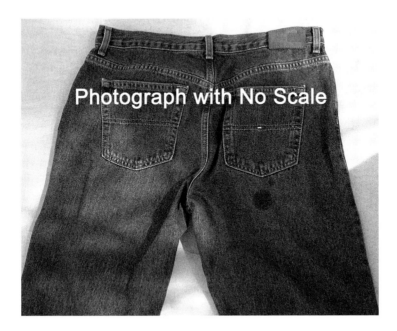

Figure C.19a Establishing view of the pants with a questioned substance below the right rear pocket.

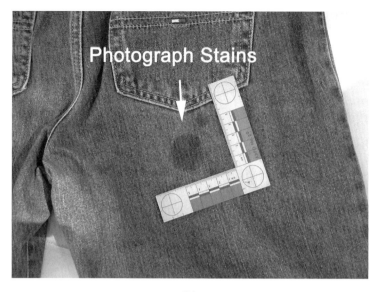

(b)

Figure C.19b   Close-up view of the questioned substance.

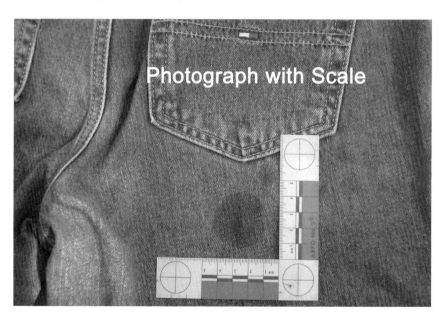

(c)

Figure C.19c   An ABFO ruler is used to show the lack of distortion.

(a)

Figure C.20a   Midrange view of the couch cushion.

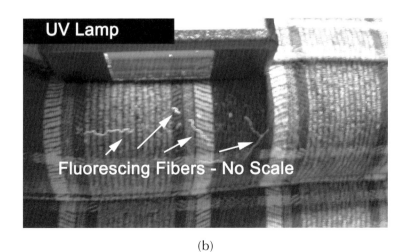

(b)

Figure C.20b   Close-up view of the fibers on the couch cushion.

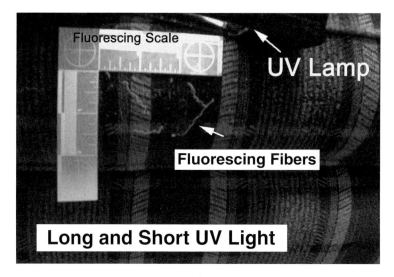

(c)

Figure C.20c   Fluorescing fibers with fluorescing scale.

Figure C.21

Figure C.22   A bulb can only be used while the camera is secured onto a tripod.

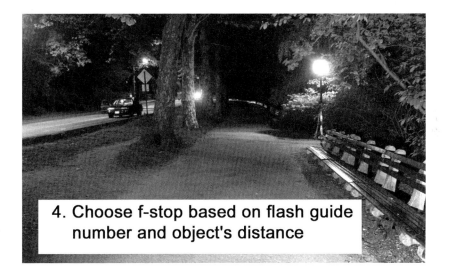

Figure C.23   If available, remove the flash from the camera and use a pop flash in various areas while the shutter release is continuously depressed.

5. Hold dark card over lens, open the shutter and take photograph with flash, cover lens with card

6. Repeat several times as needed (normally 4 exposures)

Figure C.24

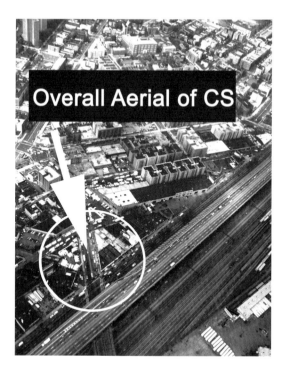

Overall Aerial of CS

Figure C.25 An overall view shows the highway and other transportation facilities.

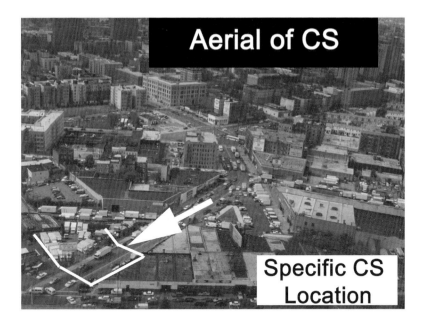

Figure C.26

Figure C.27

Figure C.28

Photographic Log

Location _____

Date _____ Time _____ Case No. _____

Digital or Film _____ Camera Model _____ Lens _____

Picture No.	Subject/Description	Date/Time	F-Stop/Shutter Speed	ISO/DIN

CSE preparing _____

Remarks _____

_____

_____

_____

_____

Appendix D: Photographic Review of Recognition and Documentation of Physical Evidence

This appendix contains photographic reviews of various types of physical evidence frequently encountered at scenes of crimes. The recognition, preliminary examination, and documentation of common categories of physical evidence are depicted. The intent of this appendix is to serve as a reminder of the types of physical evidence the investigator should be looking for at scenes of crimes. It is intended primarily for inexperienced investigators and new crime scene examiners.

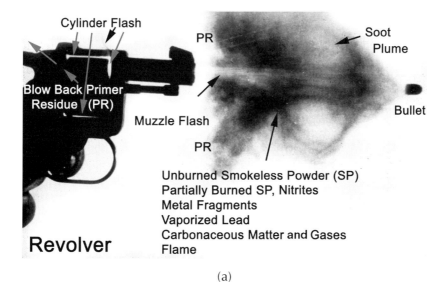

(a)

Figure D.1a Discharging a revolver. Note the flight of residue and the projectile.

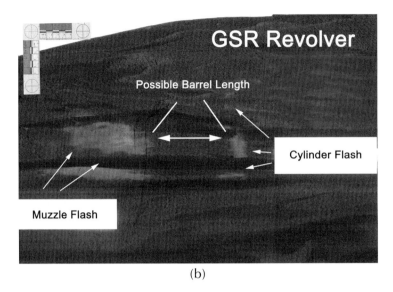

(b)

Figure D.1b Photograph with and without a scale. Package to prevent the substance from coming into contact with something else.

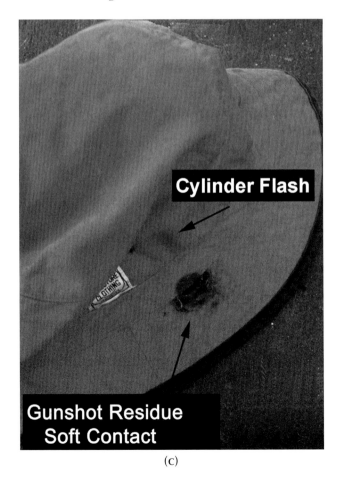

(c)

Figure D.1c

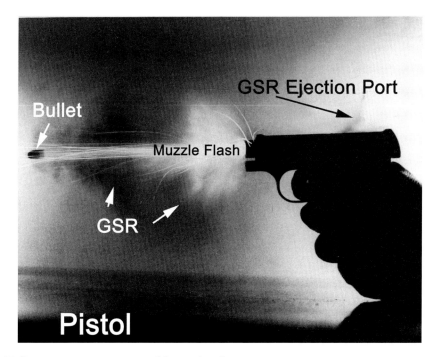

Figure D.2 Semi-automatic pistol being fired.

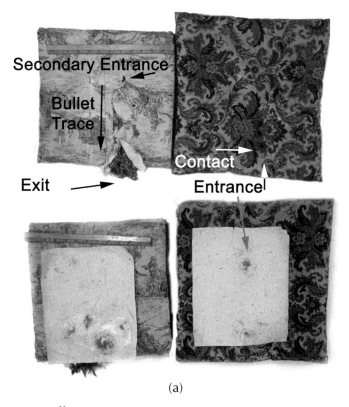

(a)

Figure D.3a GSR on pillows.

(b)

Figure D.3b   Submit the entire item, if possible. Otherwise, remove a piece with questioned anomaly and a control sample.

(a)

Figure D.4a   Microscopic view of smokeless gunpowder.

(b)

Figure D.4b Black powder grains.

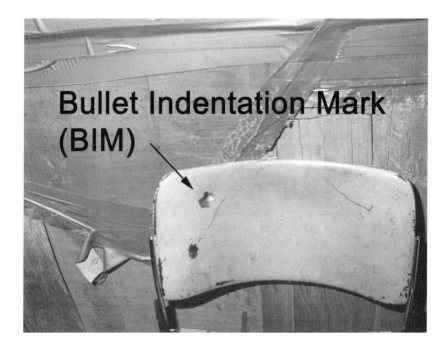

Figure D.5 BIMs need to be documented from two fixed points. Remove the entire BH and surrounding area if practical. Photograph overall and also macro to show directionality of bullet travel.

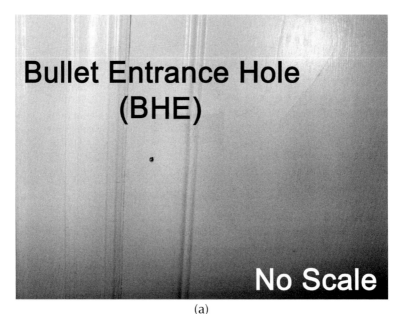

(a)

Figure D.6a   Overall or establishing view.

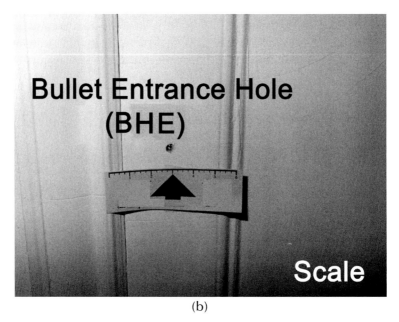

(b)

Figure D.6b   Midrange view.

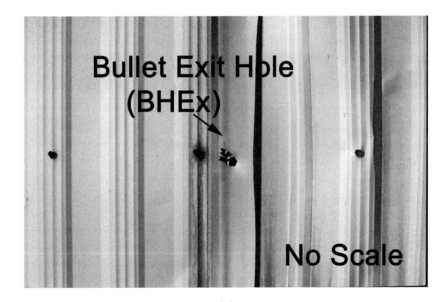

(a)

Figure D.7a Bullet hole exit point (BHEx).

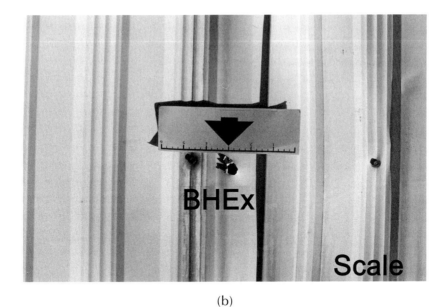

(b)

Figure D.7b Bullet hole exit point (BHEx).

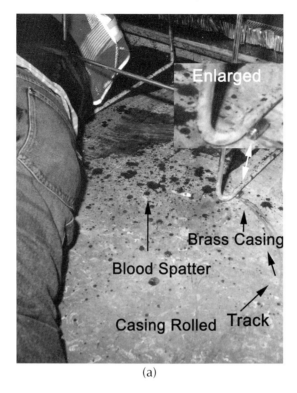

(a)

Figure D.8a   Take an overhead shot, if possible.

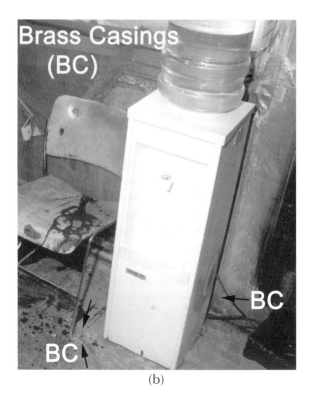

(b)

Figure D.8b   Photograph brass casing position(s).

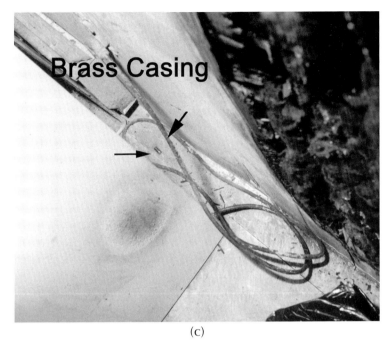

(c)

Figure D.8c Brass casing photographed at crime scene.

Figure D.9 Hairs and fibers affixed to bullet. Be mindful to document and preserve the trace evidence. DO NOT attempt to remove the TE prior to examination of evidence at the lab.

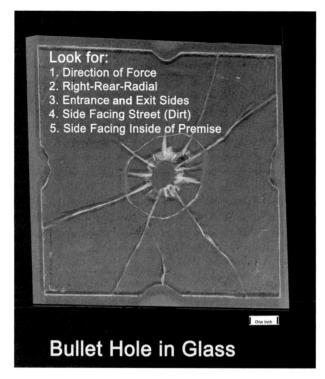

Figure D.10 Place camera on tripod, take photos without flash. Take time exposore to avoid hot spot from flash bracket exposures, be sure to include a scale.

Figure D.11 If breakage is possible, place identifying marks on each section to maintain proper orientation.

Figure D.12   Do not allow items to come into contact with each other. Examination for trace evidence (TE) would be compromised.

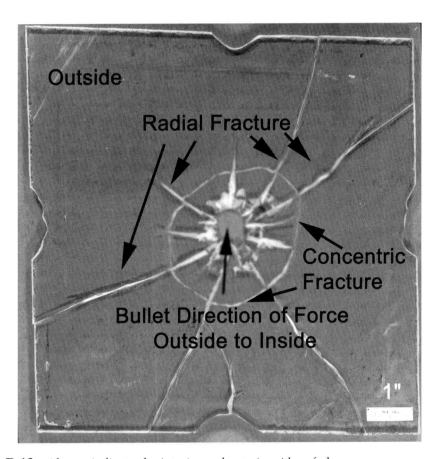

Figure D.13   Always indicate the interior and exterior sides of glass.

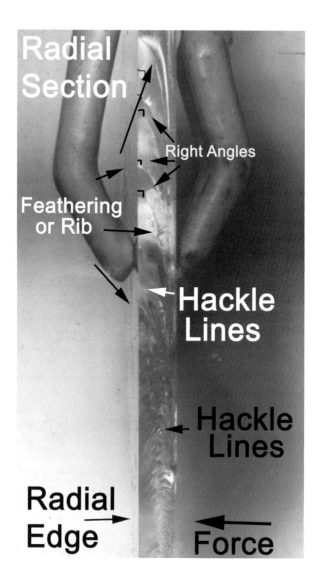

Figure D.14   The side of a glass pane shows the directionality of the force applied.

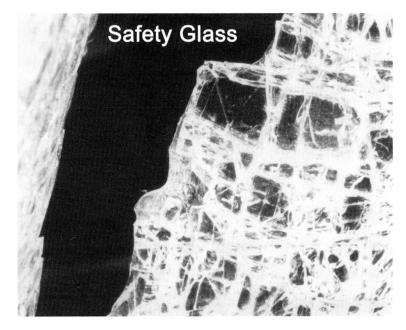

Figure D.15 Safety glass breaks into many small pieces to avoid large sections which can cause greater injury.

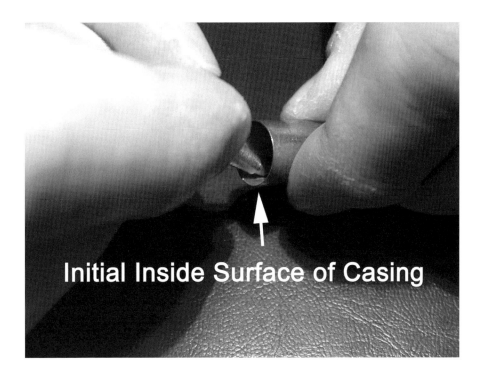

Figure D.16 Proper location to place initials to avoid damaging area being analyzed.

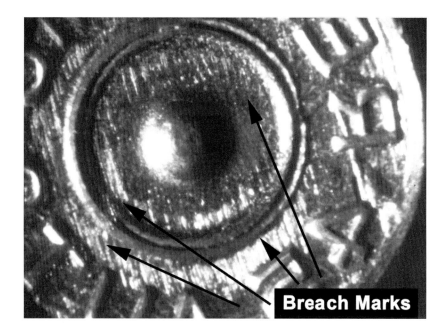

Figure D.17   Head stamp of discharged shell casing with primer hit and breach marks.

Rifle

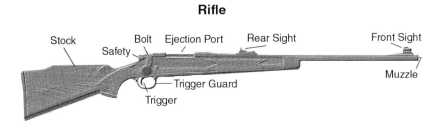

Figure D.18

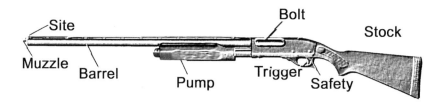

Figure D.19   Rifle and shotgun nomenclature.

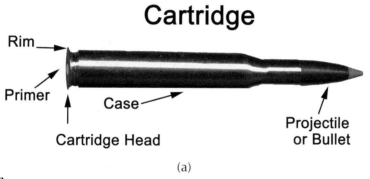

(a)

Figure D.20a

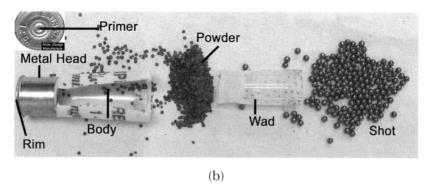

(b)

Figure D.20b   Components or shotgun shell and cartridge.

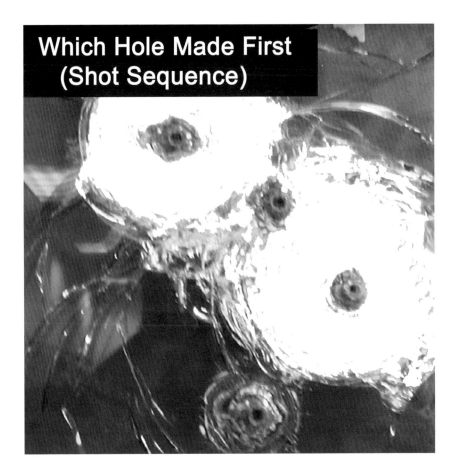

Figure D.21 A crack cannot jump over an existing crack in glass.

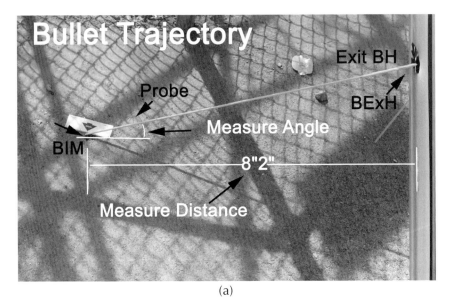

(a)

Figure D.22a Two fixed points are required to obtain a bullet path trajectory.

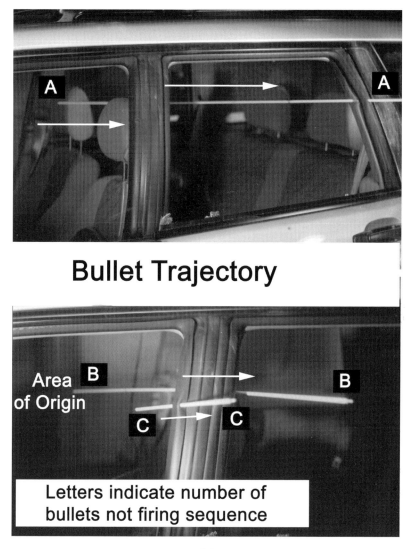

(b)

Figure D.22b   Rods show the path of travel.

Firearms **Form**

Case No._____, Time_____, Date_____

Location_____

Firearm Type_____Caliber_____

Serial No._____

Revolver: Indicate Direction of Cylinder Rotation: CW or CCW

Firearm Type: Rev.   Pistol   Shotgun   Rifle   Other_____

Rotation   Model_____, Manufacturer_____

Serial No._____

Shotgun Gauge_____

DB   Side-by-Side

SB

DB

Over-Under

Choke: Full   Modified

Derringer

Magazine Type

Indicate where cartridges were
found in weapon and their condition:

Live (L) Spent (S)   Empty (E)

Ammo: Brand_____
Caliber_____
Primer Type _____

Figure D.23   It is important to note the location of cartridges, ammunition, and also discharged shell casings inside of the cylinder.

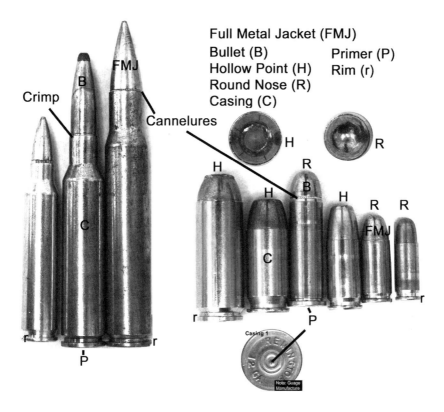

Figure D.24

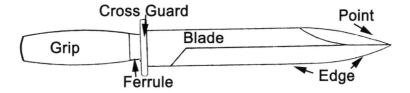

Figure D.25   Components of a dagger.

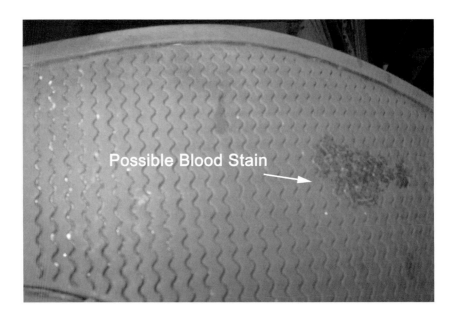

Figure D.26   A small area from this suspected blood stain will be used for a presumptive test. If the test shows a presumptive positive, a sample of the questioned substance, along with a substrate sample will be documented, collected, and forwarded to the appropriate lab for further analysis.

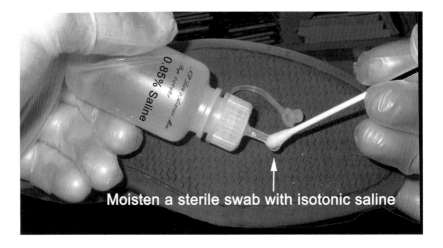

Figure D.27   Be sure not to overdampen the swab. The redder the sample, the better the sample. In cases where the sample is so minute to only allow one swab, submit the entire item to the lab.

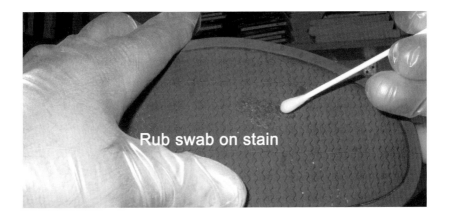

Figure D.28 Carefully collect the stain, trying not to remove the entire stain. This is especially important when a small quantity is present.

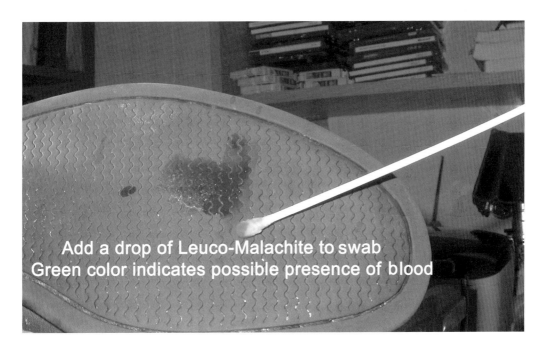

Figure D.29 A color change indicates a presumptive presence of blood.

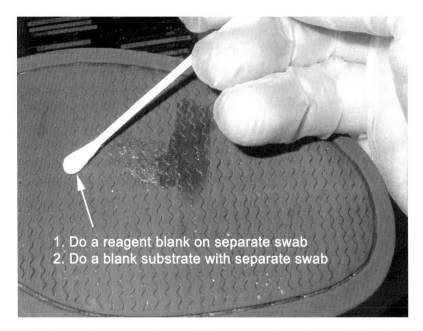

Figure D.30   Always take a control sample from an unaffected area of the substrate.

Figure D.31   Three bullets can be seen lodged in the safety glass window.

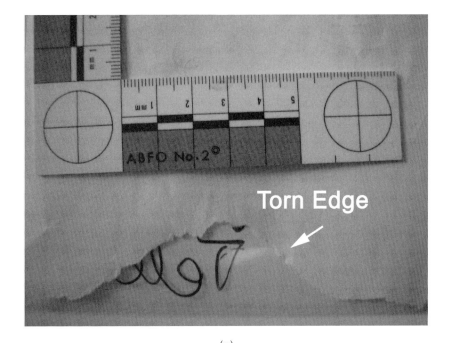

(a)

Figure D.32a Portions of a banknote with a torn edge. Be sure to maintain the morphology of the torn edge.

(b)

Figure D.32b Questioned handwriting sample recovered at the scene.

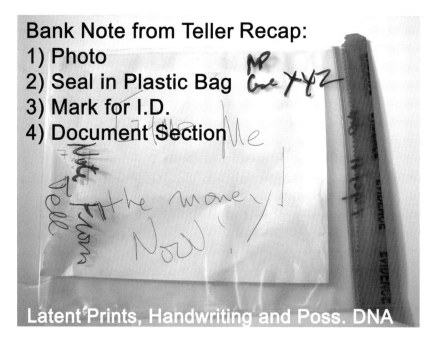

(c)

Figure D.32c   Package evidence. Label the packaging prior to placing the evidence inside to avoid possibly changing the note, i.e., you do not want to add indented writing to the note.

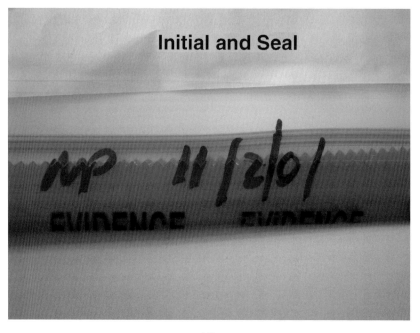

(d)

Figure D.32d   Tamper evident tape with investigator's "sign and seal" with initials and date sealed.

1. Collect Bill with Tongs
2. Place Bill in Serial Numbered Evidence Bag
3. Seal with Tape and Initial
4. Mark for ID: Date, Time, Location Collected, Case Number

INITIAL OVER SEAL AFTER SEALING BAG

AA 020845

EVIDENCE

Information in box is mandatory

ncy/Department Name:

e #: _____ Exhibit #:

d by:

(a)

Figure D.33a

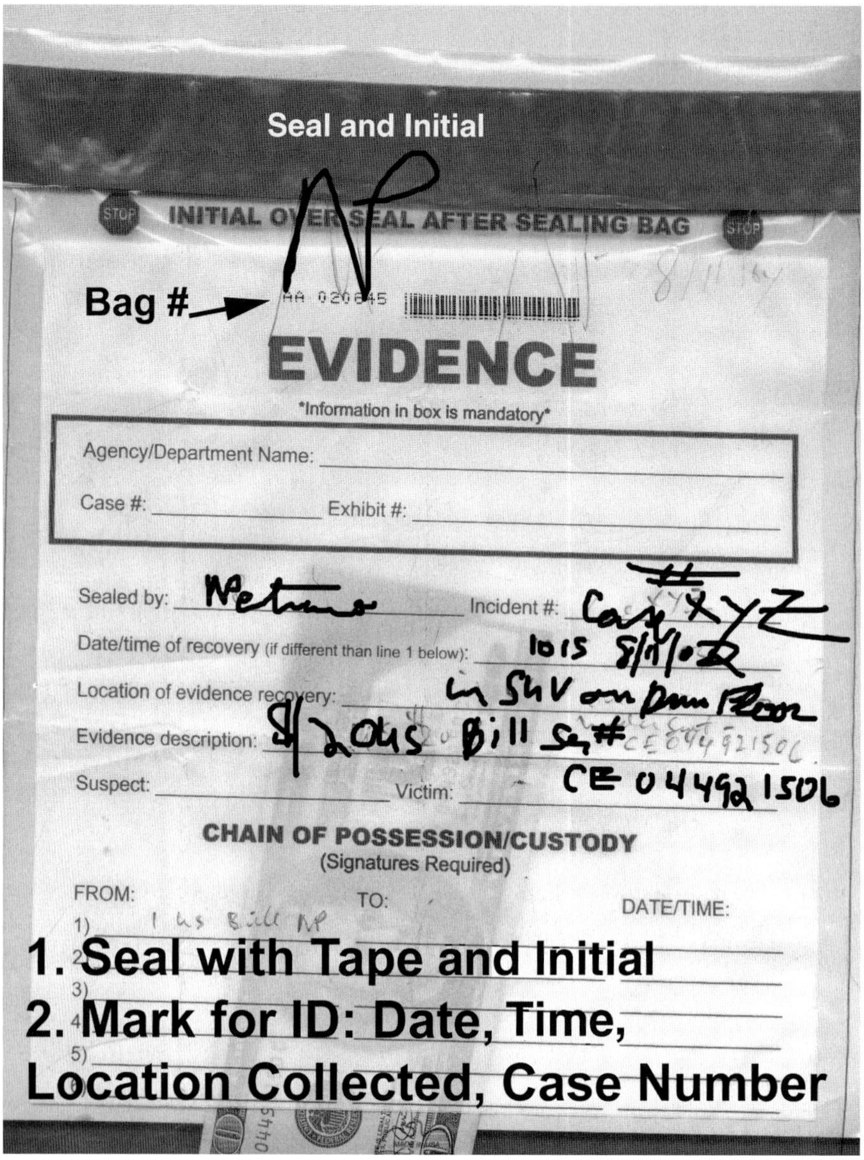

(b)

Figure D.33b

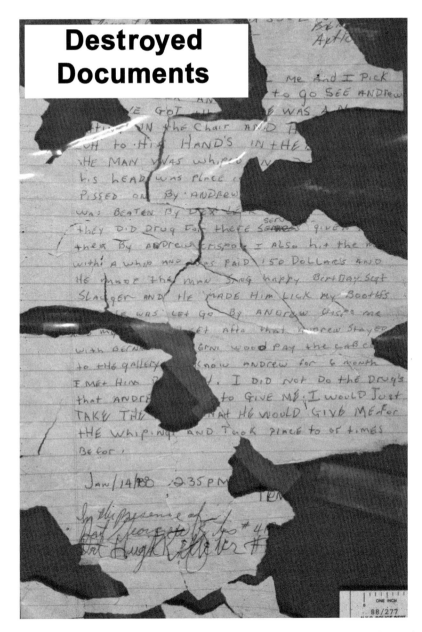

Figure D.34   Preserve destroyed documents in a bag. Be cognizant that additional examinations may be requested. Do analysis that is least destructive first. Do not tape pieces together.

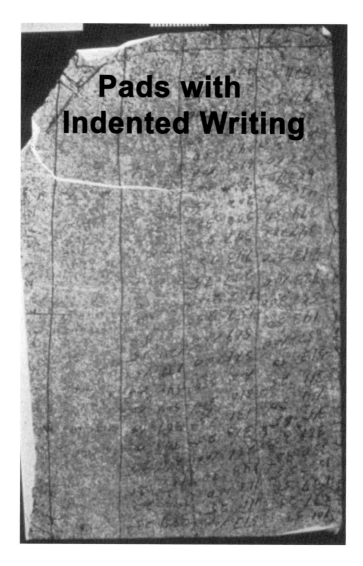

Figure D.35   Package the item, preferrably in an overpack. That would prevent any inadvertent changes to the pages that will be analyzed.

Figure D.36   Photograph, gently recover document remnants, and package. Be sure to write "Fragile, Handle with Care" on the package.

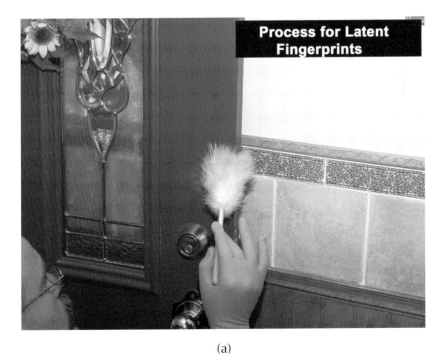

(a)

Figure D.37a   Place a quantity of contrasting powder on a brush and apply to the area being processed. Do not overapply the powder. Less is better. More powder can always be applied.

(b)

Figure D.37b

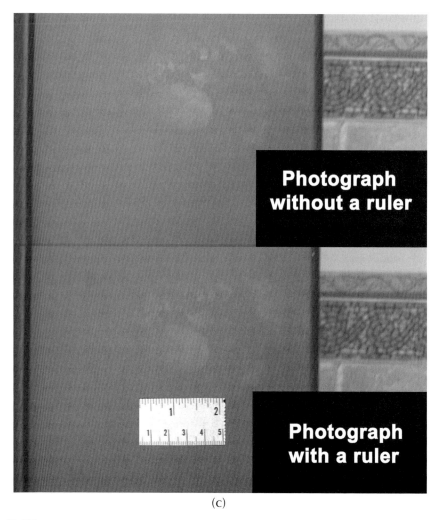

(c)

Figure D.37c

(d)

Figure D.37d Have backing in proximity to the area being processed.

(e)

Figure D.37e Apply and remove the tape in one fluid motion so you don't add any anomalies to the lift.

(f)

Figure D.37f

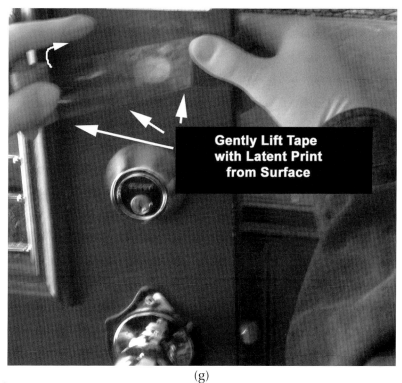

Gently Lift Tape with Latent Print from Surface

(g)

Figure D.37g

Place Lift on Backing

(h)

Figure D.37h Apply the lift to the backing. Place a portion of the tape with no lift onto the edge of the lifter, allowing the latest impression to be in the center of the lifter.

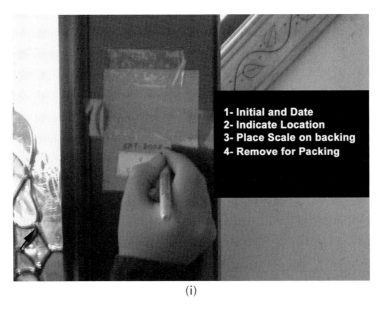

(i)

Figure D.37i

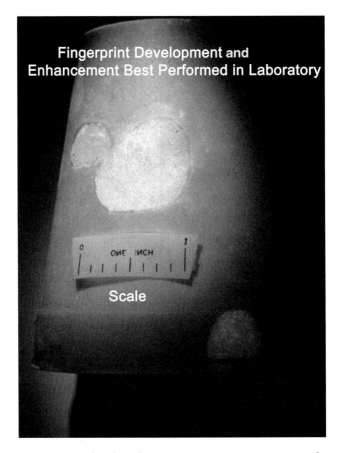

Figure D.38 Fingerprint was developed using a Copper Vapor Laser and REDWOP.

1- Lightly Spray Paper with Ninhydrin
2- Steam with Steam Iron
3- Beat Done in Laboratory Setting

Figure D.39

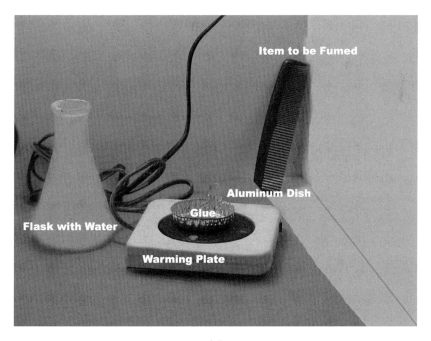

Item to be Fumed

Aluminum Dish

Glue

Flask with Water

Warming Plate

(a)

Figure D.40a Cyandacrylate fuming of object allows polymerization of the lift. The friction ridges become plasticized.

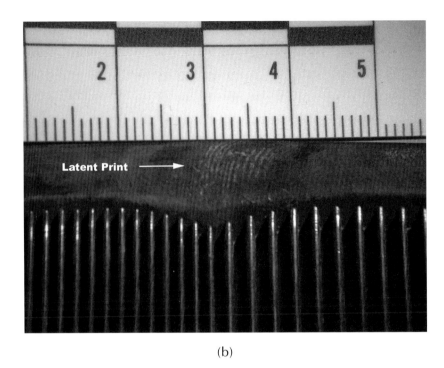

(b)

Figure D.40b   Certain objects (nonporous) are best processed using CA cyandacrylate. When forwarding to the lab, secure the item so that the potential lift is not destroyed.

(a)

Figure D.41a   Black powder is applied to a light surface and white power to darker backgrounds. Gently stroke the object because latent prints are fragile and may be destroyed if a brush is dragged across the ridges.

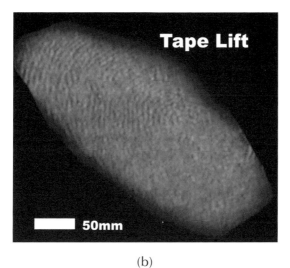

(b)

Figure D.41b Super Glue® lifted this fingerprint from a comb.

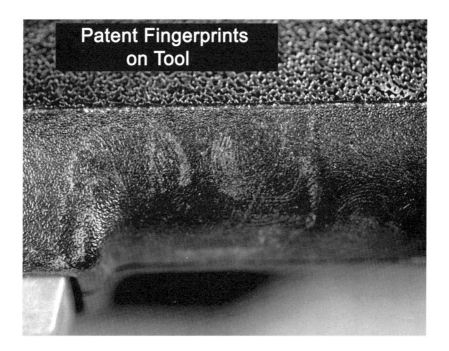

Figure D.42 Super Glue was used to develop this fingerprint on a black plastic tool handle.

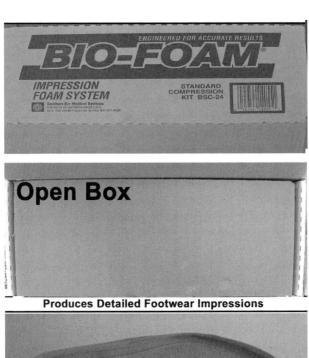

Figure D.43 Bio-Foam is an easy and useful way to obtain footwear standards.

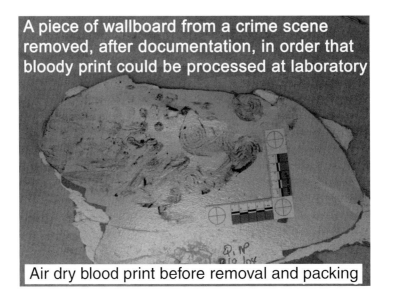

Figure D.44

(a)

Figure D.45a   If possible, remove the section of floor with dust footwear print and send to the laboratory. Cover the print with protective sheets of paper.

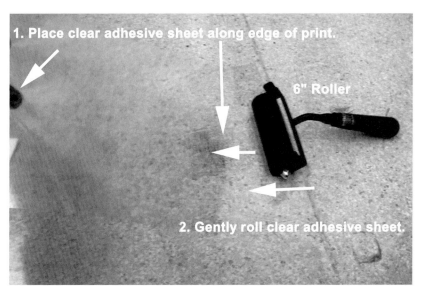

(b)

Figure D.45b   If it isn't possible to remove the floor section with the print, lift the print, as shown above.

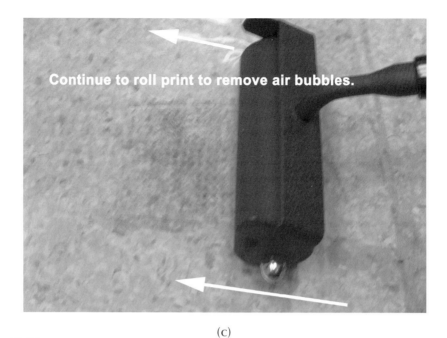

(c)

Figure D.45c

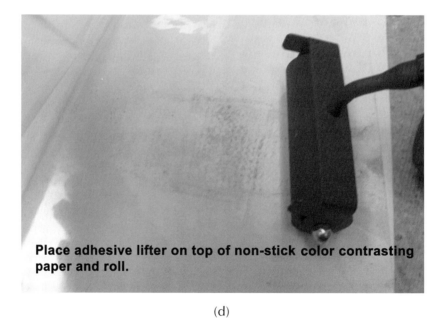

(d)

Figure D.45d

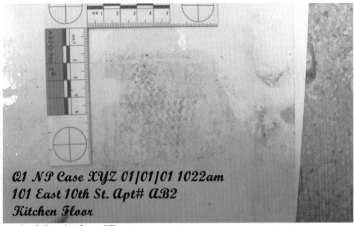

Q1 NP Case XYZ 01/01/01 1022am
101 East 10th St. Apt# AB2
Kitchen Floor

1. Mark for ID
2. Place in an Envelope
3. Seal **and** Initial the Envelope
4. Mark Envelope for ID

(e)

Figure D.45e   A spatula placed beneath the tile allows the tile to be lifted while minizing the chance for breakage. Heat applied with an acetylene torch will loosen the adhesive.

Crimescope
Enhanced with Redwop®
Blood Print on Linoleum

After

Excitation 535nm
Barrier Filter Wratten #22

Before

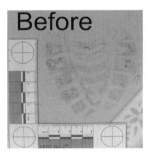

Figure D.46

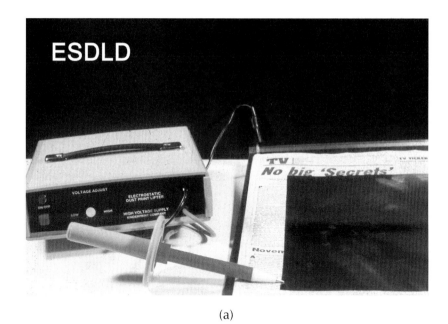

(a)

Figure D.47a Electrostatic dust impression lifting device.

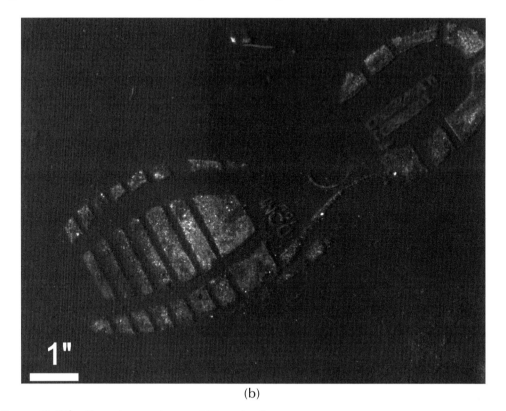

(b)

Figure D.47b Dust impression on ESDLD backing.

Figure D.48

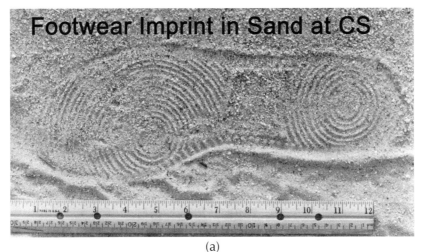

(a)

Figure D.49a   Fill film frame with important content.

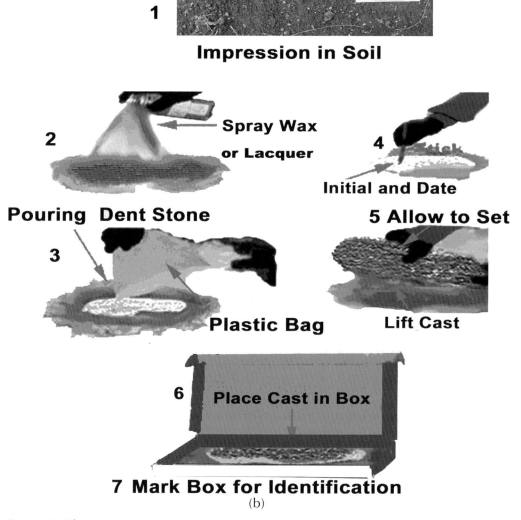

1

Impression in Soil

2 Spray Wax or Lacquer

4 Initial and Date

Pouring   Dent Stone

5 Allow to Set

3

Plastic Bag

Lift Cast

6 Place Cast in Box

7 Mark Box for Identification

(b)

Figure D.49b

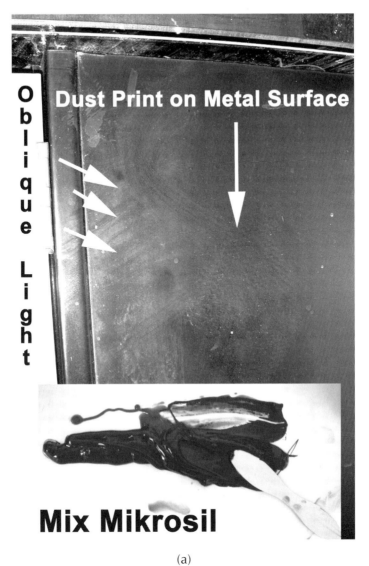

(a)

Figure D.50a

(b)

Figure D.50b Start applying Mikrosil with a spatula a short distance from the actual object being recovered. Apply a thin, even layer of the Mikrosil.

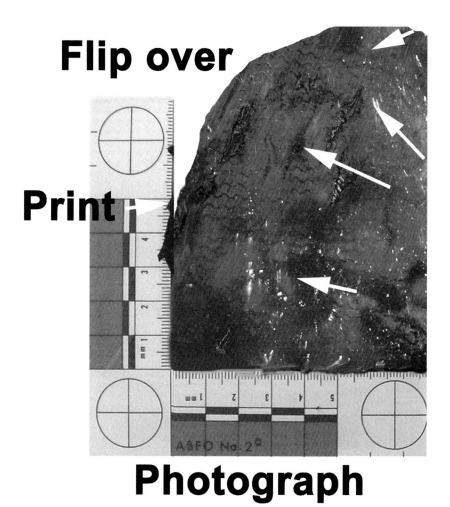

(c)

Figure D.50c   Remember: the lift has to be photographed and reversed photographically to compare to an inked print.

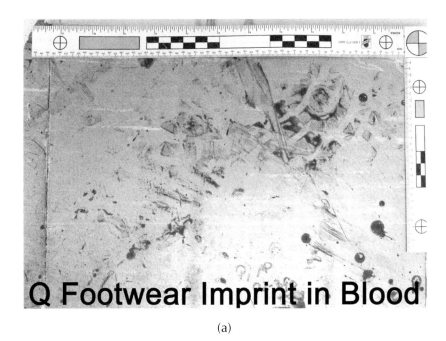

(a)

Figure D.51a Untreated floor tile. Fill the film frame and photograph with a scale.

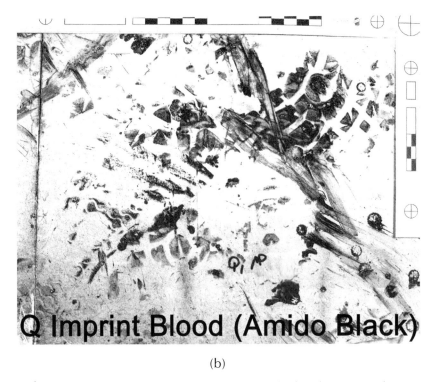

(b)

Figure D.51b After amido black, a protein stain was applied at the scene. Whenever possible, remove the item and forward to the lab to be processed under ideal conditions.

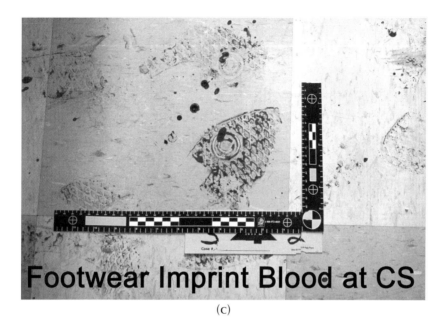

(c)

Figure D.51c

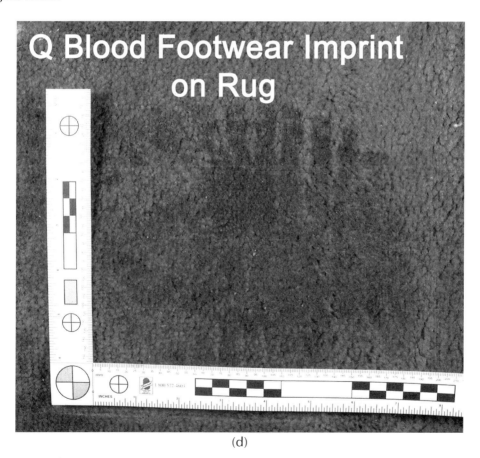

(d)

Figure D.51d Cut the section from the carpet. Keep it flat, and forward to the lab. Do not package in plastic.

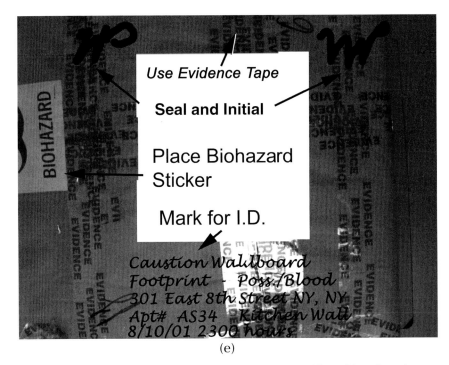

Use Evidence Tape

Seal and Initial

Place Biohazard Sticker

Mark for I.D.

Caustion Wallboard
Footprint - Poss./Blood
301 East 8th Street NY, NY
Apt# AS34   Kitchen Wall
8/10/01 2300 hours

BIOHAZARD

(e)

Figure D.51e If required, place a rigid object behind the wallboard (or object) to secure and prevent breakage.

Bullet Struck Watch Band

Bullet

Figure D.52

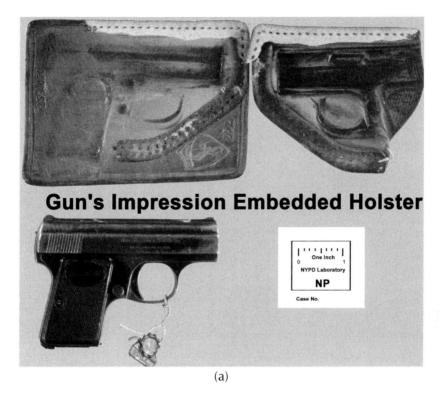

(a)

Figure D.53a   If recovered separately, do not place the weapon inside the holdster until it is documented photographically at the lab.

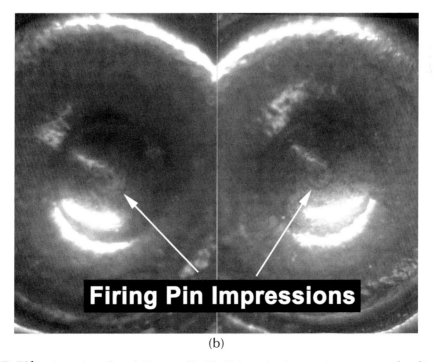

(b)

Figure D.53b   Questioned and Known (Q-K). Firing pin impressions are on the discharged shell casing.

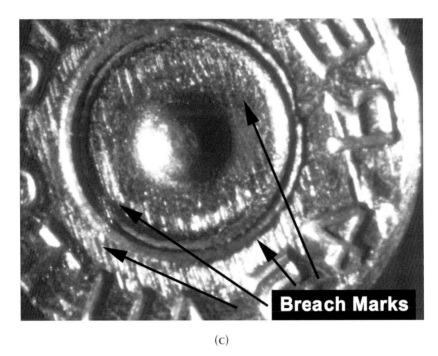

(c)

Figure D.53c Package so the breach marks do not rub or scratch against another similar object.

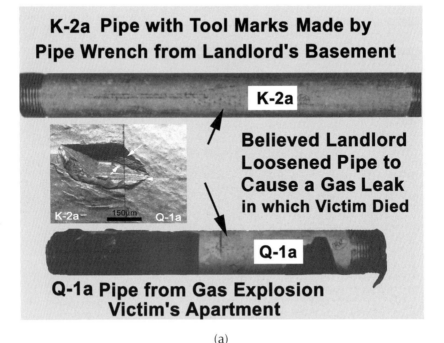

(a)

Figure D.54a Do not place the tool onto the object without ample documentation. Trace evidence might be lost or compromised. Documentation is best performed at the lab. Package each item separately.

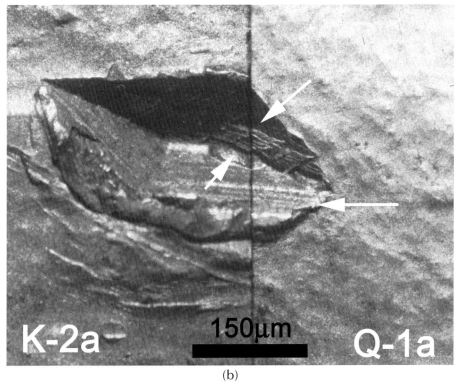

(b)

Figure D.54b   Macro view of tool mark on known and questioned pipe surface.

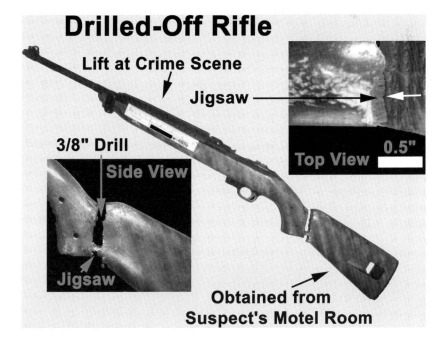

Figure D.55   Drilled-out rifle.

(a)

Figure D.56a Be aware that a scene may be staged, where a "burglary" is fabricated by a "victim."

(b)

Figure D.56b

(c)

Figure D.56c

(a)

Figure D.57a   Photograph the interior and exterior of the door as well as all locking devices.

(b)

Figure D.57b   The cylinder is removed by CSE, and documentation is performed at the lab.

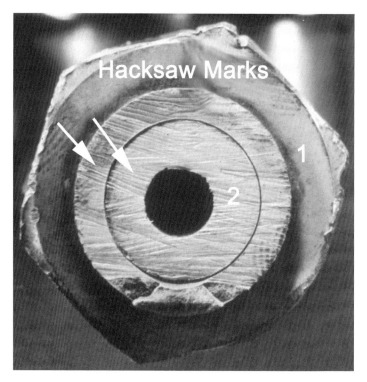

Figure D.58   The barrel of a gun. It is the CSE's function to properly preserve and package the evidence so that the minutiae are not disturbed or changed.

Figure D.59 A search warrant was executed to obtain a gun. The gun was reported to have been shot beneath a cushion on a sofa. At the time the warrant was executed, the gun was found in the backyard. The pillow was recovered. Because the proper techniques were used for packaging and preservation, the lab was able to enhance the impression and show that the weapon had been fired inside the apartment.

Figure D.60

(a)

Figure D.61a   Use a flashlight source to search for fibers.

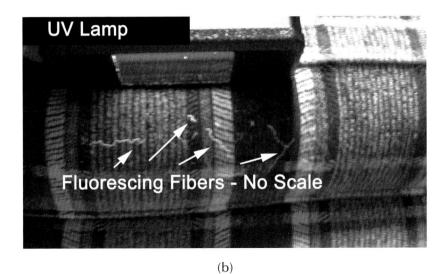

(b)

Figure D.61b   Use an alternate light source to excite the fibers and make them fluorescent.

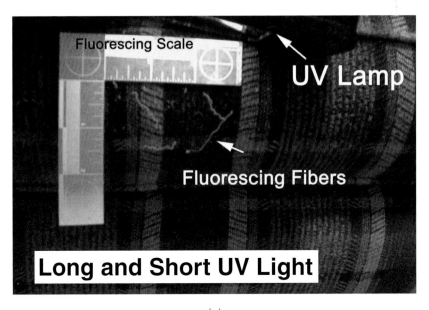

(c)

Figure D.61c

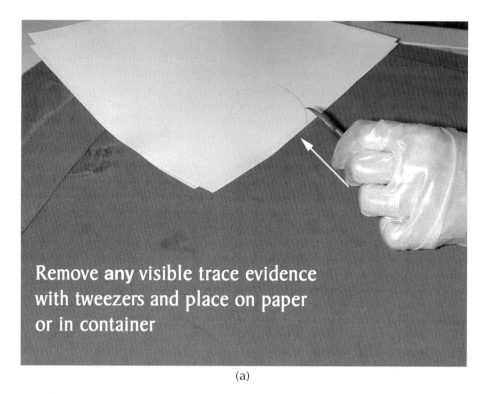

Remove **any** visible trace evidence with tweezers and place on paper or in container

(a)

Figure D.62a   Remove or recover the hair and fibers that are visible.

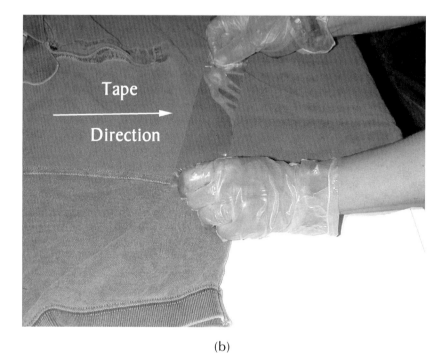

Tape

Direction

(b)

Figure D.62b   Pat the tape lift onto the surface. When the tape is no longer tacky, items will no longer adhere to the tape, and you run the risk of losing the trace evidence that was previously on the tape.

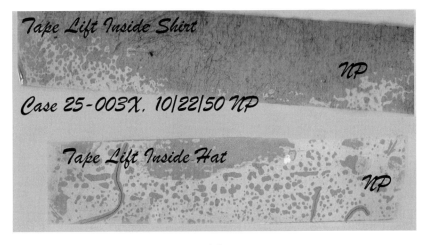

(c)

Figure D.62c Place the tape lifts from different locations into different packaging. Avoid any chance of cross-contamination.

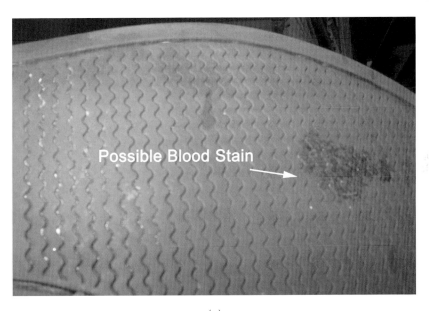

(a)

Figure D.63a Submit the entire object when practical or collect a sample. Also, collect a substrate control sample.

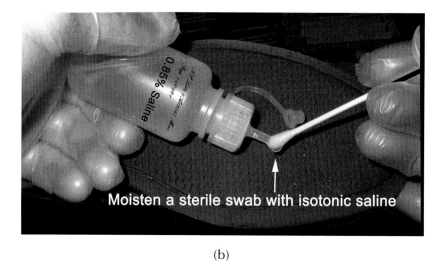

(b)

Figure D.63b Moisten the swab minimally so you don't dilute the sample extensively. The redder the sample, the better the sample.

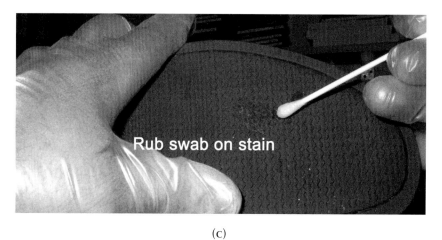

(c)

Figure D.63c

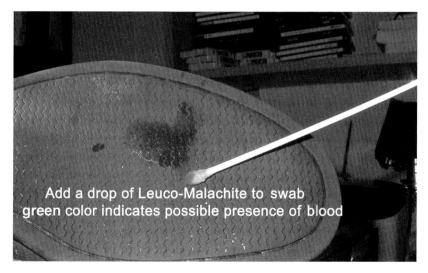

(d)

Figure D.63d

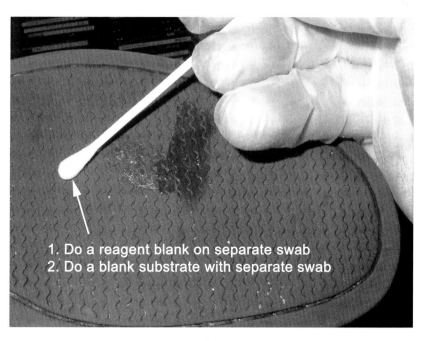

(e)

Figure D.63e

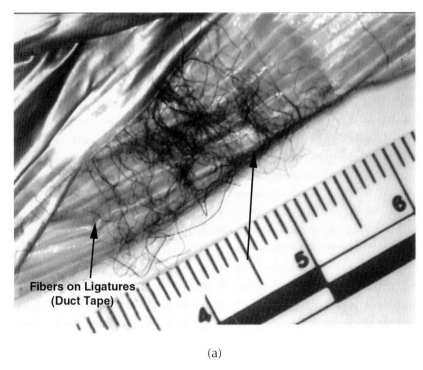

(a)

Figure D.64a The assailant was wearing gloves when he placed duct tape ligatures around the victim's hands.

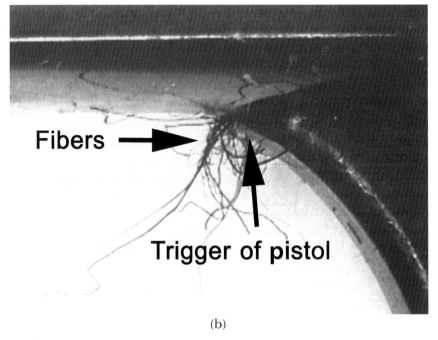

(b)

Figure D.64b Fibers consistent with those of gloves were recovered attached to the trigger guard of the weapon. The weapon was in the possession of the second subject in the killing when he was arrested.

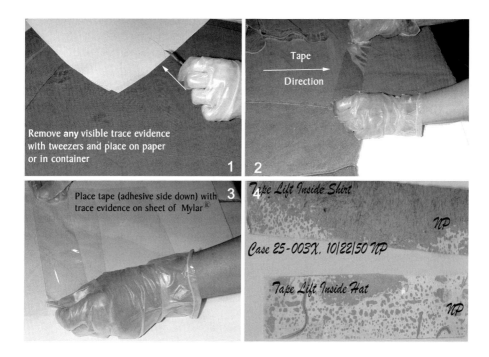

Figure D.65 Review of the collection of trace evidence with tweezers and tape lifts.

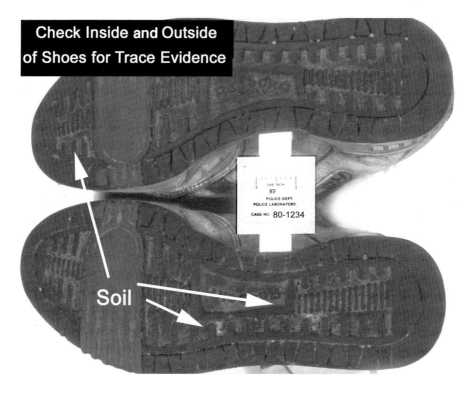

Figure D.66 Remove all trace evidence from shoes. It's best to do the work in the laboratory.

Check for Trace Evidence:
1) Outside Surfaces Front and Back (F/B)
2) Pockets F/B
3) Inside Surfaces and Pockets

Figure D.67

Check for Trace Evidence:
1) Outside Surfaces Front and Back (F/B)
2) Pockets F/B
3) Inside Surfaces and Pockets

Figure D.68   F/B = Front and Back.

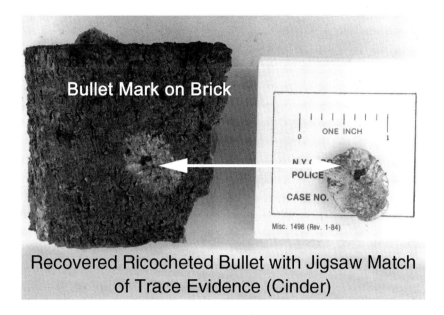

Bullet Mark on Brick

ONE INCH

0   1

N Y (
POLICE

CASE NO.

Misc. 1498 (Rev. 1-84)

Recovered Ricocheted Bullet with Jigsaw Match
of Trace Evidence (Cinder)

Figure D.69 Filter paper was placed over the impact mark on the brick to preserve the material. The bullet was packaged to ensure that the trace evidence was not lost. Both were packaged separately.

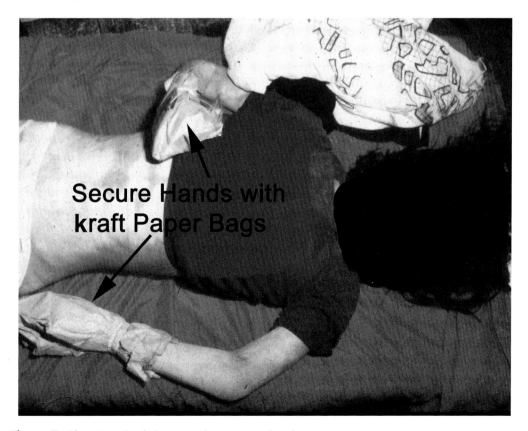

Secure Hands with
kraft Paper Bags

Figure D.70 Place kraft bags on the victim's hands.

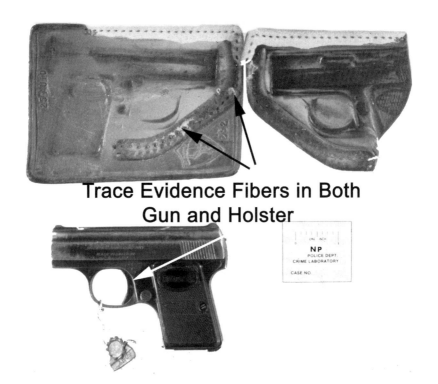

Figure D.71 Do not placed unholstered weapon into the holster. Trace evidence can be transferred, rendering analysis inconclusive.

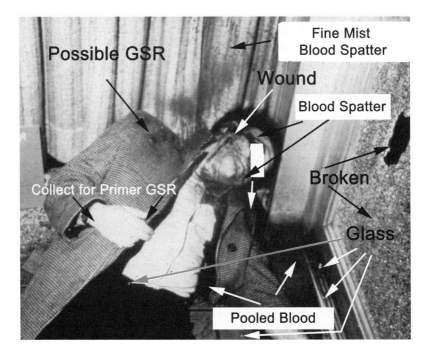

Figure D.72 Collect and fold the jacket while the area of interest is safeguarded. Use kraft paper to ensure substance is not transferred to an unaffected area.

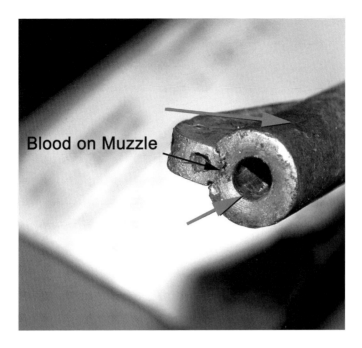

Figure D.73   Place a piece of filter paper or a manila folder over the area to prevent blood from flecking off.

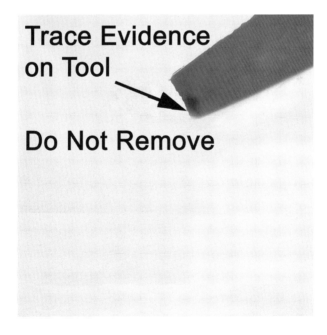

Figure D.74   A piece of clear tape can be placed over the area to ensure that the trace evidence is not lost or misplaced.

Appendix E: Crime Scene Forms and Diagrams Commonly Used

Firearms Form

Case No._____, Time_____, Date_____

Location_____

Firearm Type_____Caliber_____

Serial No._____

Revolver: Indicate Direction of Cylinder Rotation: CW or CCW

Firearm Type: Rev.   Pistol   Shotgun   Rifle   Other_____

Rotation   Model_____, Manufacturer_____

Serial No._____

Shotgun Gauge_____

DB   Side-by-Side

DB   Over-Under

SB

Choke: Full   Modified

Derringer

Magazine Type

Indicate where cartridges were found in weapon **and** their condition:

Live (L)   Spent (S)   Empty (E)

Ammo: Brand_____
Caliber_____
Primer Type _____

Figure E.1 Documentation of evidence is just as crucial as the actual evidence.

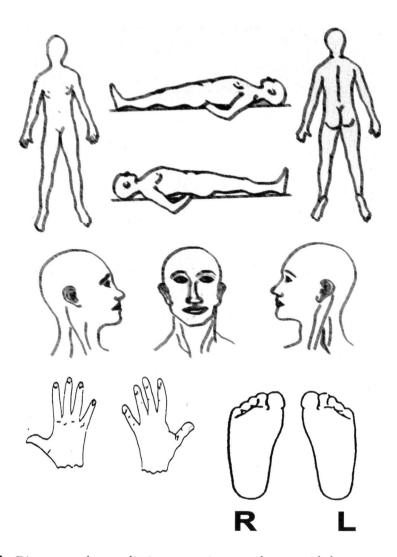

Figure E.2 Diagram to chart preliminary exterior wounds to an aided person or victim.

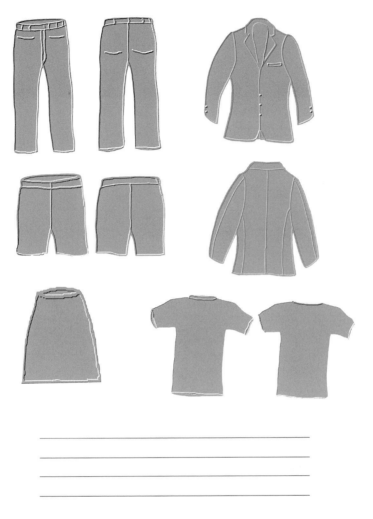

Figure E.3 Female exterior clothing documentation.

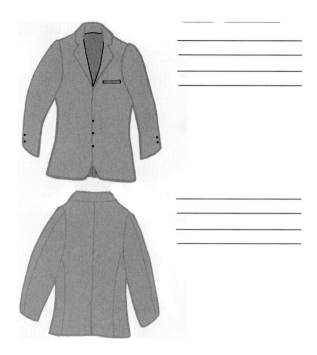

Figure E.4   Exterior jacket clothing documentation.

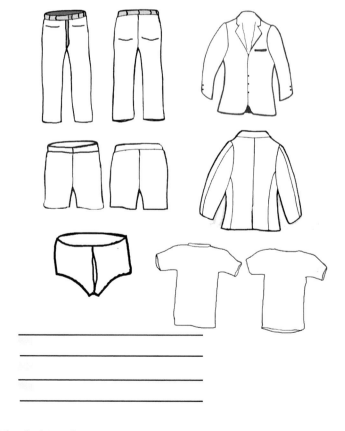

Figure E.5   Male clothing documentation.

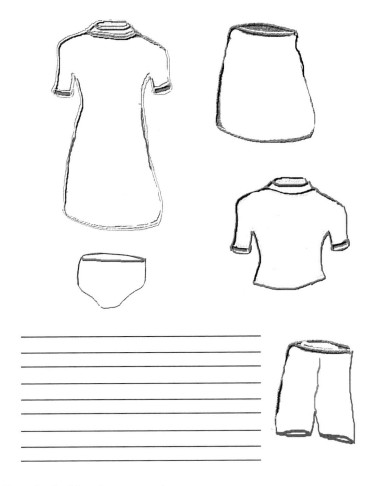

Figure E.6 Female clothing documentation.

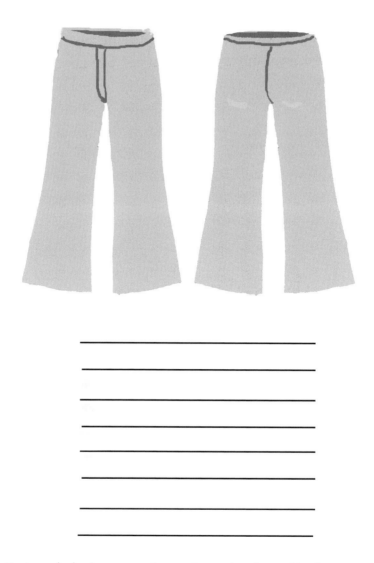

Figure E.7   Pants or slacks documentation can be used to denote blood, trace, semen, gunshot wounds, etc.

Pullover Shirt

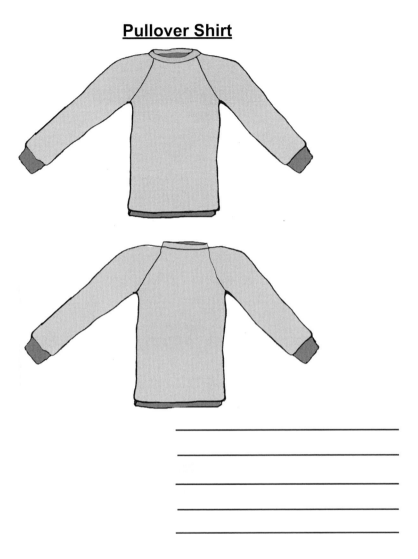

Figure E.8

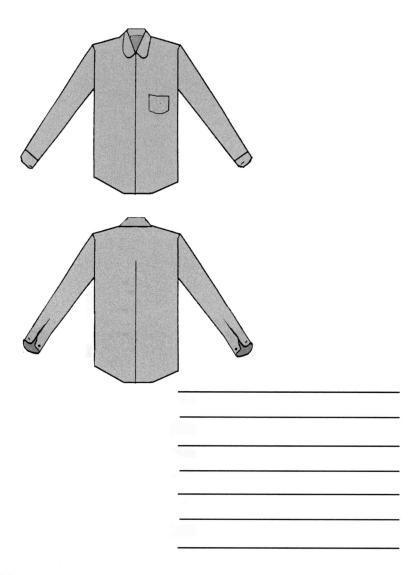

Figure E.9 Button-down shirt.

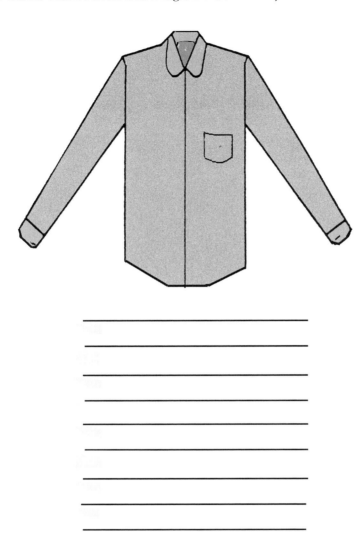

_____

_____

_____

_____

_____

_____

_____

_____

_____

Figure E.10

Figure E.11   Short pants documentation.

Coat

Figure E.12

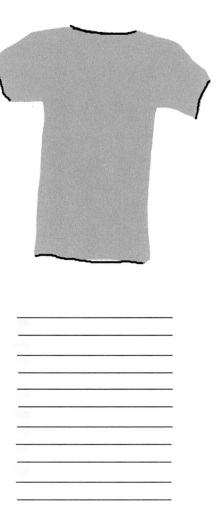

Figure E.13   Pullover shirt or blouse documentation.

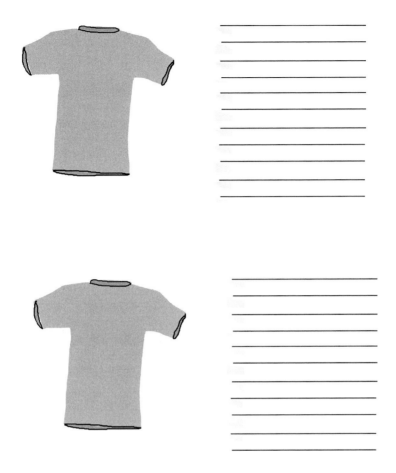

Figure E.14   Short-sleeve shirt documentation.

Figure E.15   Tank top documentation.

<u>Underwear</u>

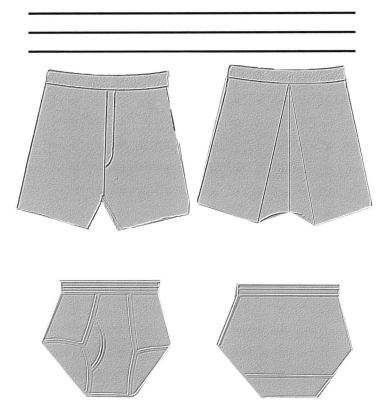

Figure E.16

_____
_____
_____
_____
_____

_____
_____
_____
_____
_____

Figure E.17 Boots, upper area documentation.

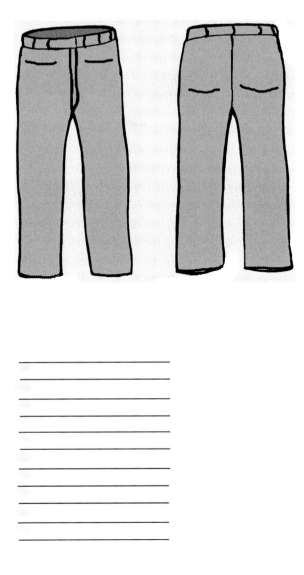

_____
_____
_____
_____
_____
_____
_____
_____
_____
_____
_____

Figure E.18

Figure E.19 Tennis shoes, top and sides, documentation.

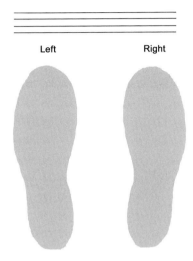

Left   Right

Figure E.20 Footwear, base documentation.

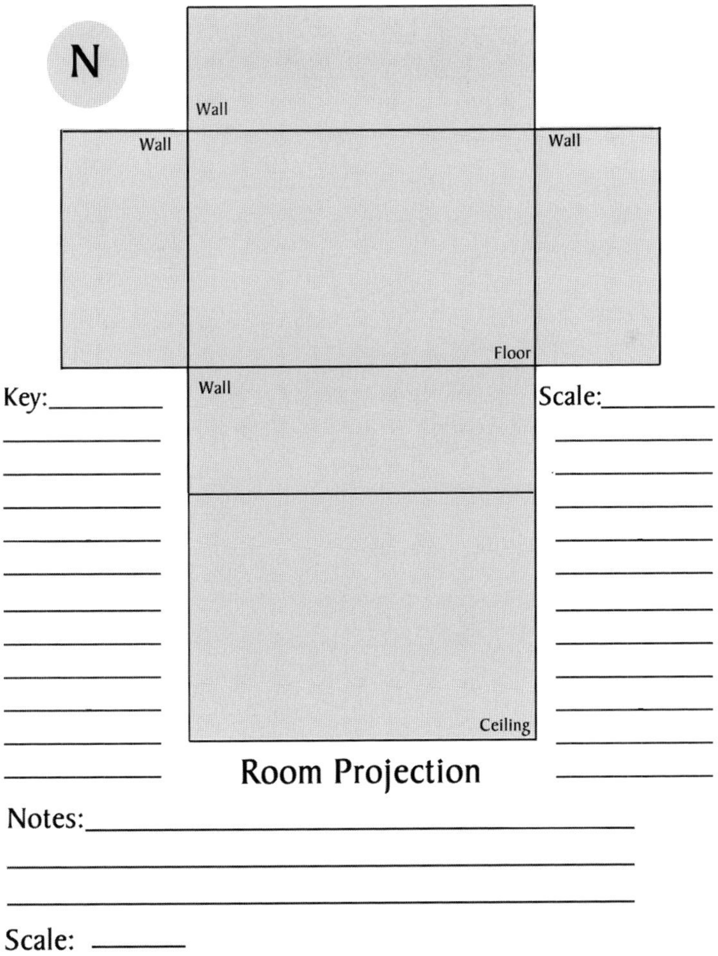

N

Wall

Wall   Wall

Floor

Key:_____   Wall   Scale:_____

Room Projection

Ceiling

Notes:_____

Scale: _____

Figure E.21

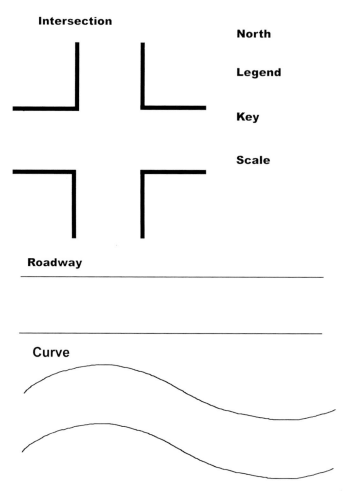

Figure E.22 Roadways documentation.

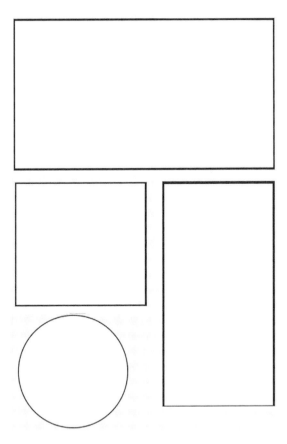

Figure E.23 Fields documentation.

Figure E.24 Field documentation.

Grave Site
Ground Level

Date _____ Time _____

Location _____

Weather _____ **Terrain/Soil** _____

_____

_____

_____

_____

_____

Top View

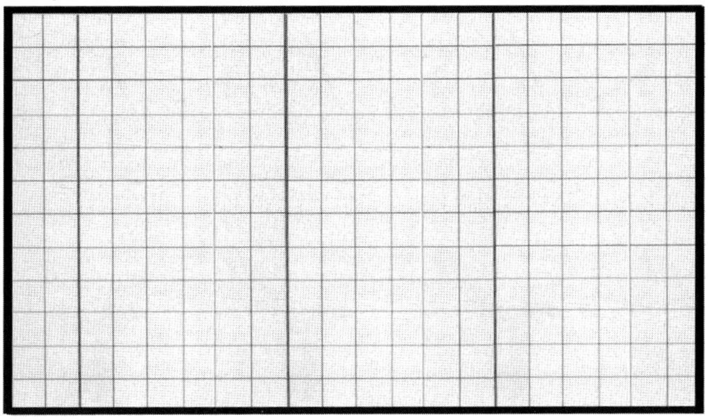

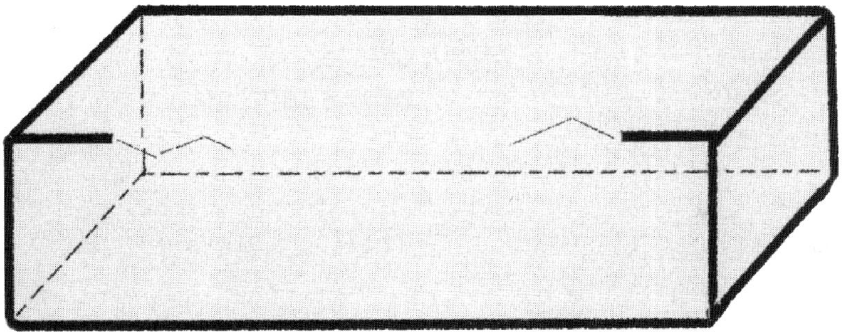

Underground

Figure E.25

Crime Scene Review Sheet   Page___ of ___

Assault Investigation

Date _____ **Time** _____ **Case#** _____

CSE_____ **Assistant** _____

Investigator Assigned _____

First Officer at the Scene _____

Occurrence Location _____
Date_____ Time_____ **Weather Condition** _____
Points of Entry/Exit _____
Victim Number _____
Address_____
Male   Female   Age___ Race___ Eye Color____ Hair Color_____   Height ___ Weight ____
Type of Injury_____
Assault Kit Prepared Serial No._____
Was Weapon Used Yes/ No   If yes, type?_____

Ballistics Evidence/Weapon
Weapon: Hand Gun   Knife   Rifle   Shot Gun   Other_____
Discharged Bullets_____ Discharged Shells_____ Cartridges_____
Safeguarded_____

Fingerprint Evidence
Latent_____ Patent_____ Plastic_____
Process: Dusted_____ Fumed_____ Chemical_____ Elimination Prints   Yes   No
Location/Item Obtained_____

DNA/Serology Evidence
Blood_____ Semen_____ Other_____

Physical Evidence /Trace Evidence
Hair/ Fibers_____ Glass _____ Paint_____ Soil_____ Other_____
Tape Lifts_____ Vacuum Sweepings _____ Other_____
Footprints____ Tire Treads____ Arson/Explosive____ Tool Marks____ Documents_____
Textile_____ Other_____
_____

Photographic/Video Evidence No. _____

Description or Comment_____
_____
_____
_____
_____
_____
_____

CSE _____   _____

Figure E.26   Assault investigation evidence review worksheet.

Crime Scene Review Sheet   Page____ of ____

Burglary Investigation

Date_____ **Time** _____ **Case#** _____

CSE_____ **Assistant**_____

Investigator Assigned_____
Occurrence Location_____
Date_____ **Time**_____ **Weather Condition**_____
Complainant_____
Address_____

Tools_____
Tool Marks_____ Safe Involved_____ Safety Deposit Box_____
Entry/Exit_____
Broken Glass_____
Alarm Defeated_____

Ballistics Evidence/Weapon
Weapon: Hand Gun   Knife   Rifle   Shot Gun   Other_____
Discharged Bullets_____ Discharged Shells_____ Cartridges_____
Weapon Safeguarded_____ Processed for Fingerprints_____

Fingerprint Evidence
Latent_____ Patent_____ Plastic_____
Process: Dusted_____ Fumed_____ Chemical_____ Elimination Prints   Yes   No
Location/Item Obtained_____

DNA/Serology Evidence
Blood_____ Semen_____ Other_____

Physical Evidence /Trace Evidence
Hair/ Fibers_____ Glass _____ Paint_____ Soil_____ Other_____
Tape Lifts_____ Vacuum Sweepings _____ Other_____
Footprints_____ Tire Treads_____ Arson/Explosive_____ Tool Marks_____ Documents_____
Textile_____ Other_____

Photographic/Video Evidence No. _____

Description or Comment_____
_____
_____
_____
_____
_____

CSE _____

Figure E.27   Burglary investigation evidence review worksheet.

Crime Scene Review Sheet   Page____ of ____

Homicide Investigation

Date_____ Time_____ Case#_____

CSE_____ Assistant_____

Investigator Assigned_____

First Officer at the Scene_____

Occurrence Location_____
Points of Entry/Exit_____
Date_____ **Time**_____ **Weather Condition**_____
Date and Time Occurrence_____
Victim Number _____
Address_____
Male   Female   Age_____   Race_____   Eye Color_____   Hair Color_____   Height _____ Weight_____
Body at Scene or Removed To_____

Weapon Used   es   No   If yes Type _____

Ballistics Evidence/Weapon
Weapon: Hand Gun   Knife   Rifle   Shot Gun   Other_____
Discharged Bullets_____ Discharged Shells_____ Cartridges_____
Weapon Safeguarded_____ Processed for Fingerprints_____

Fingerprint Evidence
Latent_____ Patent_____ Plastic_____
Process: Dusted_____ Fumed_____ Chemical_____ Elimination Prints   Yes   No
Location/Item Obtained_____

DNA/Serology Evidence
Blood_____ Semen_____ Other_____

Trace Evidence
Hair/ Fibers_____ Glass _____ Paint_____ Soil_____ Other_____
Tape Lifts_____ Vacuum Sweepings _____ Other_____

Physical Evidence
Footprints_____ Tire Treads_____ Arson/Explosive_____ Tool Marks_____ Documents_____
Textile_____ Other_____

Photographic/Video Evidence No._____

Description or Comment_____
_____
_____
_____
_____
_____

Figure E.28   Homicide investigation evidence review worksheet.

Crime Scene Review Sheet   Page____ of ____

Robbery Investigation

Date_____ Time _____ Case# _____

CSE_____ **Assistant**_____

Investigator Assigned_____

First Officer at the Scene_____

Occurrence Location_____
Date and Time Occurrence_____ **Weather**_____
Points of Entry/Exit_____

Complainant /Victim Number _____
Male   Female   Age___ Race___ Eye Color____ Hair Color_____ Height ___ Weight____
Body at Scene or Removed To_____

Force Threaten?_____ Force Used?_____
Force   Weapon Used? Yes No If yes type? _____
Assault Kit Prepared Serial No._____

Ballistics Evidence/Weapon
Weapon: Hand Gun   Knife   Rifle   Shot Gun   Other_____
Discharged Bullets_____ Discharged Shells_____ Cartridges_____
Weapon Safeguarded_____ Processed for Fingerprints_____

Fingerprint Evidence
Latent_____ Patent_____ Plastic_____
Process: Dusted_____ Fumed_____ Chemical_____ Elimination Prints   Yes No
Location/Item Obtained_____

DNA/Serology Evidence
Blood_____ Semen_____ Other_____

Physical Evidence /Trace Evidence
Hair/ Fibers_____ Glass _____ Paint_____ Soil_____ Other_____
Tape Lifts_____ Vacuum Sweepings _____ Other_____
Footprints____ Tire Treads____ Arson/Explosive____ Tool Marks____ Documents_____
Textile_____ Other_____

Photographic/Video Evidence No._____

Description or Comment_____
_____
_____
_____
_____
_____
_____
_____
_____

CSE_____ _____

Figure E.29   Robbery evidence review worksheet.

Crime Scene Review Sheet   Page____ of ____

Rape or Sex Crime Investigation

Date _____ **Time** _____ **Case#** _____

CSE_____ **Assistant**_____

Investigator Assigned_____

First Officer at the Scene_____

Occurrence Location_____
Points of Entry/Exit_____
Date_____ **Time**_____ **Weather Condition**_____
Complainant /Victim_____
Condition (circle): Unhurt   **Minor Injuries**   **Severely Injured**   **Likely to Die**   **Other**_____
Male   **Female**   **Age**___ **Race**___ **Eye Color**____ **Hair Color**_____   **Height** _____ **Weight**_____
Person Removed To Hospital_____ **Refuse Medical Aid**_____

Rape or Assault Kit Prepared Serial No. _____

Ballistics Evidence/Weapon:
Weapon: Hand Gun   Knife   Rifle   Shot Gun   Other_____
Discharged Bullets_____ Discharged Shells_____ Cartridges_____
Weapon Safeguarded_____ Processed for Fingerprints_____

Fingerprint Evidence
Latent_____ Patent_____ Plastic_____
Process: Dusted_____ Fumed_____ Chemical_____ Elimination Prints   Yes   No
Location/Item Obtained_____

DNA/Serology Evidence
Blood_____ Semen_____ Other_____

Physical Evidence /Trace Evidence
Hair/ Fibers_____ Glass _____ Paint_____ Soil_____ Other_____
Tape Lifts_____ Vacuum Sweepings _____ Other_____
Footprints____ Tire Treads____ Arson/Explosive____ Tool Marks____ Documents_____
Textile_____ Other_____

Photographic/Video Evidence No._____

Description or
Comment_____
_____
_____
_____
_____
_____

CSE_____

Figure E.30   Sexual assault evidence review worksheet.

Crime Scene Supplemental Review Form

Page ____ of ____

_____
_____
_____
_____
_____
_____
_____
_____
_____
_____
_____
_____
_____
_____
_____
_____
_____
_____
_____
_____
_____
_____
_____
_____
_____
_____
_____
_____
_____
_____
_____
_____
_____
_____
_____
_____
_____
_____
_____
_____
_____
_____

Photographs: _____
No.1_____
No.2_____
No.3_____
No.4_____
No.5_____
No.6_____
No.7_____
No.8_____

Figure E.31 Supplemental evidence review worksheet and page 1 of photo log.

Crime Scene Review Sheet   Page_____ of _____

Arson/Explosion Investigation

Date _____   **Time** _____   **Case#**_____

CSE_____**Assistant**_____

Investigator Assigned_____

First Officer at the Scene_____

Occurrence Location_____
Points of Entry/Exit_____
Date_____ **Time**_____   **Weather Condition**_____
Complainant /Victim No. _____
Condition (circle):   Unhurt   Minor Injuries   Severely Injured   Likely to Die   Dead
Male   Female   Age___   Race___   Eye Color____   Hair Color_____   Height _____   Weight_____
Person Removed To: Hospital or Morgue   Refuse Medical Aid_____

Accelerant Residue_____ Vapor Specimen_____   Explosive Residue_____
Debris Sieved_____
Parts of Device_____
Rags_____ Cans_____ Bottles_____
Other_____
Seat of Explosion or Arson Located_____
Burn Pattern_____

Ballistics Evidence/Weapon
Weapon   Hand Gun   Knife   Rifle   Shot Gun   Other_____
Discharged Bullets_____ Discharged Shells_____   Cartridges_____
Weapon Safeguarded_____   Processed for Fingerprints_____

Fingerprint Evidence
Latent_____ Patent_____ Plastic_____
Process: Dusted_____ Fumed_____ Chemical_____ Elimination Prints   Yes   No
Location/Item Obtained_____

DNA/Serology Evidence
Blood_____ Semen_____ Other_____

Physical Evidence /Trace Evidence
Hair/ Fibers_____ Glass _____ Paint_____ Soil_____ Other_____
Tape Lifts_____ Vacuum Sweepings _____ Other_____
Footprints_____ Tire Treads_____ Arson/Explosive_____ Tool Marks_____ Documents_____
Textile_____ Other_____

Photographic/Video Evidence No._____

Description or Comment_____
_____
_____
_____
_____
_____
_____

CSE_____

Figure E.32   Arson/Explosion evidence review worksheet.

Generic Crime Scene Review Sheet

Page ___of___

Crime Classification   _____

Date _____ Time _____ Case# _____

CSE_____ Assistant_____

Investigator Assigned_____

First Officer at the Scene_____

Occurrence Location_____

Date_____ Time_____ **Weather Condition**_____

Victim Number _____
Adress_____
Male   Female   Age___ Race___ Eye Color____ Hair Color_____   Height ___ Weight____
Type of Injury_____
Assault Kit Prepared Serial No._____
Was Weapon Used Yes/ No   If yes type?_____

Ballistics Evidence
Weapon: Hand Gun   Knife   Rifle   Shot Gun   Other_____
Discharged Bullets_____ Discharged Shells_____ Cartridges_____
Weapon Safeguarded_____

Fingerprint Evidence
Latent_____ Patent_____ Plastic_____
Process: Dusted_____ Fumed_____ Chemical_____ Elimination Prints   Yes   No
Location/Item   Obtained_____

Physical Evidence /Trace Evidence/DNA
Hair/ Fibers_____ Glass _____ Paint_____ Soil_____ Blood_____ Semen_____
Other_____
Tape Lifts_____ Vacuum Sweepings _____ Other_____
Footprints____ Tire Treads____ Arson/Explosive____ Tool Marks____ Documents_____
Textile_____ Other_____
Tool Marks_____ Safe Involved_____ Safety Deposit Box_____
Points of Entry/Exit_____
Broken Glass_____
Alarm Defeated_____
Property Damage_____

Description or Comment_____
_____
_____

Figure E.33   Unclassified crime/incident evidence review worksheet.

Photographic Log

Location _____

Date_____, Time_____, Case No._____

Digital or Film_____, Camera Model_____, Lens_____

Picture No.	Subject/Description	Date/Time	F- Stop/Shutter Speed	Iso/Din

CSE Preparing _____

Remarks _____

_____

Figure E.34   Photo log.

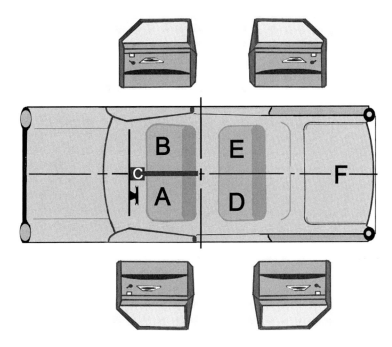

Figure E.35 Automobile evidence recovery (interior).

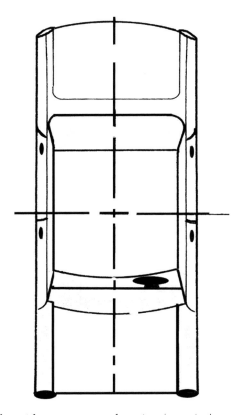

Figure E.36 Automobile evidence recovery location (exterior).

Vehicle

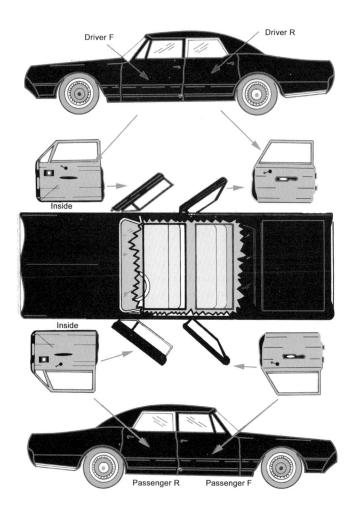

Figure E.37

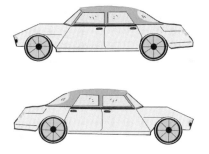

Figure E.38

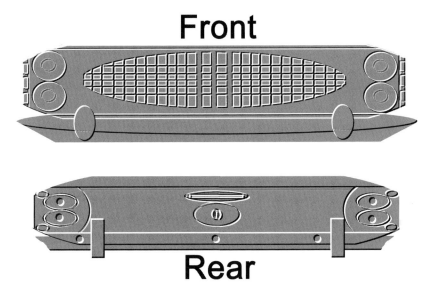

Figure E.39

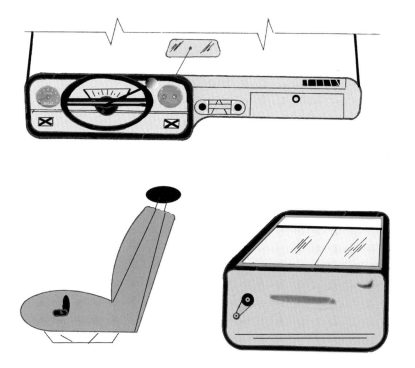

Figure E.40

Appendix F: Avoiding Potential Mistakes While Processing A Crime Scene

Figure F.1 Hot spots are caused by the reflection of the cameras's flash onto the object being photographed. By adjusting the position of the flash (and bracketing the photographs), hotspots can be minimized.

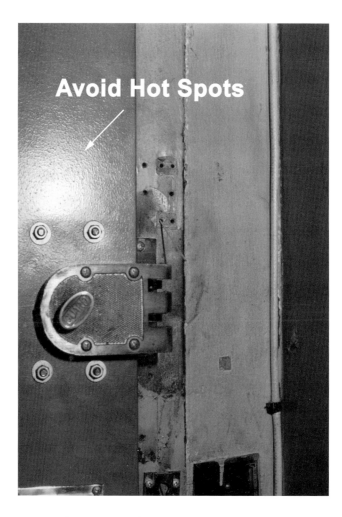

Figure F.2 Hot spots can be caused by flashlights or other items that produce light. Hot spots can also obliterate crucial photo content, and can be found to be distracting.

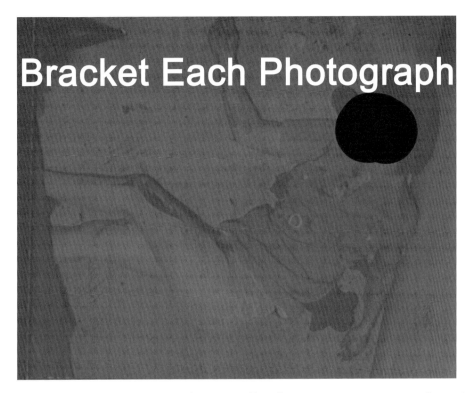

Figure F.3 Take multiple photographs, especially when important items or information is being recorded. The more important the subject matter, the more additional photographs should be taken.

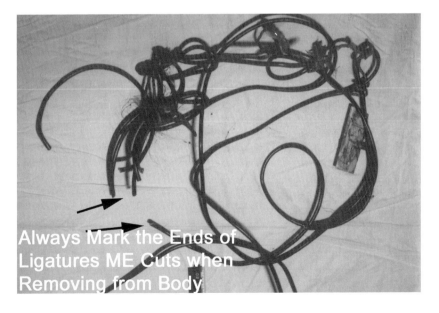

Figure F.4 Always mark the ends of the ligatures that the M.E. cuts as the ligatures are being removed from the deceased. Do not rely upon your memory to be able to reconstruct the ligature position. A small piece of tape with corresponding numbers on the ligature ends should prove sufficient.

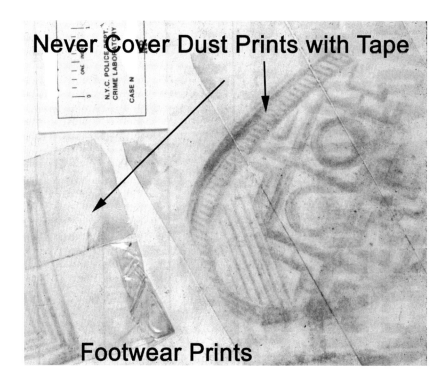

Figure F.5 Covering the impression with tape renders the evidence unable to be compared to a known impression.

Figure F.6 Bullets should be marked on their base, an area where minutiae is not present. Discharged shell casings should be marked inside of the opening, or the "neck".

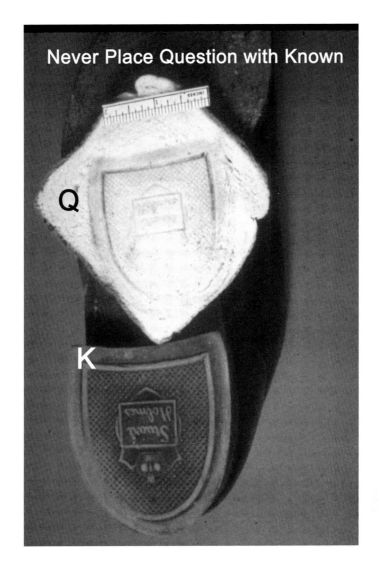

Figure F.7 Always package questioned samples and know samples separately. Never allow items that are to be compared to commingle. Trace evidence and markings may become transferred in the process.

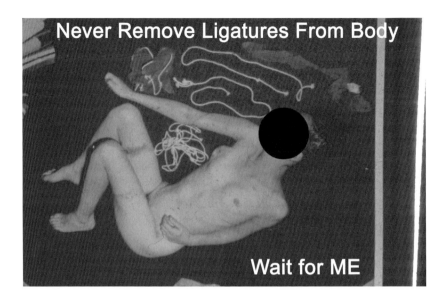

Figure F.8 Always wait for the medical examiner to view, examine, and document the deceased (in situ) prior to moving the deceased.

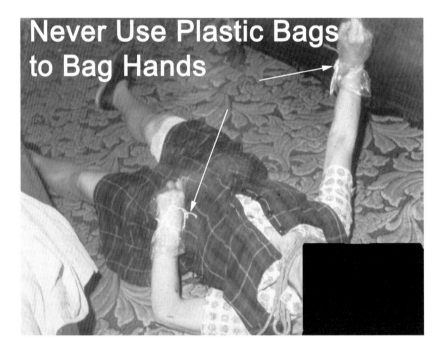

Figure F.9 Plastic bags will cause putrification to occur. This would cause unnecessary destruction of biological evidence.

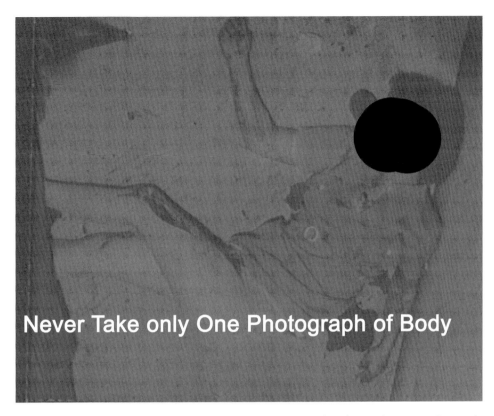

Figure F.10 Take numerous photos. The more important the photo, the more photos should be taken.

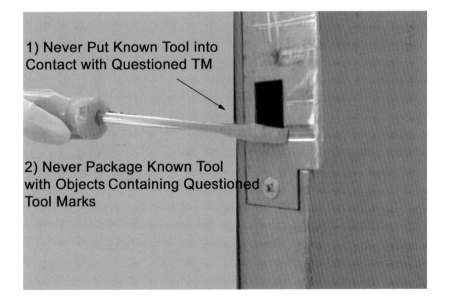

Figure F.11

Figure F.12   Photographs need be taken without and with a scale if the photos contents are to be used for comparison purposes.

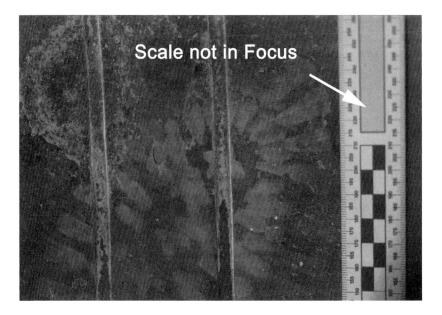

Figure F.13   Scale and content need be in focus. Remember to bracket the photograph, adjusting the aperture and lighting position when bracketing.

Appendix G: WMD Crime Scene Processing

Historically, Haz-Mat (hazardous material) day-to-day operations have most often been handled by firefighters. Many locales have teams consisting of firefighters and some EMS (emergency medical service) personnel. While traditional Haz-Mat operations or missions were handled in a professional manner, recent unfortunate, unforeseeable events have made this scenario outdated. Haz-Mat scenes have been, and are readily becoming, scenes that will require evidence processing and collection. This may necessitate that samples collected, as well as the responders' actions while at the scene, become part of judicial proceedings. While certified Haz-Mat technicians are required to respond to the scene and perform evidence gathering tasks, most have not received training with evidentiary issues in mind. In the past, life safety issues had been their sole concern, i.e., collecting samples with public safety in mind.

Technicians may now be required to work in the "hot zone, or potential hot zone" where the highest level of contamination has already, or may still occur, and perform their task operating under a different mindset and set of rules compared with traditional practice. This appendix is in no way intended to suggest that a crime scene examiner or evidence technician process a WMD (weapons of mass destruction) crime scene. One should never operate in any environment in which (s)he is not properly trained. The purpose of this appendix is to allow Haz-Mat–trained personnel to familiarize themselves with the different ways in which to meticulously document, record, and preserve/collect (potential) physical evidence while working in the hot zone. It is not the authors' or the publisher's intent to revamp any preexisting policy or protocol of your agency or department. It is more intended to serve as additional information for procedures that your agency should consider incorporating into its policies.

The following information, diagrams, and photographs depict tried and true ways to operate safely inside of the hot zone, and to successfully obtain physical evidence that will be allowed to be entered into a court of law.

In conjunction with *Suggested Guidelines for Establishing Evidence Response Teams*, as published by the Federal Bureau of Investigation, Laboratory Division, Washington, D.C., the authors have incorporated their past experiences to prepare a list of do's and don'ts at the crime scene:

There are 12 steps involved with the organization and basic stages in a search operation.

1) Preparation
2) Approach

3) Secure and protect scene
4) Initiate preliminary survey
5) Evaluate physical evidence possibilities
6) Prepare a narrative description
7) Depict the scene photographically
8) Prepare diagram/sketch of scene
9) Conduct a detailed search
10) Record and collect physical evidence
11) Conduct final survey
12) Release the scene

Each step in the FBI 12 Step Process will be explained briefly. These 12 steps can be incorporated into most any crime scene investigation in which you are involved.

1) **Preparation:** The time to prepare for a response to an emergency incident is not at the time of notification. Preparation should occur when there is sufficient "down time." Equipment should be checked to insure operability, power sources are fully charged, and collection and packaging materials are in order. Other responsibilities that need be addressed prior to responding to a possible long-term operation includes: communications, lighting assistance, shelter, transportation, food, medical assistance, scene security, and specialized equipment.

2) **Approach the scene**: Personal safety should always be of paramount importance. All personnel at the scene should make continual safety assessments. Be alert to discarded evidence, possible ingress and egress points. Establish the correct frame-of-mind to take control of the scene regardless of the circumstances observed at time of arrival

3) **Secure and Protect the Scene:** Take control aggressively at time of arrival, determine extent to which the scene has been protected and safeguarded. Be sure to check the scene for adequate security even if advised that it has been protected prior to your arrival, be mindful of the possibility of secondary devices. Obtain information from logical personnel who have entered the scene and have knowledge relative to the scenes original condition (often the first officer at the scene). Take extensive notes, do not rely upon your memory. Keep out unauthorized or unnecessary personnel from the scene, initiate a log of all persons entering and leaving the scene.

4) **Initiate a Preliminary Search:** This survey is for organizational purposes, it includes a cautious walk-through of the scene to determine what types of services will be performed. Acquire preliminary photographs to assist in the planning of the operation. Determine personnel and equipment needs, develop a general theory as to what transpired. Identify and protect any transient or fleeting evidence, and perform a continual safety assessment of the location. Any possible areas of safety concerns should be discussed with the person in charge so that he can address the problem.

5) **Evaluate the Physical Evidence Possibilities:** This evaluation begins at the time arrival at the scene, based upon the preliminary survey establishes evidence types that are most likely to be encountered. Personnel should be mindful to concentrate initially on any fleeting or transient evidence and work outwards towards the least transient evidence. Consider whether any victims or first responders may have moved the evidence or any other items inadvertently.

6) **Prepare a Narrative Description**: The narrative is a continual, running description of the condition of the crime scene that represents the scene in a general to specific reference scheme. It can also be thought of as a timeline, one that may be performed by means of written, audio, or video equipment.

7) **Depict the Scene Photographically**: Begin documenting the scene photographically as soon as possible to insure that responders do not disturb the scene or any evidence. Use a log to maintain a written record of photographs that have been taken at the scene. Insure that a progression of overall (establishing), midrange and close-up photographs are taken, both without as well as with a readily reproducible scale. Evidence should be photographed "in situ," prior to its collection and packaging. All possible points of entry and exit should be photographed, as well as windows, doors, and lighting conditions

8) **Prepare a Diagram or Sketch of the Scene:** The diagram establishes a permanent record of items, conditions, and distance at the scene. While operating in the hot-zone, it is not necessary to prepare the diagram "to scale," but rather it is important to obtain accurate measurements. The general progression of a sketch should be to: lay out the basic perimeter of the scene, place the fixed objects or location of furniture, insert evidence as it is recovered (this can be performed with the use of a number or letter designation, rather than placing all the information about the specific piece of evidence onto the diagram), record the appropriate measurements, and then insert the key/legend, note north orientation. Additional information should include the specific location of the scene, the date and time, a unique identifier or case number, the weather and lighting conditions, and any scale or notation that diagram is not prepared to scale

9&10) **Conduct a Detailed Search and Record/Collect Physical Evidence:** Search for evidence based upon the previous evaluation of the evidence possibilities, do so while searching in a general to specific manner. Photograph all items of evidence prior to its collection, remember to enter information onto the photo log. Mark the location of the evidence onto the diagram. Do not excessively handle evidence after its recovery, as it may be fragile or valuable trace evidence might become dislodged from the evidence. Consider premarking the packaging material with the necessary information prior to entering the hot zone. All packaging material must have the minimum amount of information placed upon it (location, time/date, unique or case identifier, collectors name, the type of evidence being recovered). As a result of performing steps 4 and 5 (initiate a preliminary search and evaluate the evidence possibilities), you should have a pretty good idea as to type and quantity of evidence that you plan to recover. It is always a good idea to bring some additional packaging or collection materials into the hot zone, as items have a tendency to fall or be dropped. Once on the floor, these items must be considered contaminated and should not be used to collect evidence. Remember when dealing with a complicated crime scene, or one where there are numerous entries required or personnel collecting evidence, to use an evidence custodian.

11) **Conduct a Final Survey:** This survey is a critical review of all aspects of the work up until this point. The survey addresses completeness of work, double checks documentation, and possible inadvertent errors. Check to insure that all evidence that has been collected and documentation is accounted for. Insure that all equipment and debris incurred during the investigation is collected and removed. Insure also

that a series of photographs depicts the condition of the scene, showing the final condition of the scene prior to the scene being released. The final survey can be performed by persons other than those that performed the evidence collection and documentation. Often it is more useful to use a "second set of eyes" as different people see things differently.

12) **Release of the Crime Scene:** The scene cannot be released until the final survey is completed. It must be noted to whom and by whom the scene was released, as well as the time and date of the release. The release of the scene should be made only by the person in charge and no one else. Consider the fact that a search warrant might be required to re-enter the scene.

When performing your duties, the above items need be addressed. Some agencies already use this list, but do so under a different name or order. Regardless of the order that you choose, safety should always be your primary goal.

EVIDENCE PACKAGING INFORMATION:

Whenever evidence is collected, the item(s) must be packaged properly. Evidence must be placed inside of packaging to insure that no changes or damage to the item(s) occur.

The packaging material may include plastic bags, jars, over pack containers, etc. The type of packaging that will be used is based upon the type of evidence that is being collected and submitted for analysis. Should the investigator have any question regarding the proper packaging required for the collection of the evidence, then he should contact the receiving agency's laboratory personnel to insure proper packaging procedures are followed. Do not commingle evidence by placing samples from different locations inside of common packages. Do not place control samples inside of the same packaging as samples that were collected for submission to a laboratory. Regardless of the packaging used, one thing must remain the same — the information that is placed on the outside of the container or vessel containing the evidence.

This is the MINIMUM information that should be placed onto the evidence container:

The location of the scene, be specific, not just 123 Main St., but desk in room 678 inside of 123 Main St.

The date and time of the items collection

The name and unique identifier of the person collecting the evidence

A case number or unique identifier, the number should be issued and never be used in connection with any other investigation.

The type of sample that is enclosed inside of the packaging, i.e.: powder, letter, liquid, sample swab, composite wipe, control sample, etc.

The sample number, swab no. 1, swab no. 2, etc.

Tamper evident evidence tape must be placed across the top of the bag, to insure that the evidence has not been improperly handled subsequent to its recovery. The person sealing the bag with tape needs to place his or her initials, the time, and date that the tape was affixed to the packaging across the tape.

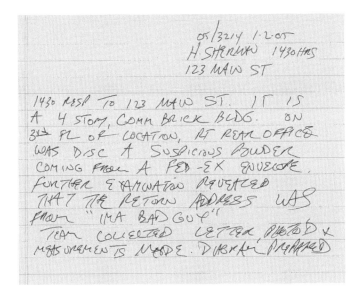

Figure G.1   Detailed notes must be taken inside the Hot-Zone, they must also be packaged, and the packaging need be decontaminated.

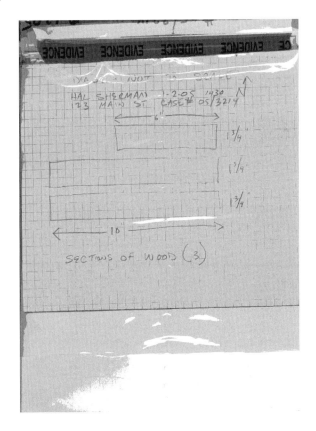

Figure G.1a   Diagrams allow a different perspective of the scene that can't be shown with photographs alone. A final diagram can be prepared with the aid of the diagram made inside of the Hot-Zone. Always retain your original notes and do not allow the notes to be discarded.

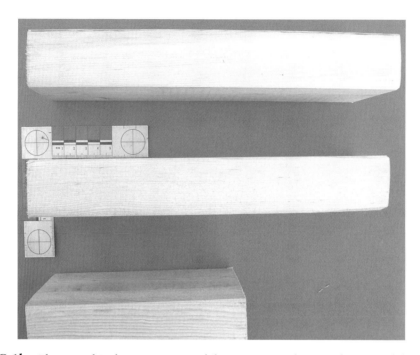

Figure G.1b   Photographic documentation of the scene provides visualization of the evidence. Photography is only a fraction of how the evidence must be documented. Diagrams (G.1a) allow the items to be viewed, but provided measurements allow greater explanation of the evidence. Notes (G.1) allow the material be explained with the use of words, or a narrative. No one method is best, but when used in conjunction with the others, allows a better perspective of that is being documented.

Figure G.2   An "establishing photograph" shows the proximity of items in overall relation with other items and areas inside of the scene. This type of photograph starts to lie the foundation of the location of the evidence as well as areas of interest.

Figure G.2a A "mid range" photograph removes much of the background (which was documented with the "establishing photo", G.2) and shows items of evidence in a general view. The location of the evidence is documented, but no attempt to individualize or depict the actual items of evidence are made.

Figure G.2b A "Close-up view" of the item shows the details of the object. This photograph should contain less background objects or areas than the "midrange view", (Figure G2.a). This photograph documents the location of the object, but does not allow for individualization of the evidence. Be mindful to take photographs without and also with placards or scales. Evidentiary photographs are used to portray a true and accurate graphic representation of the scene. Photographs taken with placards only might not be allowed into evidence, as the placard was added to the scene by the investigator.

Figure G.3 Macro views of evidence must be taken with and without a readily reproducible scale. Be certain to position the plane of the camera parallel to the item being photographed. This process will insure that distortion of the evidence is minimized. Remember the "3 F's" rule: Fill the Film Frame. Place only important items in the picture, and bracket the photographs.

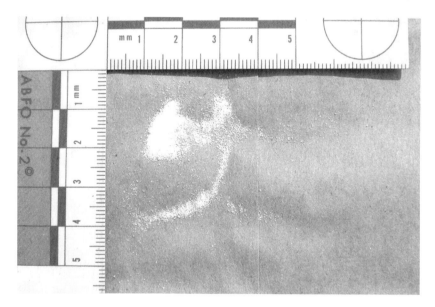

Figure G.3a Place a readily reproducible scale in proximity to the evidence when the size of the item is important. If a scale is missing from the photograph, it renders the picture useless for comparison purposes. Photos must be taken without and with a scale to insure integrity of the pictures contents. Be sure to maintain the plane of the camera remains parallel with the item being photographed.

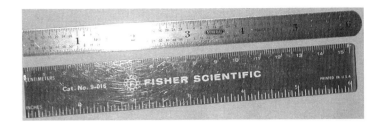

Figure G.4 Scales may be made of plastic or metal (both are easily decontaminated). Be aware of possible "hot spots" when using scales. Be familiar with your equipment, including hot spots or shadows that any items that you introduce into the scene or picture may cause.

Figure G.5 Scales may be printed on sheets of shipping labels. Be sure to keep a control sample of one of any label that you produce in case requested to in a court of law.

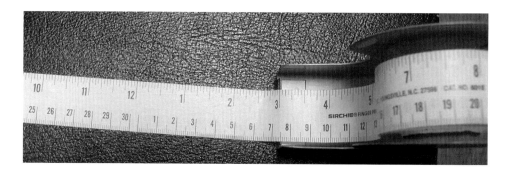

Figure G.5a Labels may be dispensed from an adhesive roll or torn from a roll similar to a tape measure.

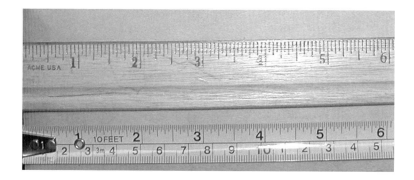

Figure G.6 Scales should not be made of material that cannot readily be decontaminated.

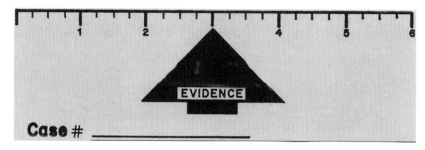

Figure G.7 Scales may be photocopied or made from cardstock. The original, or "master," of the scale must be available to be authenticated if requested in a court of law.

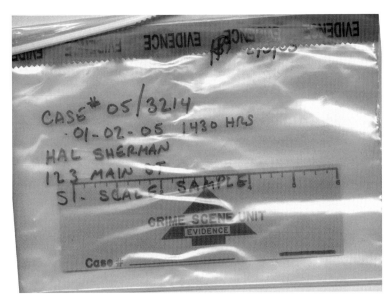

Figure G.8 If manufactured scales are used inside of the hot zone, they should be saved (as is all written material) and placed inside of a plastic bag, which must be properly sealed and decontaminated in case their authenticity is requested at a later date.

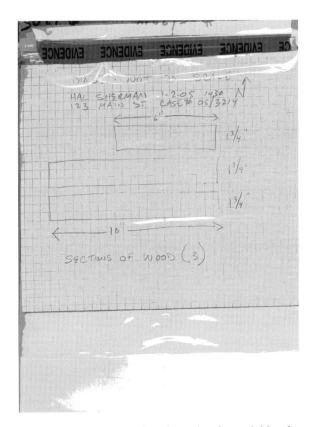

Figure G.9 Evidence and notes must be placed inside of a sealable plastic bag, with tamper-evident tape or seal being placed on the outermost bag. Tamper-evident tape can be used on packaging inside of the bag as well.

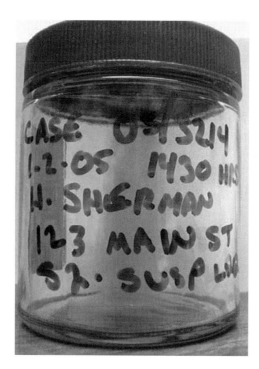

Figure G.10   The vessel or container that is being used to collect the initial sample must have certain information on the outside of the object. This includes, but is not limited to, (a) the collector's name, (b) a unique identifier or case number, (c) the date and time of the sample's collection, (d) the type of sample, i.e., swab, letter, gauze, control sample, composite swipe, or sample, (e) the location of the investigation, and more specifically the area from which the evidence was collected, e.g., top of desk in room 123, located at 456 Main St., Anytown, Anystate.

Figure G.10a   All information that was placed on the evidence must be placed on all subsequent packaging that the evidence was placed inside of. That includes jars, bags, overpack containers, etc.

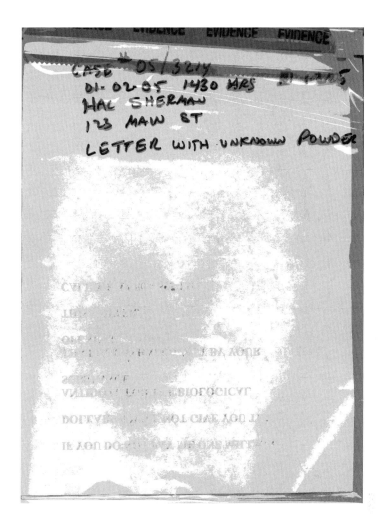

Figure G.11 Place the letter or document inside of the plastic bag, being mindful not to lose any possible trace evidence. Place the side of the document with writing facing the side of the clear plastic bag containing no writing. Remember to write the name of the collector, a unique identifier or case number, the date and time of collection, the type of sample being submitted, and the location from where the sample was obtained.

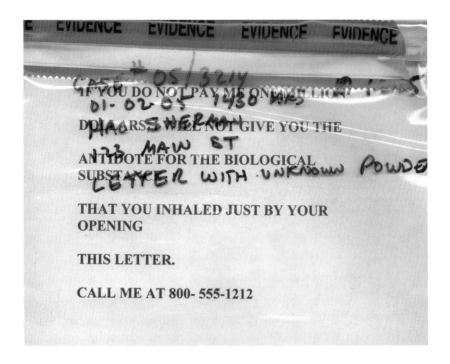

Figure G.11a Improper placement of evidence. Writing on any letters or envelopes must be clearly visible to the investigator. Do not cover or obliterate any information from the evidence beneath the information that you place onto the evidence packaging.

Figure G.12 The scene is photographed at eye level. This is the most correct view. This depiction affords the person looking at the picture to see things as they would normally view the scene.

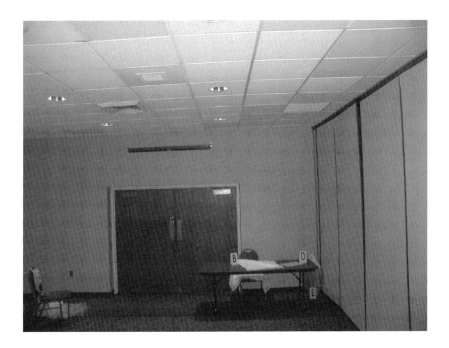

Figure G.12a This picture is taken above the photographers head. It focuses on the ceiling and draws attention away from the scene and the evidence.

Figure G.12b Avoid taking photographs at floor level. Overall photos should portray the scene as it is normally viewed. Just as in G.12A, this photo draws attention away from the table and makes the floor appear more important then it should.

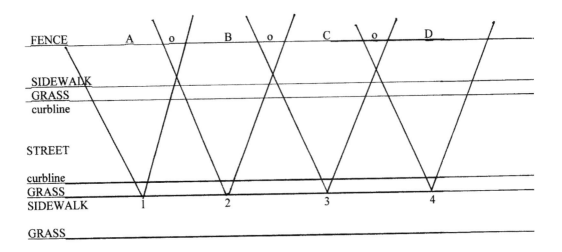

DIAGRAM EXPLANATION

1,2,3,4 are the location of the camera facing the area across the street

A, B, C, D is the content of each of the photographs

o= the area of overlap between photographs A and B, B and C, C and D

This is a procedure in which a tripod must be used, for height and also distance from the subject. What the photographer is doing is having the ability to "stitch" the photographs together and if need be create a panoramic view of the scene.
ALWAYS use an imaginary line, insuring that the plane of the camera is not only parallel to the object, but that the distance from the camera to the subject is consistent throughout the entire process.

Figure G.13 The diagram depicts photos being taken at a perspective along an imaginary plane. This allows for the photographs to be "stitched together" and viewed as one long panoramic picture. Figures G13a through G.13d will demonstrate this procedure photographically, in addition to the diagram above. This is an example where diagrams and photographs are used in conjunction with each other to demonstrate a process visually.

Figure G.13a   View of a park facing north. Note the garbage can three quarters of the way into the picture from the left side. (*location number 1 on figure G.13*)

Figure G.13b   The photo is taken along the same plane, parallel to the fence, at the same height. Note the same garbage can as in G.13a is all the way to the left side of this photo. Observe the opening of the fence on the right side of the picture. (*location number 2 on figure G.13*)

Figure G.13c   The opening of the fence is now on the far left side of the picture. The far right side of the picture has a dark object to the rear of the car, it is a storm drain and manhole cover. (*location number 3 on figure G.13*)

Figure G.13d   The far left side shows the storm drain and manhole cover that was depicted in G13.c. By overlapping the content of each photograph slightly, it allows all of the pictures to be "stitched" together, giving a panoramic view. Normally to see all the material in the above pictures, one would have to be much farther away from the object. In that instance, less detail would be visible. The photos would appear to be overall view in nature instead of midrange. (*location number 4 on figure G.13*)

Figure G.14   The use of either number or letter placards allows for easy visibility and orientation of the physical evidence for someone who did not have the luxury of being at the scene.

Figure G.15   The photo depicts how the evidence may look after being collected and stored inside of three plastic bags. Notice how the opacity of the bag distorts the evidence. Observe evidence tape along top of packaging. Information regarding collector, time, date, unique identifier and location are written on opposite side of plastic bag. This allows for a clear view of the notes and diagram by anyone that needs to view the information.

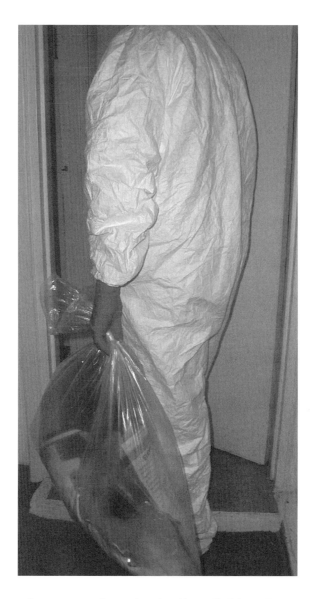

Figure G.16   Always be sure to safeguard and collect all debris that was created during the processing of the scene. "If you brought it into the scene, then bring it out of the scene."

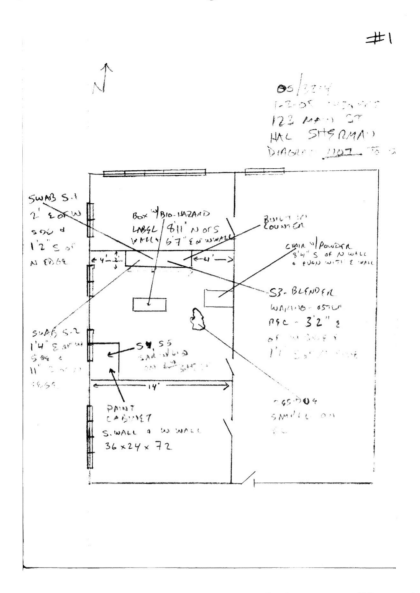

Figure G.17 Do not place too much information onto the diagram. It will have to be viewed afterward through two or three plastic bags. Make use of a key or legend; place the object, the location that it was recovered from, and any other information on another sheet of paper. Too much information makes the illustration appear "busy" and can be distracting. Also, at large scenes, consider preparing multiple diagrams, with a common point of reference, so that the illustrations can be placed together and viewed as if they were a jigsaw puzzle.

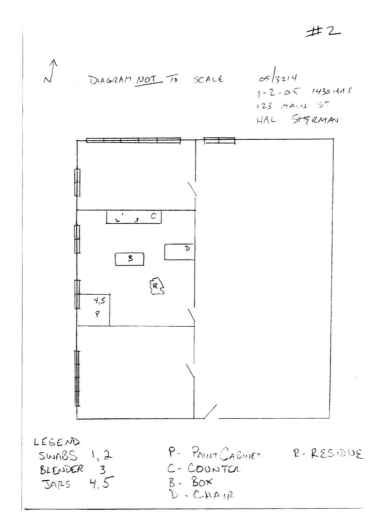

Figure G.17a Simple diagram, with compass direction pointing north, time, and date of preparation, address of scene and diagram preparer. A simple legend is placed on the bottom of the page. This diagram depicts the entire building.

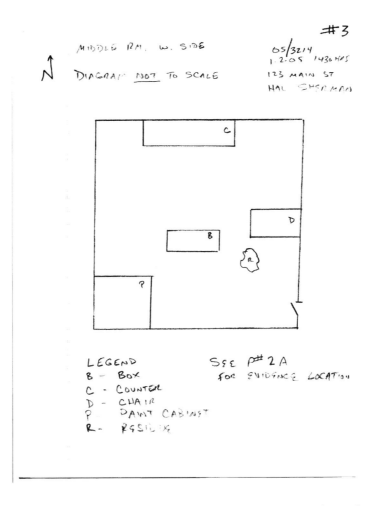

Figure G.17b Small diagram depicting the area of interest, containing the evidence. If desired, this diagram can be prepared in addition to figure G.17a. Detailed measurements of the room, its fixtures and all evidence must be taken and noted.

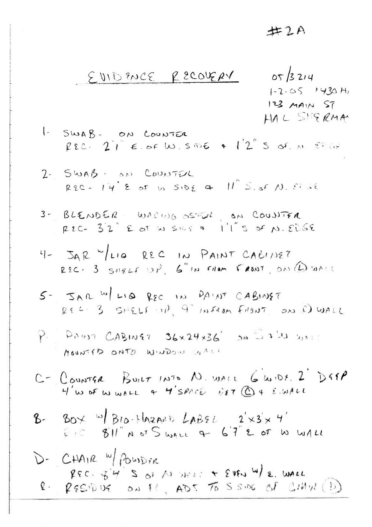

Figure G.17c Legend explanation, listing evidence and evidence location at time of recovery. Remember: Notes prepared inside of the hot zone must me placed inside of plastic bags, sealed, taped and decontaminated. It is preferable to write on 2 separate pieces of paper, instead of cramming all of the information onto one piece of paper. This information will need be transcribed afterwards to prepare a finished diagram or report. Note case number, location, time and date and personnel listed on each sheet of paper prepared during the investigation.

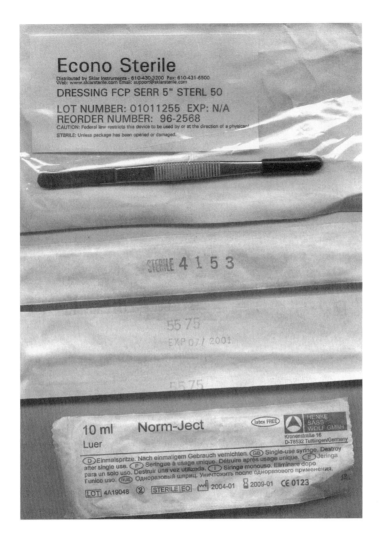

Figure G.18 Always use disposable, single-use items with lot numbers for your collection tools. Always control the tool by the handle end, not the sampling end. If the item has an expiration date, ensure that it has not passed.

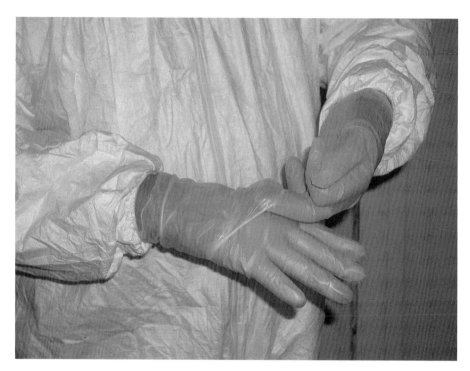

Figure G.19   Glove changes in between sample locations are a MUST. Frequent glove changes prevent the possibility of cross-contamination.

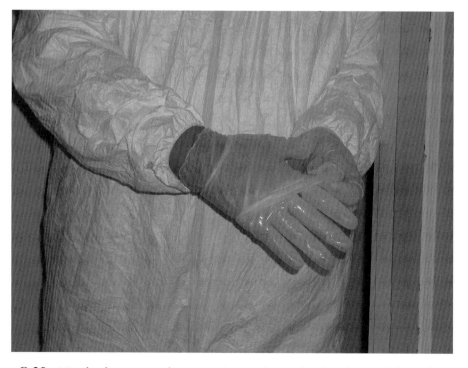

Figure G.20   Nitrile gloves worn for protection, with two (or three) sets of gloves being worn above the "protective" set of gloves. Each set of gloves is peeled off to allow a clean set of gloves to be worn while sampling takes place.

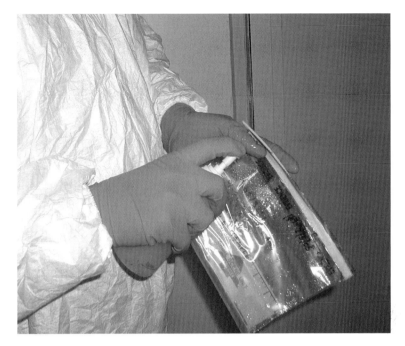

Figure G.21   Evidence must be decontaminated prior to being passed along to the next "cooler" zone. Circumstances will dictate what type of decon solution will be used. This based upon what type of contaminant is present. A 10% bleach and water solution is being used in this instance.

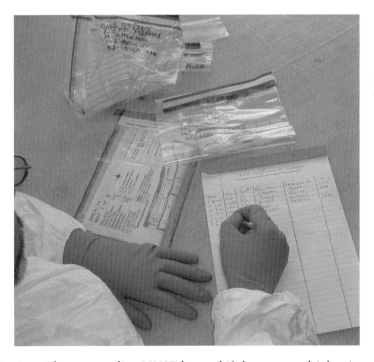

Figure G.22   An evidence custodian MUST be used if there are multiple trips made into the hot zone, or if multiple persons are collecting evidence. Maintaining a strong chain of custody is of the utmost importance.

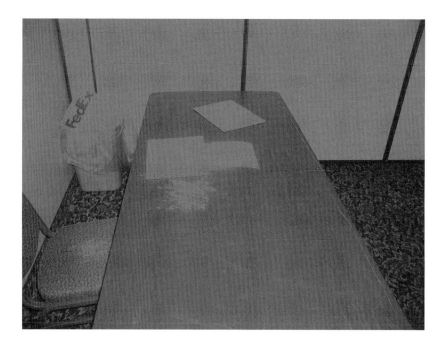

Figure G.23 Items must be measured from two fixed points. If an item is on a movable object such as a table or a chair, that item is not to be considered as being at a fixed point. Walls, doorways, stairs, etc., are fixed points.

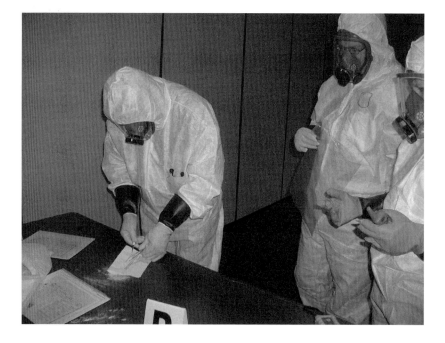

Figure G.24 Work in conjunction with at least one other person, so that you are not in an unfriendly environment alone. Always use the "buddy system."

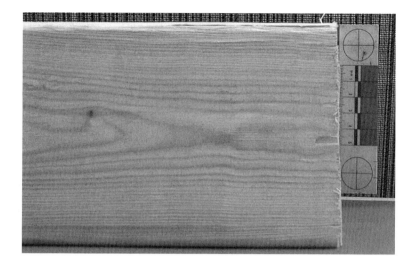

Figure G.25   Photography alone does not allow for an accurate depiction of this object.

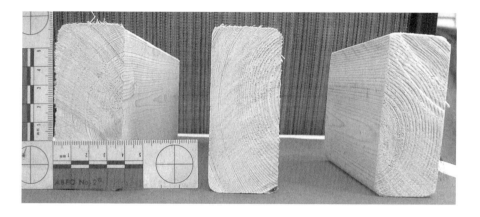

Figure G.25a   Photograph of the adjacent side of the object gives a different perspective, showing three items, but cannot determine which of the three items is the largest.

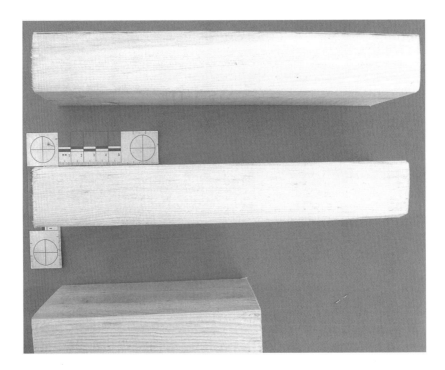

Figure G.25b   An overhead view provides the ability to see all three items, and allows their actual size to be recorded. Overhead views are not always possible, therefore vary the angle of the subject and take the photograph showing different perspectives. If size of evidence is important, or comparison to another object is necessary, take photos with and without a scale.

Figure G.25c   Photo of same items at a 45-degree angle also do not allow an accurate depiction of the size of the objects.

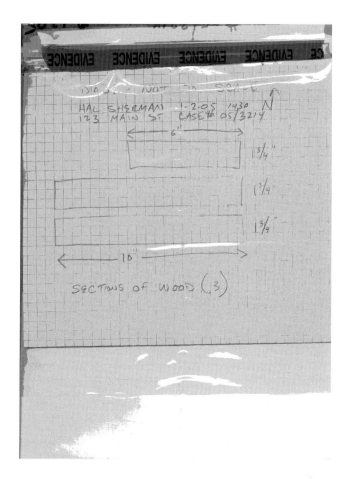

Figure G.26 This diagram shows the distance between the objects. Accurate note taking can help to alleviate any misconceptions that documentation with photography alone may cause.

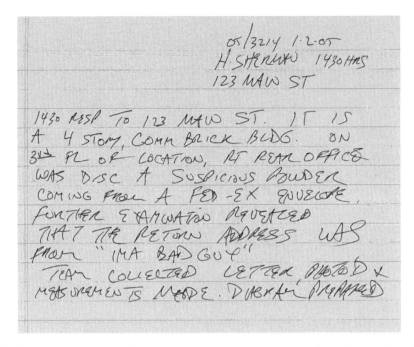

Figure G.27   Accurate note taking is essential to any investigation. Remember that many people other than yourself will be reading and examining the notes. Be accurate, if a mistake is made, line out the mistake, initial and date the error and then write the correct information. Obliteration of written material does not appear professional and is often suspect in a court of law.

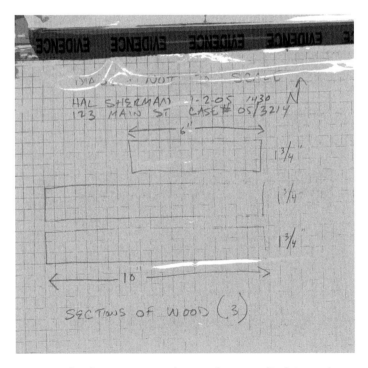

Figure G.28   Preparing the diagram, remember to place any disclaimers (not to scale) that are required onto the page. Necessary measurements describing the diagram will insure that the information will not be misinterpreted.

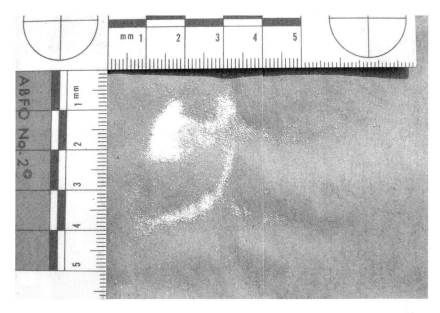

Figure G.29 Photography is extremely important. Take sufficient pictures, bracket the exposures, vary the angles and lighting position. When documenting evidence take photos without and with a scale, and be sure to keep the plane of the film parallel to the object to minimize distortion of the subject.

Figure G.30 Safeguard and retain all written material that has been prepared in connection with the investigation. Do not discard any written material as these items are considered "discovery material." Discovery is a pretrial procedure that mandates that previously unknown material that is possessed by one side of the case must be presented to the opposing side.

Figure G.31   Attempt to locate items or areas that possess unique identifiers on the packaging or container. Credit card and tracking numbers are very important to document. Postmarks and return addresses are all information that must be conveyed to incident command so that law enforcement may initiate an investigation based upon this information.

Figure G.32   When placing information on the evidence bag or packaging, use a permanent marking device (sharpie, etc). Do not rely upon labels, as they can fall off or the information may become obliterated during the decon process. Interior plastic bags will have a large quantity of humidity inside of the bags due to the decon solution. Poor marking or labeling of evidence would diminish the integrity of the evidence.

Figure G.33 United States Postal Service's suspicious letter and package tips poster.

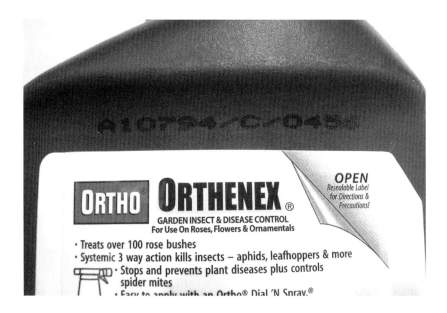

Figure G.34   Container information need be obtained. Until the contents are examined, the item should be listed as "one green plastic bottle, with a yellow cap, with a label possessing the following writing." Many people reuse plastic containers. Do not identify the contents of a container based soley on the affixed label.

Figure G.34a   Unique identifiers must be noted and recorded.

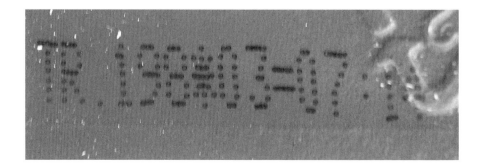

Figure G.34b   Manufacturers codes and lot numbers can provide a great deal of information to investigators. Certain substances are sold in a specific area only. If these items are found in a area that they normally are not found, that would potentially provide some useful intelligence. Expiration dates are also useful to note. Document any unique identifiers that you observe.

Figure G.35   Sony underwater camera housing. A camera placed inside of a waterproof housing allows investigators to take photos inside of the hot zone. The housing can then be decontaminated prior to entering the cold zone. Officials at the incident command can view the hot zone photographically, while establishing a collection plan while remaining in the cold zone.

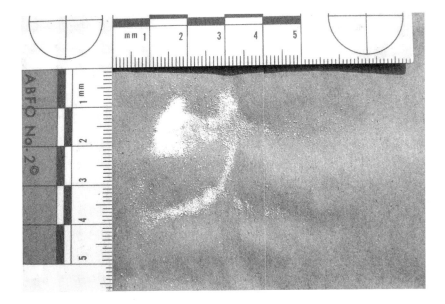

Figure G.36   The more important the photographs content, the more important it is to bracket the photo. Changing the lighting conditions of the subject will provide different nuances or subtleties of the information being documented. Attempt to take some photos using a flashlight and not the cameras flash when taking a macro view of evidence. The flash can produce "hot spots" on shiny objects or when the camera is very close to the object being photographed.

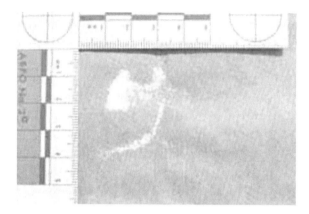

Figure G.36a   Changing exposures will produce different photographic highlights.

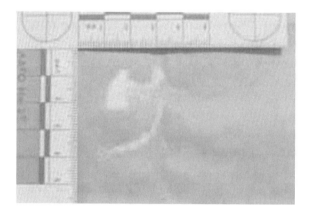

Figure G.36b

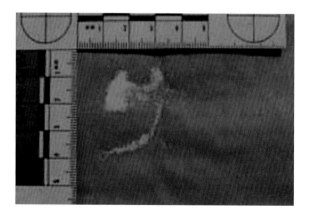

Figure G.36c

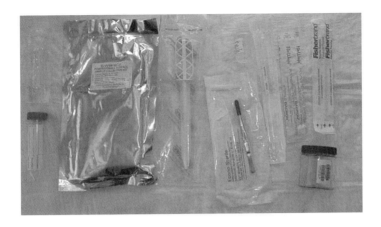

Figure G.37   Submit control samples or trip blanks to the lab. Always keep control samples inside of the cold zone, inside of their wrappers. This procedure is used to prove that the collection equipment was not contaminated prior to its being used to collect the evidence. This helps to insure that integrity in the collection/analysis process is maintained. Control samples need possess the same lot number as the actual equipment that was used to collect and package the evidentiary sample.

Glossary

AFIS   Automated Fingerprint Identification System.

Ammunition   Live cartridges.

Ballistics   Study of the flight of projectiles.

Druggist's or paper fold   A clean piece of paper folded for the containment of trace evidence.

Biohazard   An item of physical evidence that contains, or in itself may be, a material of biological origin that poses the threat of spreading AIDS, hepatitis, or some other blood-borne pathogen to its handlers.

Biological evidence   Any material of human or animal origin, such as blood, saliva, urine, semen, vaginal secretions, and any other physiological fluids, as well as hair, tissue, skin, bones, and teeth.

Bullets   Spent projectiles without their casings.

Cartridge case   A shell without its projectile and load.

Case file or case folder   A collection of documents containing information concerning a particular investigation, including but not limited to: reports of investigation interviews, work notes of all investigators, rough crime scene sketches, laboratory requests and report of findings, photographs, videotapes, and audiotapes.

Case number   The alphabetic and/or numeric characters used to identify a particular case.

Cast   A mold or replica of a questioned impression produced by pouring in or otherwise applying a material that will solidify and provide an exact replication of the query imprint. Examples of impressions are footwear imprints in soil, tire tread imprints, tool marks, and bite marks.

Chain of custody   A record of the people who have collected, processed, and otherwise had custody of the physical evidence, along with the written chronological record of the evidence acquisition and possession.

Charred document   A burned written record.

Collection   The process of recognizing, documenting, gathering, and packaging physical evidence.

Contamination   The transfer of foreign material to items of physical evidence.

Control samples   Pieces of unstained or known material removed from areas adjacent to questioned stains, or that represent the substrate containing the questioned stain or trace evidence. Control samples are normally tested to ensure that the background material does not interfere with the testing procedures.

Cross-contamination   The inadvertent transfer of trace evidence between two or more items of physical evidence.

DNA   The molecule that encodes genetic information.

DNA analysis   The procedure(s) used in testing to identify DNA patterns or types.

DNA profile   The pattern of the relative positions of DNA sequences at several locations on the molecule.

Document   Any typed, printed, copied, or otherwise-produced written communication, letter, note, or memorandum produced during, or used in the commission of, a crime.

Documentation   Written, visual, and audio records containing information concerning a particular investigation, including but not limited to: reports of investigation interviews, work notes of all investigators, rough crime scene sketches, laboratory requests and report of findings, photographs, videotapes, and audiotapes.

Evidence   Something that can be used to identify the people, places, and things involved in an event, to prove or disprove an element of an event, and to reconstruct the crime or events themselves.

Exculpatory evidence   Elements of proof that can be used to prove that someone or something was not involved in an event or crime.

Fiber   A structure that is at least ten times longer than it is wide.

Firearms   Any loaded or unloaded weapon.

First responder   The initial responding law enforcement officer arriving at the crime scene.

Forensic science   The application of the various scientific disciplines to the analysis of physical evidence involved in criminal or civil litigation.

Fragile evidence   Evidence that will lose its value if not adequately preserved or protected.

Known or reference samples   Terms used to describe samples of known source taken for elimination purposes.

Latent print   A fingerprint that is not readily visible on the surface on which it was deposited.

Perimeter   The border surrounding the crime scene.

PIPE   Personnel investigative protection equipment.

Residue   Minute trace of gas, liquid, or solid matter that can be used to identify inorganic compounds or organic molecules.

Safety equipment   Articles such as disposable (latex) gloves, masks, shoe covers, and eye protection that are utilized to provide a barrier to keep biological or chemical hazards from contacting the skin, eyes, and mucous membranes and to avoid contamination of the crime scene. See also PIPE.

Scale   An object showing standard units of length used in photographic documentation of an item of physical evidence.

Trace evidence   A small quantity of any matter or substance, whether gas, liquid, or solid, that can be collected and used to prove or disprove an element of a crime.

Walk-through   A preliminary assessment conducted by walking into and out of a crime scene to evaluate the scene, establish points of entry and exit, identify potential evidence, and determine the best plan for processing the scene.

Bibliography

Abbott, J. R., *Footwear Evidence*, Springfield, IL, Charles C. Thomas, 1964.

Bass, W. M., *Human Osteology: A Laboratory and Field Manual*, 3rd ed., Columbia, MO Archaeological Society, 1995.

Bevel, T., and Gardner, R. M., *Bloodstain Pattern Analysis — with an Introduction to Crime Scene Reconstruction*, 2nd ed., Boca Raton, FL, CRC Press, 2002.

Bisbing, R. E., The forensic identification and association of human hair, in Saferstein, R., ed., *Forensic Science Handbook*, Englewood Cliffs, NJ, Prentice Hall, 1982.

Bodziak, W. J., *Footwear Impression Evidence*, 2nd ed., Boca Raton, FL, CRC Press, 2000.

Byers, S. N., *Introduction to Forensic Anthropology — a Textbook*, Boston, MA, Allyn & Bacon, 2002.

Cassidy, M. J., *Footwear Identification*, Public Relations Branch of the Royal Canadian Police, Ottawa, ON, 1980.

Catling, D. M., and Grayson, J. E., *Identification of Vegetable Fibres*, London, Chapman Hall Ltd., 1982.

Crown, D., *The Forensic Examination of Paint and Pigments*, Springfield, IL, C. Thomas, 1968.

Davis, J. E., *An Introduction to Tool Marks, Firearms and the Striagraph*, Springfield IL, C. Thomas, 1958.

De Forest, P. R., Gaensslen, R. E., and Lee, H. C., *Forensic Science: An Introduction to Criminalistics*, New York, McGraw–Hill, 1983.

DeHaan, J. D., *Kirk's Fire Investigation*, 4th ed., Englewood Cliffs, NJ, Prentice Hall, 1994.

Di Maio, V. J. M., *Gunshot Wounds: Practical Aspects of Firearms, Ballistics and Forensic Techniques*, 2nd ed., Boca Raton, FL, CRC Press, 1998.

Fisher, B. K. J., Svensson, A., and Wendel, O., *Techniques of Forensic Science Investigations*, 5th ed., Boca Raton, FL, CRC Press, 1993.

Frei-Sulzer, M., Coloured fibres in criminal investigations with special reference to natural fibres, in Curry, A. S., ed., *Methods of Forensic Science*, vol. IV, New York, Interscience, 1965, pp. 141–175.

Given, B. W., Nehrich, R. B., and Shields, J. C., *Tire Track and Tread Marks*, Houston, TX, Gulf, 1977.

Graves, W. J., Mineralogical soil classification technique for the forensic scientist, *Journal of Forensic Sciences*, 24, 1979, pp. 331–337.

Grieve, M., Fiber Committee Chairman, *Forensic Fiber Examination Guidelines*, Fiber Subgroup, TWGMAT, Washington, DC, US Dept. of Justice, 1998.

Gross, H., *Criminal Investigation,* adapted from Adams, J. C., *System der Kriminalistik,* London, Sweet & Maxwell Limited, 1924.

Hamm, E. D., The individuality of class characteristics in Converse All–Star footwear, *Journal of Forensic Identification,* 39, no. 5, Sep./Oct. 1989, pp. 277–292.

Hamm, E. D., Track identification: A historical overview, *Journal of Forensic Identification,* 39, no. 6, Nov./Dec. 1989, pp. 333–338.

Hatcher, J. S., Jury, J. R., and Weller, J. A. C, *Firearms Investigation Identification and Evidence,* 2nd ed., 1977, Harrisburg, PA, Stackpole Co., Copyright 1935.

Hicks, J. W., *Microscopy of Hair,* Issue 2, Washington, DC, U.S. Government Printing Office, 1977.

Hilton, O., *Scientific Examination of Questioned Documents,* New York, Elsevier, 1982.

James, S., and Nordby, J., eds., *Forensic Science: An Introduction to Scientific and Investigative Techniques,* Boca Raton, FL, CRC Press, 2003.

Kirk, P. L., *Crime Investigation,* New York, Interscience, 1953.

Krogman, W. M., *The Human Skeleton in Forensic Medicine,* Springfield, IL, Thomas, 1962.

Kubic, T., and Petraco, N., Microanalysis and examination of trace evidence, in James, S. H., and Nordby, J. J., eds., *Forensic Science: An Introduction to Scientific and Investigative Techniques,* Boca Raton, FL, CRC Press, 2003.

Kubic, T. A., and Petraco, N., *Forensic Science: Laboratory Experiment Manual and Workbook,* 2nd ed., Boca Raton, FL, CRC Press, 2005.

Lee, H. C., and Gaensslen, R. E., eds., *Advances in Fingerprint Technology,* New York, Elsevier, 1991.

Lesko, J., Torpey, W. F., and Kelly, J. P., *Crime Scene Technicians Manual,* New York City Police Dept., 1977.

Locard, E., The analysis of dust traces, Part I, *American Journal of Police Science,* 1, 1930, pp. 276–298.

Locard, E., The analysis of dust traces, Part II, *American Journal of Police Science,* 1, 1930, pp. 405–406.

Locard, E., The analysis of dust traces, Part III, *American Journal of Police Science,* 1, 1930, pp. 496–514.

London, B., and Stone, J., *A Short Course in Photography,* 3rd ed., New York, HarperCollins College Publishers, 1996.

Longhetti, A., and Roche, G. W., Microscopic identification of man-made fibers from the criminalistics point of view, *Journal of Forensic Sciences,* 3, no. 3, July 1958, pp. 303–329.

Margot, P., and Lennard, C., *Fingerprint Detection Techniques,* 6th ed., Institut de police scientifique et de criminologie, Lausanne, Switzerland, 1994.

Miller, E. T., Forensic glass comparisons, in Saferstein, R., ed., *Forensic Science Handbook,* Englewood Cliffs, NJ, Prentice Hall, 1982.

Murray, R. C., and Tedrow, J. C. F., *Forensic Geology,* New Brunswick, NJ, Rutgers University Press, 1975.

Nash, S., Race, T., Hare, K., and Robitaille, M., *Crime Scene Investigation Guidelines,* Rochester, MN, IAI, 1999.

National Police Agency, Tokyo, An electrostatic method for lifting footprints, *International Criminal Police Review,* 272, Nov. 1973, pp. 287–292.

Nause, L., *Forensic Tire Impression Identification,* Canadian Police Research Centre, 2001.

NFPA 921, *Guide for Fire and Explosion Investigators,* Quincy, MA, NFPA International, 2001.

O'Hara, C. E., and Osterberg, J. W., *An Introduction to Criminalistics,* New York, Macmillan, 1949.

Olge, R. R., Jr., *Crime Scene Investigation and Physical Evidence Manual,* 2nd ed., n.p., Cal., author, 1995.

Olsen, R. D., Sr., *Scott's Fingerprint Mechanics,* Springfield, IL, Charles C. Thomas, 1978.

Osterberg, J. W., and Ward, R. H., *A Method for Reconstructing the Past: Criminal Investigation,* Cincinnati, OH, Anderson Pub. Co., 2000.

Palenik, S. Microscopy and microchemistry of physical evidence, in Saferstein, R., ed., *Forensic Science Handbook,* vol. II, Englewood Cliffs, NJ, Prentice Hall, 1988, pp. 165–167.

Palenik, S. J., Microscopical examination of fibers, in Robertson, J., and Grieve, M., eds., *Forensic Examination of Fibers,* Philadelphia, PA, Taylor & Francis, 1999.

Petraco, N., Trace evidence — the invisible witness, *Journal of Forensic Sciences,* 31, Jan. 1986, pp. 321–328.

Petraco, N., Resua, R., and Harris, H. H., A rapid method for the preparation of transparent footwear test prints, *Journal of Forensic Scien*ce, 27, 1982, pp. 935–937.

Petraco, N., and De Forest, P. R., A guide to the analysis of forensic dust specimens, in Saferstein, R. , ed., *Forensic Science Handbook,* vol. lll, Englewood Cliffs, NJ, Prentice Hall, 1993.

Petraco, N., and Kubic, T., *Color Atlas and Manual of Microscopy for Criminalists, Chemists and Conservators,* Boca Raton, FL, CRC Press, 2003.

Pickering, R. B., and Bachman, D. C., *The Use of Forensic Anthropology,* Boca Raton, FL, CRC Press, 1997.

Robertson, J., ed., *Forensic Examination of Fibers,* New York, Ellis Horwood, 1992.

Robertson, J., The forensic examination of fibres: Protocols and approaches — an overview, in Robertson, J., ed., *Forensic Examination of Fibres,* Chichester, UK, Ellis Horwood, 1992.

Robertson, J., ed., *Forensic Examination of Hair,* London, Taylor & Francis, 1999.

Robertson, J., and Grieve, M., eds., *Forensic Examination of Fibers,* Philadelphia, PA, Taylor & Francis, 1999.

Russ, J. C., *Forensic Uses of Digital Imaging,* Boca Raton, FL, CRC Press, 2001.

Sansone, S. J., *Police Photography,* Cincinnati, OH, Anderson Inc., 1977.

Scott, C. C., *Photographic Evidence,* 2nd ed., vol. 1, St. Paul, MN, West Publishing Co., 1969.

Skoog, D. A., Holler, F. J., and Nieman, T. A., *Principals of Instrumental Analysis,* 5th ed., Philadelphia, PA, Harcourt Brace College Publishers, 1998.

Smith, E. J., *Principles of Forensic Handwriting Identification and Testimony,* Springfield, IL, Charles C. Thomas, 1984.

Söderman, H., and O'Connell, J. J., *Modern Criminal Investigation,* New York, Funk & Wagnalls, 1936.

Söderman, H., and Fontell, E., *Handbok I. Kriminalteknik,* Stockholm, 1930.

Svensson, A., and Wendel, O., *Crime Detection — Modern Methods of Criminal Investigation,* 1st English ed., Amsterdam, Elsevier, 1955.

Svensson, A., Wendel, O., and Fisher, B. A. F., *Techniques of Crime Scene Investigation,* 3rd English ed., Amsterdam, Elsevier, 1982.

TWGBSI Committee, *A Guide for Explosion and Bombing Scene Investigation,* NIJ Research Report, Washington, DC, US Dept. of Justice, June 2000.

Zeno, G., Use of computers in forensic science, in James, S. H., and Nordby, J. J., eds., *Forensic Science: An Introduction to Scientific and Investigative Techniques,* Boca Raton, FL, CRC Press, 2003.

Index